THE
A.B.C. OF
GARDENING

by

W.E. SHEWELL-COOPER

M.B.E., N.D.H., F.L.S., F.R.S.L., F.R.H.S., M.R.S.T., Dip. Hort. (Wye),
Director, The Horticultural Educational and Advisory Bureau, and
Principal, The Horticultural Training Centre.
Command Horticultural Officer, Eastern and S. Eastern Commands,
1940–49.
Late H. Superintendent, Swanley Horticultural College
Sometime Horticultural Adviser to the Warwickshire
and Cheshire County Councils and
Garden Editor, B.B.C. North Region.

ENGLISH UNIVERSITIES PRESS LTD,
ST. PAUL'S HOUSE, WARWICK SQUARE,
LONDON, E.C.4.

To
MY DEAR WIFE
IRENE R. SHEWELL-COOPER
who typed every word of this book
and
very patiently !

First printed . . 1937
Post War Edition . 1946
Sixth impression . 1952
New edition . . . 1954

*Made and Printed in Great Britain for The English Universities Press Limited
by C. Tinling & Co., Ltd., Liverpool, London and Prescot*

CONTENTS

THANK YOU

No gardening author can ever claim that the whole book is his own ! He has learnt so much from others ; so many have helped with advice, that a gardening book becomes the experience of a large number of people, welded together by one—in this case by one who has gardened for quarter of a century and more.

The author specially thanks, Miss Gweneth D. Wood, Dip. Hort. (Swanley), F.R.H.S., the Technical Assistant at The Horticultural Educational and Advisory Bureau, who has corrected the proofs, taken care of the drawings, and in fact generally helped to " put the book to bed."

He also thanks Miss Diana Marks, a Student, at The Horticultural Training Centre, for her drawings and Mr. Leslie L. Stead the publisher's artist.

May I also thank the officers and men in the South Eastern and Eastern Commands, who worked so hard during the 1939–1946 War in the gardens and allotments when I was Command Horticultural Officer.   Many have written since asking for another book and here it is.

The photographs were all taken by The Horticultural Photo Supply Service.

W. E. Shewell-Cooper,
Principal.

The Horticultural Educational and Advisory Bureau,
    Thaxted,
        Essex.

ILLUSTRATIONS

PLATES

7

LINE ILLUSTRATIONS—*continued*

CHAPTER I

SOILS

I answer the following questions :—

1. What do bacteria do in the soil ?
2. How shall I treat my sticky clay soil ?
3. What does Humus mean ?
4. I want to dig properly this winter. How can I set about it ?
5. What kind of hoe should I use ?
6. How does one drain land ?

THERE are large numbers of people in the world who look upon soil as an inert mass, and rather a dirty inert mass at that. If this is your conception of the material that you are going to deal with during your efforts at gardening, then the sooner you get the idea out of your head the better.

It is true that the soil is a place where roots can grow and so " anchor " the plants down, and it is true also to say that it is a reservoir from which the roots may extract the dissolved mineral substances ; but the best way, perhaps, to regard soil is to think of it as a very large manufacturing centre where millions of living organisms are working all the time. Some of them will work so as to break down plant foods and turn them into a form that the root hairs can take into use, while others, if they are given the chance, will try and build up these materials into a form useless to the plant. Our main object, then, in treating the soil (from the cultural point of view) will be to see that the bacteria that are working to help us are given the conditions they like, so that they can multiply and work unrestricted.

If bacteria – for this is what we call these living organisms – were not present, the soil would be sterile, and could not support plant growth at all. If, then, we are out to get the best out of our gardens, we must encourage the bacteria by seeing that the soil is well aerated, sufficiently moist, that

A*   9

enough lime is present, and that it is warm enough. The organisms work at their best at 65 degrees F., and cease to work above a 100 degrees and below 10 degrees.

SOIL ORIGIN

Without a doubt soil has been produced by various agencies that have been at work for thousands of years disintegrating rocks. This " weathering " has been caused by the heat and the frost, by rain and running water, by the cracking and pounding of rocks by the glaciers, and so on. Further than this, the material so produced may have been carried down to the plains by floods or by gravity, and so, in its turn, new types of rock have been produced. These rocks, thus produced, may, in their turn, have been pulverised ; so you find, in consequence, many varied types of soils produced all over the country. Because of the movement of soil, it is quite possible to have the surface soil quite unrelated to the rock down below. For our purposes it will be sufficient to accept the soil as we find it, and we must learn to treat it in the best manner possible.

TYPES OF SOIL

The modern soil surveyor can talk to us very learnedly about soil series, and he is doing more to classify soils, in the way the botanist does plant life, than anyone has ever attempted in past years.

But we need not bother our heads about this. It should be sufficient for us to learn that there are five main types of soil which we may have to deal with. These are the clay, the loam, the sand, the calcareous or lime, and the peat. Of course even these soils differ, and you can have combinations of one or more of them ; thus there are clayey loams and sandy loams. Again, you can have the soil itself consisting of one type and what is commonly known as the subsoil of perhaps another.

If we take each group one at a time, and discuss them, we shall perhaps learn their essential differences, both in texture and treatment.

Sandy soils contain less than 10 per cent of clay, and consist of very small particles of silica and quartz. Of course the amount of humus present will alter the colour and the texture. Sand may be said to be light and, of course, dry. It is one of the warmest soils in that, because of its dryness, it warms up much more quickly in the spring. For this reason it is useful in producing early crops. One of the advantages of a sandy soil is that it can be worked at any time of the year and it is comparatively easy to cultivate. On the other hand it is poor in plant foods, coarse-grained, and does not retain moisture easily.

Clay may be likened in some ways to putty. It is very fine-grained, and smooth and silky to the touch. Even when well drained, it is wet, and so is difficult to cultivate during rainy periods and in the winter months. In fact, if it is dug or forked when wet, it has the nasty habit of settling down – or " panning," as it is called – like cement, and then it is very difficult to work afterwards. Clays should be dug in the autumn, if possible, and left rough, so that the action of the frost and wind can pulverise them, and make them into an easily workable condition in the spring. Such soils are said to be late, because it is impossible to get on them as early as sandy soils in the spring, and so the crops produced are later also. On the other hand, clay soils are much richer in plant food than sand, and this, in addition to their water-retention properties, makes them valuable in a dry season. It is most important to see that clay soils are drained, and this is one of the best ways of improving them. Lime should be applied to clay soils regularly, as it prevents them from becoming so " sticky," and " opens " them up.

Loam.—The best way of describing loam is to say that it is an ideal blend of sand and clay. The sand being present to keep the soil open, and the clay, in its turn, ensuring that sufficient moisture-retention properties are there. Obviously there are various types of loams, depending on the proportion of clay or sand present. In all gardening books the word loam appears continuously as being the best soil for large numbers of plants. Of course the ideal loam has all the advantages of of sandy and clay soils, and none of their disadvantages. The sand present allows the plant roots to work easily throughout it ; the clay present helps to look after the plant food side, and prevents rapid drying out. In wet weather the water can percolate through quite quickly, and so the soil does not become waterlogged, and in dry weather it does not become too hard for the roots to work through.

Calcareous or chalky soils, more often than not, are very deficient in plant food and rather shallow. They are often very lacking in humus, and as much organic matter as possible should be added every year. They are more often calcareous by reason of the fact that they overlie chalk or limestone, and the fine particles of these substances may be found every time the land is cultivated. When wet, they are often very sticky and unpleasant, and so are difficult to work during rainy periods. In dry seasons they are disappointing, as they soon suffer from lack of water. Because of the chalk present, the leaves of plants often become bright yellow in colour, owing to what is known as chlorosis. This yellowing may not affect the plants in any other way, but it usually means stunted growth. Chalky soils have the advantage that it is seldom necessary to lime them, and in them the clubroot disease of cabbages, etc., does not flourish.

Into this group one ought perhaps to put what are known as the **marls,** though these are really a chalky clay. In the garden they are therefore treated in the same way as clay soils, except that, again, heavy dressings of lime are not usually necessary.

The last group refers to **peaty soils,** and the most outstanding feature of them is that they are usually absolutely void of lime, and so are very " sour." This sourness is produced by the decaying of the vegetable matter present, as soils such as these contain more than 20 per cent of humus. Peats have usually been derived from marsh land where there has been continuous growth for thousands of years. They are often low-lying, and so may be waterlogged and may need pipe draining. Certain crops, like celery, for instance, do very well on peaty soils, and what are known as the moss lands of Lancashire and Cheshire are evidence of this. The brown peat is more easy to bring into cultivation than the black, heavy bog-like peat. Once peaty soils are well worked and limed, they can prove very valuable – in fact some plants, like rhododendrons and azeleas, prefer these soils to any other.

SOIL COLOUR

Soils differ in colour, as stated previously, according to the amount of humus they contain, but moisture plays its part in giving a darker or lighter appearance also. Soils that are full of organic matter are naturally dark and warm up quickly (that is one of the reasons it's so important to dig in plenty of well-rotted organic matter each year), while soils with little organic matter are light. Sometimes there is a good deal of oxide of iron present, and this will make the soil look red or yellow. The beautiful red soils of Devon are usually in a high state of fertility, because there is a good deal of organic matter present, together with the oxide of iron, and so these soils are sufficiently moist also.

SUB-SOILS

Most soils are about a foot in depth, though many of them are no deeper than eight or nine inches. (I know some in Kent that are only 3–4 inches deep.) Below this we have what gardeners call the sub-soil, which may be similar in character to the material above, and yet which may not contain available plant foods. It is important to try and get the soil to as great a depth as possible, and so, when describing digging operations, we shall aim at deep cultivation. Of course there are places where the layer of soil may be only a few inches over hard rock, and, on the other hand, in districts of the Transvaal in South Africa one can find stretches where the potential soil is up to forty feet in depth. Sub-soil affects the gardener, chiefly because it either allows or impedes drainage. For instance, if you have a light loam over gravel or sand you can be assured that all excessive moisture will be quickly carried away. It is unfortunate to have an easily workable loam over clay, as then the movement of water is stopped and the surface is apt to be waterlogged. We must take notice, then, of both the soil and the sub-soil, as the one is the complement of the other.

DRAINAGE

In small gardens pipe drainage is often difficult to arrange, as the work is complicated by the fact that near-by neighbours may not have the same ideas on the subject and it may be difficult in consequence, sometimes, to get the water away. Soils that are well drained are much warmer than those undrained, and, as we have said that we must have warm soils to ensure fervent bacterial activity, we can see how important this operation is. In early days, before pipe drains came into vogue, drainage was arranged for by raising the surface of the soil to be cultivated, and by allowing ditches on either side to take the excess water away. Even to-day there are allotments in some parts of the country which have to be raised above the surrounding ground because pipe drains have not been laid. The modern pipe drain is usually laid 2 feet 6 inches deep, and so allows of deep hand cultivation. When arranging to drain a garden, there are three types of drains to be considered – the mains, the sub-mains, and the small drains which themselves lead into these. The main drain is usually laid in the direction of the greatest slope, and the sub-mains enter into this. At the junction where the sub-mains enter the main drain, a hole is made in the larger drain, and the small one fits loosely into it. See that these drains enter at an angle in the direction of the flow of the water, so that there is no silting up. The pipes are laid down end to end, and are not joined by cement. In this way the water passes into the system at the open joints. Latterly special porous concrete pipes have been made which can be laid down joining one another, as, because of their porosity, the water percolates into them readily. These drains have another advantage in that they do prevent the roots of trees getting into them. In the ordinary field drain, after a number of years such roots may become a nuisance.

It is well to arrange that the " fall " is at least 1 in 100 for the mains, and 1 in 75 for the sub-mains. Under certain conditions, owing to difficulties in the outfall, it is possible to get water away with as slight a fall as 1 in 300, but this is by no means ideal. When draining is carried out under this system the whole scheme looks rather like the proverbial " herring-bone," or series of herring-bones, should the garden be large. The illustration on page 16 explains this more clearly.

Always start laying the drains from the lower end, as it is only in this way that you can ensure an even fall. At this end, you must, of course, have a ditch, or some similar gully, to take the water away, and, if this is impossible, a well should be dug (this may be square), which should be lined with brick. Such a well may be useful in supplying water during dry periods.

If tile drains are found to be too expensive, it is possible to use stones instead of pipes, and a trench dug out to the depth of 2 feet 6 inches, say 4 to 6 inches wide, may then be filled up to a depth of 9 inches with stones, tin cans, and other insoluble rubbish. Such makeshifts work quite satisfactorily. Even on top of the drainpipes it is a good plan to place clinkers and suchlike – especially in clay soils, which are apt to seal up the spaces in between them.

It is impossible to over-emphasise the importance of drainage, and this is the very first job that should be tackled if the soil water does not drain away naturally.

HUMUS

We have already referred to humus, and we shall do so from time to time throughout the book. We must try, then, to understand the exact meaning of the word. Humus may be said to be a brownish black " jam " or " jelly " which results from the decaying and rotting vegetable matter in the soil. This is produced also from the dung that has been purposely added, and from the leaves and roots of former plants. One of the reasons that farmyard manure is so popular is that it not only adds plant food to the soil, but it increases the organic or humic content also. Humus tends to act like a

BASTARD TRENCHING

TRUE TRENCHING

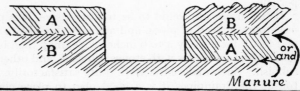

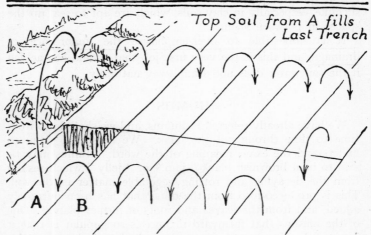

Top Soil from A fills Last Trench

Top Soil from B fills A and so on

HOW RIDGING IS DONE

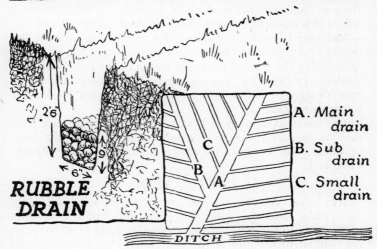

RUBBLE DRAIN

2'6" 9" 6"

DITCH

A. Main drain

B. Sub drain

C. Small drain

sponge and to hold moisture for the plant roots. In itself it produces plant foods, and the acids and gas given off during the process of the rotting of the organic matter help to free and preserve other plant foods, that would otherwise, be useless and not available to plants. Humus darkens soil, and tends to warm it. It is vital to build up the Humus content of a soil.

MULCHING

The movement of water in soil is both upward and downward. The excess water gradually percolates through, and, if the drainage is perfect, is carried away. Because of the porosity of soil the water in it may rise also, and when the water gets to the top of the soil the heat of the sun may evaporate it, and the wind carry it away. In this way soils can, in hot weather, soon be dried out. To prevent this evaporation of soil moisture the operation known as mulching is carried out. This can take two forms : (1) the continued cultivation of the top half-inch or inch of soil – known as dust mulching, and (2) the application of some organic material – often dung, straw, sedge peat, or lawn mowings. Either of these methods has the same effect in helping to keep the water where it is required – round about the roots of the plants.

Mulching is carried out during the summer months for this definite purpose, and there is no excuse for putting on rotted material at the base of trees and plants in the late autumn or winter. In the same way do not be in too great a hurry to mulch early the following year, as it is necessary for the soil to get warm first.

The constant reminders that are given in this book from time to time about hoeing, not only refer to the keeping down of weeds, but to the dust mulching that we have already explained.

CULTIVATION

We have already referred to the necessity for deep cultivation, and we must now, therefore, outline definite methods as to how this can be achieved. First of all we must get hold of the meaning of two operations : (a) trenching, and (*b*) bastard trenching. These operations will be referred to as necessary throughout the book. In trenching, the layers of the soil are reversed and in bastard trenching they are kept in the same relationship, the one to the other. It is said colloquially that trenching is being done to one or two " spits," deep, and the same is true of bastard trenching (the word spit really refers to a spade's depth).

) In bastard trenching to two spits deep, the bottom spit remains at the bottom and the top spit at the top. This is perhaps the most commonly practised digging operation of all where deep cultivation is a necessity. The very fact that the top spit of soil contains plant foods in an available form, and that the under spit has in all probability never been weathered or improved, encourages gardeners to keep these at their normal levels.

The method adopted is to mark out on the piece of ground to be dug a strip 2 feet wide, and then to remove the top spit and wheel it to the end of the plot, where the digging will finish. You then get into the trench thus made, and dig it up well, leaving the dug soil where it is ; if the soil is apt to be heavy, a fork is perhaps the best tool for this purpose. On top of the forked ground the manure is placed, together with annual weeds and any other rotted material to hand. The line is then moved back another 2 feet, and, spadeful by spadeful, the first trench is covered in with the top soil from this area. In this way another trench, similar in size to the first one, is formed, and this is treated in the same way. This operation is then continued until you reach the other end, where you will find the heap of soil to fill in the last trench made.

It is possible to divide with a line the piece of ground to be dug into two portions as in the diagram, and then to dig down the whole of one strip round the end of the plot, and come up to the top of the other strip, where you will have placed the pile of soil from the first trench marked A in bottom diagram on page 16. If you want to increase the fertility of the lower soil you can not only place the manure on top of the dug-out bottom of the trench, but, when forking, actually fork manure into this as well.

TRUE TRENCHING

Here, as we have explained, the surface layers of the soil are altered, and so the operation is commenced in this way : a trench is opened up as before, and the soil is wheeled to the other end of the plot, but, instead of forking up the bottom of the trench, this is dug out to a spit's depth also, and taken to the same place but put into another pile. We should have now a trench about 2 feet deep. When the line is moved back, the top spit from this part is put into the bottom of the trench, and the second spit is then placed on top of it. Thus we have the top soil from the second trench in the bottom of the first trench, and the bottom soil of the second trench on the top of the first trench. You continue digging like this for the whole of the plot, and again when you come to the end you will find the mound of sub-soil and soil ready for you, to fill in the last trench you make.

RIDGING

Ridging has very nearly become a lost art – perhaps because the modern generation is rather lazy. It is, however, an excellent way of weathering heavy soils, and clays particularly will benefit from such treatment. The idea is to get the land into a series of ridges to expose as great a surface to the action of the weather as possible. Further, in rainy seasons excess water is readily carried away and the soil in the spring is, in consequence, much warmer. When marking out the ground, a strip 2 feet wide should be chosen, running the whole length of the plot, north and south. A trench is opened out, and the soil taken to the end of the plot as usual. The strip is now divided into three, in your mind's eye, and spadeful A is placed into the centre of the trench thus made, spadeful B on top of it, and spadeful C on top of spadeful B. If this operation is continued right the way down the strip, it will be found that a ridge has been made the whole length of the ground. Further strips are marked out with the line as before, and so a large number of ridges are formed running parallel one with another.

It is possible to do a kind of omnibus operation at one and the same time, and this is known as " ridging and bastard trenching." In this case, before the soil from the second trench is put into the ridge-like position, the bottom of the first trench is thoroughly forked over. Manure can be added as well, at the same time, if desired.

Single Digging consists of turning the ground over to one spade's depth, and is often done in the summer when you are in a hurry to prepare for another crop. A shallow trench should always be taken out to start with.

FORKING AND RAKING

Other summer operations are *forking* and *raking*, both of which are designed to get the soil down into a fine condition suitable either for the sowing of seeds or the putting out of plants. This condition is known in the gardening world as a fine tilth. In the autumn, then, we aim at digging the ground to as deep a depth as possible, leaving the land rough, and in the spring and early summer we aim at the fine tilth. The rake is specially designed to prepare the land for seed sowing, and when used properly is a very useful tool indeed. See that it is drawn backwards and forwards over the surface of the ground, leaving the land in a fine condition and yet absolutely level. It should not be used, as it so often is, for removing large quantities of small stones. These if left in the soil assist in the drainage and in the movement of air. In the summer they tend to keep the land cool – the surface stones acting as a mulch – while in the winter they help in keeping the land warmer. Do not waste your time, then, in raking your land continually for the purpose of stone removal.

HOEING

Hoes are also summer tools, there being two cheap types – the Dutch hoe and the draw hoe, sometimes called the drag hoe. In ordinary gardens the Dutch hoe is to be recommended, and should be used continually between rows of seedlings to keep down weeds, and everywhere in the garden to provide a mulch. In operations connected with the movement of the top inch of soil or so for purposes such as " earthing up," the plate hoe is invaluable. It is also useful after weeds have grown rather tall, as when hoeing they can be cut off at the root. (A draw hoe is often very useful when you return from your summer holiday !)

A two-pronged hoe, known as the Canterbury hoe, is often used for earthing up potatoes, in order to keep the tubers from turning green. It may be necessary, to earth up peas, especially autumn-sown ones, before the frosts or cold winds worry them.

The only other operation that should be mentioned is that of *treading* or *rolling*. Light soils often need consolidating, and certain crops, like onions, need firm ground below. After forking, then, it may be necessary to tread the ground all over methodically, or else to roll lightly, and then to hoe the land over to produce a tilth on the top inch or so only.

Watering.—As most plants are composed of 80 per cent of water and as many of them will transpire 300 or more lbs. of water during each season of their life time, it is very important to ensure that there is plenty of moisture present in the soil during the growing season.

If when bastard trenching the sub-soil is found to be dry, it is a good plan to put in the dung or well rotted compost and then flood the trench. No Water Board will be against the using of water for the garden in the winter.

When watering in the summer it is better to use an overhead sprinkler like a " Brosson " and to leave this in position for at least an hour so that the ground is properly soaked. If every part of the garden is given such an overhead watering once a week during the drought periods all should be well.

Hoeing is done after watering – not before.

CHAPTER II

MANURES AND MANURING

A difficult problem, manures and fertilisers. What can I say about them ?

1. Nearly all soils lack four plant foods
2. There are many kinds of organic manures.
3. Instruction is given as to how to use such useful organic materials as Seaweed, Hops, Hoof and Horn, etc.
4. Many artificial manures are described and their uses discussed.
5. Details are given as to how to mix artificials to get the best results with various crops.
6. Lime is used as a plant food and to counteract acidity. There are various types of lime.

In order to keep up the fertility of the soil it is necessary to add manure regularly. Manures and fertilisers may be grouped, first of all, into two main sections : (1) organic, and (2) inorganic. The organic manures are the various forms of farmyard manure, poultry manure, composted vegetable refuse, fish guano, meat refuse, shoddy, etc. While the inorganic fertilisers are what some people call the chemical manures, or " bag " manures.

Too often there arises an argument at lectures which I attend, or give, between people who are supporters or opponents of one type or another. I have known gardeners who boast that they have never put any artificial manures on their gardens, and there is no doubt that this is possible, and many would say advisable.

The great thing is to build up the humus content of the soil first – and it is then you can add "extras" as tonics, if necessary.

The plants themselves have to build up their " bodies " both from materials they extract from the air and from the minerals they take up from the ground. It is actually a combination of these two that provides for the starches and the sugars that are necessary in crop production.

In the soil one finds all kinds of minerals necessary to plant growth, and actually there are ten that are essential. Fortunately for us, six of them are present in sufficient quantities in practically every soil one comes across, and so there are only four that we may have to apply from time to time. These four are : nitrogen, phosphorus, potash, and calcium, or, as we commonly apply it, lime.

We shall be dealing with lime later on, because it not only supplies plant food, but sweetens up the soil, and so, for this reason, it is only usual to talk about three necessary plant foods.

This is the secret of all good systems of manuring, and all gardeners must realise that all plants require these three foods in the correct proportions. It is absolutely useless to apply a greater quantity of the one in the hope that it will make up for a deficiency of the other. Obviously some plants want more potash than others, while others, in their turn, require a heavier dressing of nitrogen, and so on. For this reason suggested formulæ are given at the end of the chapter.

The first thing all prospective gardeners should learn about manures is how to classify them into their correct groups, and for this reason the different types are put under their correct headings later on.

If, then, these three plant foods are necessary, what function does each of them have ?

NITROGEN

The function of nitrogen is to build up the green leaves and stems of the plant. When nitrogen is withheld, the leaves tend to be light green in colour and smaller in size. When nitrogen is applied to growing crops in a quickly available form, the speed at which the plant is growing will increase. An overdose of nitrogen will cause coarse, strong, luxuriant, and sappy growth. This makes the plant liable to attacks of fungus diseases and defers ripening of the crop. Nitrogen, then, is useful for crops where one desires large, succulent green leaves, as in the case of cabbages.

PHOSPHORUS

Phosphorus – or phosphates, as components of phosphorus are commonly called – seems to possess the power of causing fruitfulness, and is valuable in increasing root production. Plants starved of phosphorus make little root growth, and, in consequence, during times of drought they suffer tremendously.

If you want to keep your plant growing steadily, firmly, and continuously, then, phosphates will help you. Another point in favour of this group is that it tends to hasten the ripening of plants.

POTASH

The main value of potash is in the way it " tones up " a plant. Soils that have had sufficient potash applied to them grow plants with firmer leaves, more resistant to disease, and generally hardier altogether. Potash, for instance, assists in forming strong fibre, and with fruit it certainly plays a part in producing fruits of a better colour which tend to keep longer. It is useful in the case of lighter soils, as these are normally deficient in this food. It is even claimed that potash appears to increase the scent in flowering plants.

SOIL CULTIVATION

Whatever kind of manuring is going to be carried out, it will be absolutely useless unless the soil is well worked. The deep cultivation advised in the previous chapter goes a long way towards producing the perfect plant. Unless you are prepared to stir the soil deeply and regularly, and to turn it from time to time, it is useless to bother to take advice on manuring. It seems hard to continue impressing this point, but shallow cultivation and heavy manuring never go hand in hand – anyway successfully.

ORGANIC MANURES

All soils will be improved by the addition of organic material. What is known as the physical condition is definitely helped by bulky, organic refuse. Not only does this supply plant food but it adds substances that have the power to act on insoluble compounds in the soil, and so reduce them to a form that the plant can use. Perhaps the only soil that does not require the addition of organic material is the peaty soil, though this will appreciate artificial manures and lime. Heavy soils are improved by organic manuring as they become lighter and easier to work. Light soils are made to retain moisture more readily, and so it helps them to withstand drought periods. There are people who believe that dung is very rich in plant food, but in point of fact it contains relatively small quantities.

FARMYARD MANURE

This is the oldest and perhaps the most popular type of organic manure used. It consists, of course, of the animal excrements, both liquid and solid, and of the litter put down for the animals to lie on. The value of dung varies according to the way the animals have been fed and looked after. Further, the value differs according to the way it has been stored. The most valuable manure is old manure that has been made and kept in a covered-in yard. If manure is left exposed to the action of the sun, the wind, and the rain for many months, its value may be reduced by half. Litter can play an important part in altering the value of dung – as, for instance, manure containing peat is richer in nitrogen than a similar quantity containing straw. In comparing the dung produced by various animals, we find that horse manure is more valuable than cow manure, though in fairness one must say that it loses its value, if kept in the open, more quickly than the other. Pig manure is richer in nitrogen, and so is sheep manure.

If it can be obtained, and is not too dear, dung should be applied every year to the crops that require it. Some lands will need heavier dressings than others ; generally, 1 good barrow load to 10–15 square yards is sufficient.

Be careful not to buy dung that has been made with saw-dust or wood chippings – this is inferior to any other kind, and the wood itself is often very harmful.

It is a good plan to dig in the farmyard manure, in the case of heavy soils, in the autumn and winter, and in the case of light soils in the spring. For heavy soils, use strawy manure, and for light soils well-rotted material.

COMPOST HEAPS

An excellent substitute for dung may be made by the gardener with all the vegetable refuse from the garden or allotment and from the house. Many experiments have been and are being done in this very vital and interesting work. But, as a matter of fact, composting is no new method of fertilizing the soil. It has been practised for hundreds of years by the Chinese, who are experts at the intensive culture of vegetables.

Sir Albert Howard has had excellent results from the " Indore " method of composting. The John Innes Institute advocates a method of composting which does not include the turning of the heaps. Miss Maye Bruce, another expert, uses a bin made of old railway sleepers, which are sprayed with a clay solution. The material to be composted consists of vegetable refuse, but little hard woody material. When it is filled the heap is treated with a potion of herbs. The Bio-dynamic method also includes the addition of a herbal mixture.

It is impossible to go into details of all the processes, but one which has given excellent results and used at The Horticultural Training Centre for a number of years, is as follows :

The Bin Method.—A bin made of wood or wire netting is used to hold all the vegetable refuse from the house and garden – potato peelings, tea leaves, dead flowers, rotting leaves, hedge clippings, etc., and litter from the rabbit hutches and poultry runs.

These materials are put in to a depth of 6 inches and are well trodden. A fish fertiliser is then sprinkled on at the rate of 3 ozs. per square yard and watered in. The quantity of water added being controlled by the dampness of the material composted ; it should never be sodden, but thoroughly moist. (Water should not ooze out of the compost when squeezed in the hand.) Successive layers are made in this manner as material becomes available. Every fourth 6-inch layer should be limed instead of treated with the fish

COMPOST HEAP

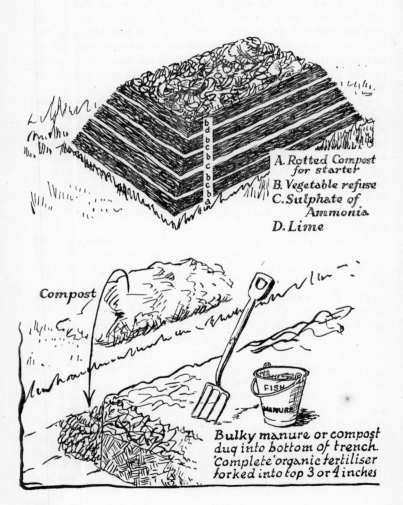

A. Rotted Compost
    for starter
B. Vegetable refuse
C. Sulphate of
    Ammonia
D. Lime

Compost

Bulky manure or compost
dug into bottom of trench.
'Complete' organic fertiliser
forked into top 3 or 4 inches

COMPOST BIN arrangement of Layers

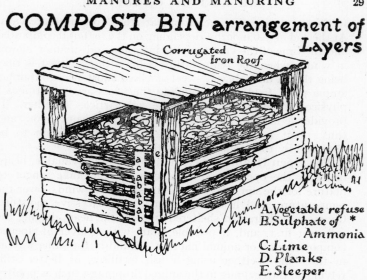

Corrugated Iron Roof

A. Vegetable refuse
B. Sulphate of *
   Ammonia
C. Lime
D. Planks
E. Sleeper

SOAKING PEAT

* Better still use rabbit droppings or poultry manure.

fertiliser.   Use carbonate of lime at 4 ozs. to the square yard.
At the end of 3–6 months, depending on the material composted
and the time of the year (quicker in spring and summer, slower
in winter when the temperature is low), the compost is ripe,
being then a dark, black, sweet-smelling substance, containing
ample plant foods and providing the necessary " glutinous "
physical property for binding the soil particles together.   It
provides a medium for the soil bacteria to work upon, and
thus, plant food is produced in the right condition to be
absorbed by the roots and utilised by the plants.

The Open Heap.—Where no protection is available, heaps
made in the open are quite successful, but take longer to
mature for the sun dries out the moisture, the winds lower the
temperature, and heavy rains may give excessive moisture.
Choose a well-drained sheltered spot for the heap, digging the
soil over first, and, if possible, start with a layer of ripened
compost, straw or animal manure.   Build in the same way as
in the " bin " either using a fish fertiliser, or better still,
relying on the enzymes in the animal droppings, such as poultry
or rabbit manure, to serve as the activator every 6 inches.   A
dusting of lime (preferably powdered lime) should be given
for every 2 feet, or even 3 feet when the animal manure is
used.   A one-foot depth of brittle material, such as straw
and the dead stems of herbaceous plants, should be sandwiched
between layers of fresh green material, such as grass mowings
and cabbage leaves.   Where a large quantity of green material
is to be composted, it should be allowed to wilt first, otherwise
the water content of the heap may be too high and an acid
slime will be produced, excluding air and retarding the work of
the bacteria.

While making the heap cover with sacks to keep in heat and
moisture.   Protect if possible from excessive rain, and when
the heap is finished, a casing of 4–5 inches of soil should be put
on.   The heap should be from 9 foot–12 foot wide at the base,
sides sloping to 6 foot–8 foot at the top, and 5 foot–6 foot high.
The length can be as desired.

Testing for Condition.—To test the condition of the
compost, make a hole with a trowel in the side of the heap.

If it is slimy, wet and sour-smelling, it will be as well to strip off the covering and turn the heap and add drier material and a sprinkling of lime. If it is brittle and smells musty, either add dilute liquid manure or water, or, if possible, turn the heap during rain. The compost is ready for use when it has a pleasant, earthy smell.

POULTRY MANURE

There is really little definite information available as to the value of this manure. It should be free from sawdust and disinfectants, and should be stored in a dry place. When applied wet, its value is only about half that of similar material stored and kept dry. When dry it should be used with caution, at the rate of about 1 lb. to the square yard, and may be dug in or used as a top dressing in the spring or early summer and hoed in.

It is however excellent as an accelerator and should be used on the Compost Heap at 2 ozs. to the square yard for every 6-inch layer of refuse.

Pigeon Manure contains more plant food than poultry manure, and is approximately twice as valuable.

FISH MANURE

This is a popular manure, and is offered by manufacturers free from objectionable odour. It is made from waste fish and fish residues, and if the makers have removed the oil it is quite quick-acting. Without any additions it is rich in nitrogen and phosphates, but contains no potash. Some manufacturers do, however, add potash during the process of drying and packing, and then it becomes a complete manure. Fish guano is comparable to all true guanos in that it is able to yield nitrogen to the growing crop throughout the whole season. The analysis of a high grade fish guano is remarkably constant. The nitrogen varies between 6 per cent. and 9 per cent, and the phosphate from 13 per cent to 20 per cent. Fish manure rapidly rots down and feeds the soil. By the addition of humus it also stimulates bacterial action.

Some fish manures have other substances added to them in order to increase their value. The following substances have been found incorporated with first-class fish guanos ; dried blood, finely ground hoof and horn, bone meal, potash nitrate, sulphate of potash and sterilized humus. It is usually applied at 2 to 4 ozs. to the sq. yd. as in the case of meat and bone meal.

SHODDY

This is the waste left behind during the manufacture of various materials. Wool shoddy is more valuable than cotton shoddy. The former contains nitrogen only, and, like fish manure, its value depends largely on the amount of oil present. The greater the amount of oil the less its value. All shoddies rot down slowly, and are applied at the rate of, say, 1 large barrow load to 12 square yards. Shoddy is dug in in the autumn, and is more often used on heavy soils than on the lighter kinds. It lasts a long time, and is slow in its action.

SPENT HOPS

Various kinds of hop manure are for sale, and are quite a good substitute for dung. Normally they contain a little nitrogen, but no phosphates or potash, a good application being a large barrow load to 10 square yards.

SEAWEED

Those readers who live close to the sea will find seaweed quite useful. It is nearly as valuable as farmyard manure, though low in phosphates. It is, however, richer in potash. It should be applied at the same rate as dung.

PEAT

Prepared sedge peat is now being sold as an alternative to animal manures. Be sure and see that the normal acid properties of this substance have been neutralised during the process of manufacture, so that it can be applied to the land with safety. Apply at the rate of 1 large bucketful to the square yard when dug in a spade's depth and at half a bucketful to the square yard worked in to the top 2 or 3 inches.

Putting a little sulphate of ammonia on to weeds on a lawn is an effective way of killing them when there are only a few.

As the bulbs reach maturity the tops should be bent over
to enable them to ripen off properly. Note the way this
is done so that one row is bent away from the other.

OTHER SUBSTITUTES

Other substitutes are – dried blood, which is too dear to use out of doors, though it is very rich in nitrogen ; Ground Hoof and Horn, which is slow in action, containing nitrogen and phosphates, but no potash, a normal dressing being 5 cwt. an acre. Soot contains nitrogen, and is valuable because it darkens the soil. It contains no phosphates or potash, and is useful on heavy soils, in making them easier to work and more porous.

GREEN MANURING

This should come under the heading of the bulky manures such as we have been already mentioning, and can be an excellent substitute for dung.

The scheme is to sow a crop purely for the purpose of digging it in while it is still fresh and green. Various crops are suitable, the commonest being mustard, rye, spinach and tares. If it is desired to add nitrogen in large quantities, then peas, tares, clover, or lupins are sometimes used. It is important to dig the crops in before they get to the flowering stage. They not only add humus to the soil, but help to retain the soluble plant foods which were present when the crop was sown. Such foods may easily be washed away during a rainy period. Directly the ground is free of a crop, one of these green manures can be sown instead of leaving the land bare. Spinach, for instance, is often sown in September and October, and so is rye, while mustard and tares are often sown in April. Mustard has its advantages in that it may be dug in, in less than eight weeks' time ; but has its disadvantages, as it is liable to get club root, and so keep the disease going in the ground.

Far too little green manuring is done, and good gardeners should make it a practice to have suitable " green manure " seed by them, so that directly a patch of ground is vacant, and is not required definitely for anything else, this may be sown and the resultant crop dug in. Never complain that you cannot get organic manures all the time that you can sow green manures, and rot down your own vegetable refuse.

B

ARTIFICIAL MANURES

Artificial, chemical, or bag manures are far more concentrated than the organic manures we have already
mentioned.   They must only be used as a " tonic " and cannot
be regarded as " main foods."

Most artificial manures may be classified into the three big
groups we have already discussed, though some, it is true,
overlap from one group into another.

THE NITROGENOUS FERTILISERS

These are sulphate of ammonia, nitrate of soda, nitro chalk,
nitrate of lime, calcium cyanamide, and so on.

Sulphate of ammonia is retained in the soil, and is
not easily washed away.   It will release nitrogen steadily,
and may be applied as one dressing in the spring.   It is neutral,
dry, and in powder form, and so is easy to apply on the
ground.   It is not usually applied as a top dressing when the
crops are growing, as not only is it slow in action, but it can
burn the foliage.

Nitrate of soda does not contain quite so much nitrogen
as sulphate of ammonia, but is the most rapid in action of
those used commonly.   It comes from the mines of Chile, and
being in the form of a nitrate is immediately available to plant
roots.   For this reason, also, it is easily washed out by rain,
and so should be applied in small dressings – say 1 lb. to 40
square yards.   It is often used in the spring, to hurry plants
into growth after the cold winter.   It can be used in the
summer, when it is thought that an extra fillip of nitrogen is
required.

Nitro chalk.—This is British made, and contains the same
amount of nitrogen as nitrate of soda.   The lime or calcium
carbonate present in this manure is valuable also ; it is quick-
acting, and, because it is sold in a granular form, it is easy
to apply.   It does not scorch the leaves of plants, even when
scattered rather indiscriminately, as the little granules roll off

the leaves.   It is advised by some for use on acid soils, and is sometimes used to give a " fillip " like nitrate of soda.

Nitrate of lime is similar to nitro chalk, and is perhaps nearer to the form in which the plant takes up nitrogen in nature.   It seems to have no harmful effects on the soil, but its great disadvantage is that it soon absorbs moisture from the atmosphere, and so becomes sticky and difficult to apply.

Calcium cyanamide is equal to sulphate of ammonia as far as the nitrogen content, but is rich in calcium oxide (lime) also.   It is a black fine dust, and, because of its corrosive action, must not be used on growing crops.   It is applied at about 2 ozs. per square yard.

PHOSPHATIC FERTILISERS

These are superphosphate, basic slag, mineral phosphates, steamed bone flour, and bone meals, etc.; of these, the only really soluble manure is superphosphate.

Superphosphate.—Although superphosphate is soluble, it does not wash out easily from soil.   It will burn leaves when applied to a growing crop, and so is always put on before a crop is sown – when the land is being prepared.   It should be dry and look like a grey powder.

Basic slag is a by-product produced during the manufacture of steel.   It should be applied early in the winter if it is to be of value next spring, and is used at the rate of 2 ozs. per square yard.   It is much recommended on heavy soils, or in soils rich in organic matter.   Like some of the artificial nitrogenous manures, it contains a certain amount of lime as well.

Mineral phosphates are not as effective on the young plants as superphosphate.

Steamed bone flour.—This is the residue that is left after bones have been robbed of the fat and gelatine during the making of glue.   It is a slow-acting manure, but will provide a regular supply of phosphates throughout the season and as the plant requires them.   It is usually applied at 2 ozs. to the square yard, and more often to glasshouse, pot, or permanent crops.   It is organic in origin and can be recommended.

Bone meals are sold, and differ from steamed bone flour in that they contain gelatine but not the fat. They are much slower in action than steamed bone flour, and give good lasting results.

POTASSIC FERTILISERS

Experiments seem to show that potash is one of the most important fertilisers used. Plants showing potash starvation are usually stunted, and often have brown scorched edges to their leaves. The potassic fertilisers are sulphate of potash, muriate of potash, and kainit.

Sulphate of potash is the most expensive fertiliser of this group, but it is undoubtedly the safest to use, and the most valuable one where good quality is required. There is an excellent type of sulphate of potash made from grape skins. It can be used in the spring, for it is not easily washed away. By itself it is usually applied at 1 oz. to the square yard.

Muriate of potash.—This is a much impurer product than sulphate of potash, and never seems to give good quality. It should not be applied to growing crops, as it can injure them easily. It is not a recommended fertiliser.

Kainit.—A cheap form of potash, and one that contains a high percentage of salts. In the garden it is only used for crops that can tolerate salt—such as beet, celery, and asparagus. It is very dangerous to use on heavy and silty soils.

WOOD ASHES

Wood ashes should not be called an artificial, though they are being included under this heading because they can be applied similarly. They are about a twelfth as valuable as sulphate of potash, and so very heavy dressings have to be applied if they are to act as a substitute for this. They are *very useful* in improving the texture of soils, and because plenty of bonfire ashes are available they are much used in gardens. (In this connection it is necessary to point out that *coal ashes* can do a great deal of harm and so should be avoided.)

COMMON ARTIFICIALS THAT CONTAIN MORE THAN ONE PLANT FOOD

Nitrate of potash.—This contains nitrogen and potassium, but, because it is so dear, it is not much used as a manure. It is recommended by some for growing vegetables for exhibition, or for special use in pot-work under glass.

Phosphate of potash.—Like nitrate of potash, this is very highly concentrated, and is rather expensive. It is sometimes used to make up a concentrated liquid manure for watering pot-plants.

MIXING ARTIFICIALS

It is possible and advisable to buy complete fertilisers ready mixed, in an organic form like fish manure. It is, however, within every gardener's power to mix up his own artificials. A complete fertiliser consists of nitrogen, phosphates, and potash, and perhaps the commonest of all the general mixtures is the following :

> 1 part sulphate of ammonia
> 3 parts superphosphate
> 1 part sulphate of potash.

This may be altered to suit various types of crops. In the case of sweet peas, for instance, the mixture might be altered to :

> 1 part sulphate of ammonia
> 4 parts superphosphate
> 2 parts sulphate of potash.

For more permanent crops, and for those needing larger quantities of phosphates, the formulæ might be altered to :

> 1 part sulphate of ammonia
> 2 parts superphosphate }
> 2 parts steamed bone flour } phosphates
> 2 parts sulphate of potash.

In the case of a very light soil, where it is desired to retain moisture, or for salt-loving plants, a mixture used by some is :

     1 part sulphate of ammonia
     3 parts superphosphate
     3 parts Kainit.

All these mixtures would be applied at the rate of 3 oz. per square yard.

WARNING

Amateurs keen on mixing their own manures are advised to stick to the ones that have been mentioned. It is dangerous, for instance, to mix superphosphate with nitrate of soda, as the nitrogen will be lost and the superphosphate will revert, that is to say, be in a form that the plant cannot use. For the same reason sulphate of ammonia must never be mixed with basic slag.

LIME

When discussing lime previously, we said that the calcium lime was useful as a plant food. This is not the only importance of lime, as it can do a great deal to improve the workability of soils. Lime can make clay easier to work. Lime helps to set free other plant foods – particularly potash. Lime counteracts the acidity in the soil. Lime helps to build up the salts which are used by the plant as food, and it is very useful in helping to decompose organic material. Not only does it do all these valuable things, but if it is applied regularly it can prevent attacks of that dreaded disease, club root.

Though most plants require lime, there are some that are lime haters, the most important of which are, perhaps, rhododendrons, azaleas, ericas, gaultherias, kalmias, pieris, several primulas, and several of the gentians.

Some wild plants will only flourish under acid conditions, and so are taken as indicators of sour soil. These are spurry, sheep's sorrel, corn chrysanthemum, and stinking May-weed.

HOW TO APPLY

Lime should be applied on the surface of the ground, and
it does not need to be dug in. It washes down very quickly,
and there is no need to fear that it will not get to the roots
of plants. Unfortunately, this washing away means that
applications of lime have to be made regularly to keep land
sweet. Never put lime on at the same time as you are
applying farmyard manure or any of the acid artificial manures
we have described. It is, however, quite safe to dig manures
in and then to apply lime on the surface.

TYPES OF LIME

There are three main kinds of lime which can be used, and
these are :

(1) **Chalk or limestone.**—These may be ground and sold as
   ground limestone, and contain about half their weight in
   oxide of lime. Use at from 5–7 ozs. per sq. yd.

(2) **Oxide of lime.**—This is sold as quick lime, lump lime, and
   so on. It can also be ground, and is then sold as ground
   lime. (Please notice the difference between ground limestone and ground lime.) 3 ozs. per sq. yd.

(3) **Hydrate of lime.**—This contains about three-quarters of
   the amount of oxide of lime as quick lime, though it is
   very conveniently handled and does not burn. This is the
   lime that is sold in bags under various proprietary names.
   Use at from 4–6 ozs. per sq. yd.

Quicklime is, then, the most active of the limes. If ground
limestone is used, nearly twice the amount is necessary, and
with hydrated lime, $1\frac{1}{2}$ times the amount.

CHAPTER III

ANNUALS AND BIENNIALS

Most people want to have beauty without much expense.
Annuals and biennials fulfil this desire.

1. Did you know that annuals could be sown in the autumn ?
2. Had you any idea that you could get a beautiful border of annuals, just like a herbaceous border ?
3. Had you thought of an idea of how to recognise annuals from weeds when they are in the seedling stage ?
4. Do you realise the importance of raking the ground down very fine before sowing the seed ?
5. Have you thought that many perennials are grown as annuals ?
6. What about climbing annuals. Do you want them ?

THERE are far too many people who believe that in order to have a beautiful flowering garden it is necessary to spend large sums of money. This is definitely a fallacy, and those who have grown annuals for years will give this statement the lie gladly.

Do not forget that the life of an annual is limited to twelve months, and so you must not expect it to grow up and bloom again the next year.

One of the great advantages of annuals is that they are quite easy to grow and yet give beauty of flower, and even scent, over a long period.

Do not be satisfied with growing the commoner annuals such as Nasturtiums, Virginia Stock, Candytuft, Cornflower, etc., though these can be very beautiful in themselves, but try and grow the annuals that are less known, whose names you will find in the seedsmen's catalogues.

There are two kinds of annuals – the hardy and the half-hardy. The hardy annuals can be sown out of doors either in the autumn or in the spring, while the half-hardy annuals should be raised in frames or under continuous cloches.

Soil.—If you have any choice at all, choose a light soil in preference to a heavy one. Clay soils can be improved by digging in burnt refuse, strawy manure, sand, and organic material like spent hops, or rotted leaves. Some plants, like the annual Larkspur, Sweet Pea, the Canary Creeper, and Convolvulus, will do well in heavy soils.

Preparation of the soil.—In the first place see that the land is well drained and deeply cultivated. Annuals do like a cool root run and hate waterlogging. Dig in a barrowful of well-rotted farm manure – in the case of light soil – or strawy manure – in the case of heavy soil – for every ten square yards. See that this is put in below the top spit. The soil should be dug a long time before the seeds are to be sown, so that it may settle down and become firm. It is a good plan to tread the surface down and then give a light raking over afterwards. This prevents the seed disappearing into deep " crevices."

The preparation of a fine tilth before sowing the seed is extremely important.

If the ground is known to be poor, a good fish manure should be applied to the surface at 3–4 ozs. to the square yard and forked in lightly at least a month before sowing the seed. If it is impossible to do this, see that they are given as a top dressing afterwards, when the plants are several inches high.

Lime may be given in normal cases, especially if the ground is acid. Do not forget that there are some plants that dislike lime.

There is no need to sow deeply or thickly – most of the annual seeds are very small, and so they only need to be just covered. Some people mix sand with seed to be sure of sowing them thinly enough. If you do this, use ten times the amount of sand to seed.

After sowing either rake the bed over, shallowly, or else sift a little soil over by means of a fine-meshed sieve. Pat the ground lightly with the back of a spade.

Sow annuals on a fine, dry day when the soil is in a friable condition.

Sow the seed in rows, a foot apart, in patches or clumps. Be sure, in this case, not to have the clumps too close together.
B*

CHOOSING ANNUALS
with Regard to Shape

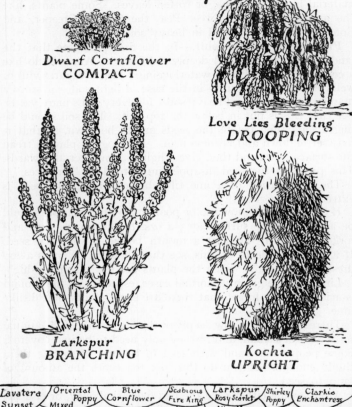

Dwarf Cornflower
COMPACT

Love Lies Bleeding
DROOPING

Larkspur
BRANCHING

Kochia
UPRIGHT

Lavatera Sunset	Oriental Poppy Mixed		Blue Cornflower	Scabious Fire King	Larkspur Rosy Scarlet		Shirley Poppy	Clarkia Enchantress
					Nigella Miss Jekyll		Linum Grandiflorum	Godetia Lavender
Larkspur Blue Spire	Gypsophila Elegans	Lupin Hartwegii Azure Blue	Bartonia Aurea	Coreopsis Tinctoria				
					Viscaria Mixed			Sweet Sultan Yellow
Mignon-ette	Silene	Candytuft Deep Rose	Alyssum	Nemo-phila	Golden Gleam	Eschscholtzia	Candytuft Lavender	Lanaria Mixed
					Phacelia Campanularia			

PLAN OF TYPICAL ANNUAL BORDER

A plant that is going to grow to a foot in height really needs a square foot of space in which to grow to perfection. The clumps will then have to be sown a good distance the one from the other.

It is quite a good plan to scratch, with a pointed stick, rings of varying shapes into which the seeds of the different kinds are going to be sown. I like to arrange " drifts " as shown in the plan on the opposite page.

Whatever the width of the border, the dwarfer plants may be sown, generally speaking, to the front and the taller varieties at the back. Occasionally some of the taller varieties will be allowed to come to the front in order to prevent the monotony of outline.

Time of sowing the seed.—It is usual to sow annuals in the spring, any time from the end of March to the end of April, according to the soil, season, and district. Some people, because they live in the north or in an exposed situation, sow the seed in frames in the spring and either allow them to flower there or transplant the plants they raise as soon as the weather is more open.

If possible autumn sowing is always to be preferred, as the plants grow better and flower much earlier in consequence. In this case the seed is sown any time between mid-August in the North and mid-September in the South. It is not possible to sow all varieties of annuals in this way, as many of them are killed by the frost in the winter, or by the damp. For this reason a list of those that normally live through the winter is given **as** a guide to those who wish to take advantage of it.

Cloches are ideal for covering annuals in the winter – in fact, cloches enable a far greater variety of annuals to be autumn sown.

Thinning.—This is a very important operation indeed, and must be done very early.

Some people can transplant annuals quite successfully, and some varieties are easier to move than others. As the seed is cheap, this is usually unnecessary, but if you have a miss here and there it is well worth while trying, in order to " fill up."

Such annuals as Cornflowers, Calendulas, and Nigella will usually transplant well.

You may have great difficulty in recognising the annuals from weeds, especially in their young stage. It is quite easy to pull out all the plants and just leave the weeds there ! To help you to recognise them, if you are new to the game, why not sow a few seeds in boxes and grow them in a frame, or even indoors, so that they come up a fortnight or so before those outside ? Having seen what they are like in the box, you will be able to thin those in the garden without any trouble.

If thinning can be done when the soil is moist, so much the better. In a dry time, the roots of the little plants you leave in may easily get disturbed and damaged.

Thin early, thin rigorously and thin to a distance of half the height of the plant concerned when fully grown, and you will have good plants that will flower freely.

When the annuals are sown in the autumn, it is very debatable whether they should be thinned before the winter sets in or not. Very often they succeed better if thinning is left until early in the spring.

Staking.—The great mistake most beginners make is that they do not stake early enough. Another fault is staking with straight, soldier-like sticks such as bamboos. Bamboos are all very well for plants with stiff, strong stems, but for the feathery kinds, and those that branch out, twiggy sticks like pea-sticks are much preferable. If you put these in very early on, the plants will grow among the twiggy bits and get all the support they need. Further than this, the twigs are quickly hidden, and the beauty of the plant is not marred by an " unbeautiful " support. Such things as Sunflowers can have a long straight bamboo if you like, and the climbers, like the Sweet Pea and the Tropaeolum, can clamber up quite tall sticks.

Watering.—Do not water until the plants are well through. Never give light sprinklings, but soak the ground well either in the evening or early in the morning. Give a mulching of lawn-mowings, rotted leaves, or old hot-beds directly the hot weather starts, and this will save both hoeing and watering.

General cultivation.—Hoe the ground continuously, and

so keep it free from weeds. A certain amount of hand weeding may have to be done also. After all operations such as staking, cutting off the dead blooms, etc., the ground should be hoed or raked in order to remove the footmarks and provide a dust mulch. Never allow the plants to go to seed, and so cut off the dead flowers directly they appear. It is not a bad plan after one batch of flowering to cut the plant back, and so let it throw out new shoots and flower again. People often complain to me that the annuals seem to be coming to the best just as they are going on a summer holiday, and when they come back they seem all dead and useless. The tip here, is clip the plants back a little to prevent seeding, the day you go away, so that when you come back the annual border is a blaze of colour again.

A BORDER OF HARDY ANNUALS

The following is a short list of some of the more useful and beautiful annuals:

Name	Height	Colour
Agrostemma	2½ ft.	*Crimson*
Alyssum (sweet)	½ ft.	*Lilac and white*
Asperula	1½ ft.	*Blue*
Bartonia aurea	1 ft.	*Bright yellow*
Calendula	2 ft.	*Orange, yellow, apricot golden*
Calliopsis	1½ ft.	*Yellow*
Candytuft	1 ft.	*Crimson, lilac, rose, white*
Centranthus	2 ft.	*Red*
Chrysanthemum (annual)	1 to 3 ft.	*Yellow, white, crimson, bronze, etc.*
Clarkia (single and double)	2 ft.	*Red, rose, pink, white*
Collinsia	1 ft.	*Lilac, white, rose*
Cornflower	1 to 3 ft.	*Blue, purple, rose, white*
Erysimum	1½ ft.	*Yellow and orange*
Eschscholtzia (single and double)	1 ft.	*White, lemon, crimson, orange*
Gamolepis Tagetes	½ ft.	*Yellow*
Godetia	¾ to 2 ft.	*Crimson, pink, white*
Helichrysum (everlasting)	2½ ft.	*Orange, yellow, pink, violet, white*
Jacobaea	1 ft.	*Crimson, purple, white*
Larkspur	3 ft.	*Red, white, rose, blue, mauve*
Lavatera	4 ft.	*Pink, white, red*
Leptosiphon	½ ft.	*Purple and lavender*
Limnanthes	½ ft.	*Yellow and white*

Name	Height	Colour
Linaria	1 ft.	*Purple, pink, white, yellow*
Linum grandiflorum	1 ft.	*Blue, red*
Love-lies-bleeding	2 ft.	*Red*
Lupins (annual)	2 ft.	*Blue, white, scarlet, yellow, pink*
Mignonette	1 ft.	*Lilac, white and red*
Nasturtium (single and double)	dwarf & climbing	*Yellow, red, rose*
Nigella	1½ ft.	*Blue, white*
Oenothera Drummondii	1 ft.	*Yellow*
Phacelia	1 ft.	*Blue*
Poppies (all kinds)	2 ft.	*All colours*
Portulaca (single and double)	½ ft.	*White, crimson, scarlet, primrose*
Saponaria	½ to 2 ft.	*Pink, white*
Scabious	2½ ft.	*Mauve, yellow, white, red*
Silene	¾ to 1½ ft.	*Rose, pink*
Statice (everlasting)	1½ ft.	*Blue and rose*
Sweet Sultan	1½ ft.	*Yellow, white, mauve*
Ursinia	¾ ft.	*Orange*
Viscaria	1 ft.	*Crimson, pink*
Xeranthemum (everlasting)	2 ft.	*Purple, white, yellow*

Climbers.—Convolvulus ; Tropaeolum Canariense (the Canary Creeper) ; Nasturtium, and Sweet Peas.

HALF-HARDY ANNUALS

In addition to the large-group described above, there are a very large number of half-hardy annuals which, with a little care and attention, will make a bold show in the summer. The only trouble about them is that they have to be raised under glass either in a greenhouse or in a frame.

The following is a list of the more attractive half-hardy annuals :

Name	Height	Colour
Acroclinium (everlasting)		*White and rose*
Ageratum	1 ft.	*Blue, white*
Antirrhinum	1 to 2½ ft.	*White, yellow, pink, red*
Arctotis	1 ft.	*Yellow, mauve, white*
Balsam	1½ ft.	*Rose, scarlet, white*
Brachycome	1½ ft.	*White, mauve, purple, blue*
Celosia	2 ft.	*Crimson, yellow, rose*
China Asters	1½ to 2 ft.	*Blue, rose, scarlet, pink, white*
Cosmos	2½ ft.	*Pink, white, crimson, mauve*
Dimorphotheca	1 ft.	*Yellow, orange white*

Name	Height	Colour
Gilia	1 ft.	*White, violet and scarlet*
Marigold (French and African)	1 to 2 ft.	*Lemon, orange, striped*
Martynia	2 ft.	*Mauve*
Nemesia	1¼ ft.	*Blue, carmine, orange, pink, and white*
Nicotiana (scented)	2½ ft.	*Red, white*
Perilla	1½ ft.	*Beautiful bronze foliage*
Petunia (single & double)	1 to 2 ft.	*Various*
Phlox Drummondii	1¼ ft.	*Scarlet, white, rose, violet, yellow, many with a white open eye*
Rhodanthe	1 ft.	*Pink and white*
Salpiglossis	2 ft.	*Various*
Schizanthus (single and double)	2 ft.	*White, pink, red and yellow, variegated*
Statice (everlasting)	2 ft.	*Mauve, white, yellow*
Ten-Weeks-Stocks	2 ft.	*All colours*
Venidium Fastuosum	3 ft.	*Brilliant orange, dark centre*
Verbena	1 ft.	*Rose, blue, scarlet, etc.*
Zinnias	3 ft.	*Crimson, purple, scarlet, sulphur, violet, white, very large*

Beginners are often worried as to which annuals to use for varying purposes. It may be useful, therefore, to give one or two more tables, grouping the plants together under different headings.

Hardy Edging Plants.—Alyssum ; Asperula ; Dwarf Gilias ; Dwarf Candytuft ; Kaulfussia ; Leptosiphon ; Dwarf Nasturtium ; Nemophila ; Phacelia ; Dwarf Saponaria ; Silene ; Ursinia ; and Virginia Stock.

Varieties that can be autumn sown.—Cornflower ; Candytuft ; Calendula ; Nigella ; Larkspur ; (others, like annual Chrysanthemum, Linaria, Sweet Sultan, may live through the winter).

Annuals suitable for cutting.—Cornflower ; Candytuft ; Calendula ; Nigella ; Larkspur ; Clarkia ; Godetia ; Gypsophila ; Linaria ; Saponaria ; Sweet Sultan.

Annuals for autumn blooming.—It is often necessary to try to get plenty of bloom in the autumn, and the following annuals, if sown at the beginning of July, will flower freely at the late end of the year : Alyssum ; Cornflower ; Candytuft ;

Clarkia ; Godetia ; Gypsophila ; Limnanthes ; Nasturtium Sweet Sultan ; Virginia Stock.

Half-hardy annuals for edging.—Ageratum ; Arctotis ; French Marigold ; Nemesia ; Phlox Drummondii ; Portulaca.

BIENNIALS

The true description of a biennial plant is one which completes its life's cycle, i.e., grows, flowers, and seeds all within the second year from germination. When they are sown one year, they bloom, ripen their seed, and die the following year.

A large number of other plants, including the Canterbury Bells, Hollyhocks, Gaillardias, Sweet Williams, and Wall-flowers, are really perennials, but are grown as biennials as they are best treated as such.

Many amateurs have difficulty in recognising the difference between annuals and biennials, and even confuse them with perennials. Presumably the reason is that many of the annuals seed themselves, and so come up again of their own accord the next year, while some of the perennials are apt to die at the end of the first year, owing to bad treatment.

Sowing the seed.—The seed of the various biennials is sown during the months of May, June, and July. The time of sowing differs according to the type of soil, season, and locality. It is usually unnecessary to sow under glass ; shallow drills are drawn out a foot apart on friable soil, and the seed is sown in these. Directly the plants are 3 inches high they are planted out into further prepared drills, or put into permanent beds or borders.

They will transplant quite easily, especially after a showery period.

Preparation of the ground.—The ground where biennials are to grow should be dug to a good depth and be well drained. Dig in a heavy dressing of farmyard manure deeply, and give a good mixture of artificials the following spring. Do not give the young plants too much nitrogen or else they will find it difficult to live through a hard winter.

Some biennials, like the Brompton and East Lothian Stocks have to be covered with a cold frame during the winter.

As a general rule the earlier sowing outside is preferable to the later sowing.

LIST OF BIENNIALS

Name	Height	Colour
Brompton Stocks	2 ft.	*Violet, yellow, rose, pink, mauve, white*
Canterbury Bells (single and double)	2½ ft.	*Blue, mauve, rose, white*
Foxglove	2–6 ft.	*Mauve, white*
Gilia	1 ft.	*Scarlet*
Hollyhock	6–8 ft.	*Red, pink, yellow, flame*
Honesty	2 ft.	*Purple and white*
Penstemon	2½ ft.	*Red, pink, purple*
Poppy, Sunbeam and Iceland (single and double)	1 ft.	*Orange, yellow, white*
Sweet Rocket	2 ft.	*Purple and white*
Sweet William	2 ft.	*Various*
Wallflower	1½ ft.	*Brown, yellow, red, orange, white, mixed*

Antirrhinums and Pentstemons are often treated as biennials as well.

CHAPTER IV

PERENNIALS, HERBACEOUS BORDERS AND BULBS

There is something very permanent and pleasing about a herbaceous border. Cut flowers too are useful for the house. Shall we think about :—

1. The way that we can propagate our herbaceous plants at home ?
2. Which plants grow well in shade ?
3. How to keep slugs away from Delphiniums ?
4. The varieties that can be grown, when they flower and where they ought to be planted ?
5. How are we going to plan our herbaceous border ?
6. What bulbs we are going to grow ?

OF all the plants that are grown in the garden the perennial is usually the most popular. This term, of course, strictly speaking, refers not only to herbaceous perennials, but also to trees and shrubs. This chapter will deal with herbaceous perennials only, and, because they live more than two years and grow up every year without much trouble, they are indeed the gardener's friend.

Herbaceous perennials can be bought to suit all tastes. They give flowers of all colours, and can be arranged in gardens to keep up the supply of bloom from, say, April until October. Many of the perennials will stand dry periods far better than annuals, and on the whole are stronger and " firmer " than these.

Like the annuals they can be grown purely for cutting or can be planted in a border (usually known as a Herbaceous Border), and they are here soon the most beautiful part of the garden.

It will be necessary, in the first place, to discuss the growing of the perennial, and then to explain how it can be used in the border.

PROPAGATION

Perennials can be propagated in various ways. Firstly by sowing seeds, secondly by root cuttings, thirdly by division and occasionally by stem cuttings.

Seed sowing.—The seeds are sown either in the open, in a sheltered place, or in a cold frame about the beginning of June. It is an advantage if the soil is on the light side, so if you have heavy land try to dig in some sand to lighten it.

Shallow drills, a quarter of an inch deep, are taken out six inches apart, the seed being sown thinly in these. Should the weather be dry and the soil also, it is a good plan to water the bed well the afternoon before sowing. Try to raise sturdy seedlings by sowing sufficiently thinly to obviate thinning. Having sown the seed, rake the ground over lightly, making certain to rake in the same direction as the drill so as to prevent there being any chance of the seed being distributed in the rows. It may be necessary, after sowing, to water through a fine rose.

If you have to sow in a frame, keep this closed down until the young plants are through, when you may ventilate. Continue the ventilation whenever the weather is warm enough, but, should it be too sunny, shade the frames by putting whitewash on the glass, or just by covering over with sacking or Archangel mats.

There is always a danger when sowing the seed outside that the young seedlings may be damaged by birds and insects. You can prevent the former by putting in little bamboos at definite intervals and stretching black cotton in a zigzag fashion in between them. In the latter case, spray regularly with nicotine and soft soap or else with Derris (*see* Chapter XV).

Directly the plants are 3 inches high – and this may be within a month or 6 weeks from the time of seed sowing – they can be planted into their permanent position. This is not, however, usual, and they are generally, therefore, transplanted into other beds 9 inches or so square, in order that they may grow on until big enough to use in the herbaceous border. The new bed should be well dug, and

CUTTINGS of MICHAELMAS DAISY

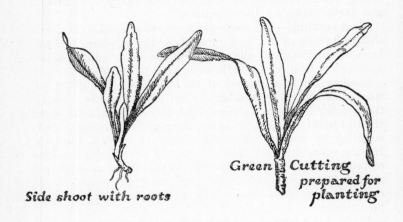

Side shoot with roots

Green Cutting
prepared for
planting

ROOT CUTTINGS

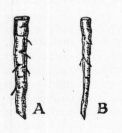

A

B

A. A good root cutting
prepared for planting

B. Bad cutting,
Root is too thin

Cuttings
in
Position

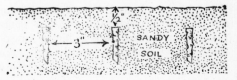

½"
3"
SANDY
SOIL

farmyard manure incorporated between the top and bottom spit.

Sandy soils should have a good fish manure added at the rate of 4 ozs. to the square yard, and many people use bone meal, at the rate of 2 ozs. per square yard, as well. These are forked in some time before the plants are put out.

Do not make the mistake of planting carelessly. Spread the roots out evenly, give them plenty of room, and see that they are firmed. It is dangerous to make a hole with a dibber, as too often an air-pocket is left underneath the plant after it has been planted. When the plants are all in, give the bed a good soaking with the watering-can. This bed will need regular hoeing throughout the growing season so that the plants can have every chance.

The transplanted perennials will thus be ready to put out into their permanent positions in the autumn of the second season.

Root cuttings.—There are many varieties of perennials that do not come true from seed. For this reason it is necessary to adopt other methods, and a favourite one is the root cutting. A much larger number of plants can be raised from the original, as the roots are cut up into quite small portions, each one of which will make a plant. Unfortunately it is only the plants with fleshy roots that respond to such treatment. The most common example being the Anchusa, though others, like the Delphinium and Lupin, are often propagated in this way.

The plants are dug up immediately after flowering – and dug up very carefully. The roots are then cut into portions 3 inches long, being sure to make a square cut at the top and a cut slanting wise at the bottom end. This enables you to know for certain, after the cuttings have been prepared, which way up they ought to be planted. It is no good planting roots upside down !

The root cuttings are then placed in sandy soil – some people use coarse silver sand alone – each cutting being 2 or 3 inches away from its neighbour, and, if in rows, these may be from 4 to 6 inches apart. Place them in position so that they are covered with not more than $\frac{1}{2}$ inch of sand.

Root cuttings may be inserted in pots, and, if so, these can be placed in a frame or in a cool greenhouse. More often the cuttings are placed direct into the sandy compost placed in a cool frame.

The young plants that result can be planted out the following spring.

Division.—Perhaps the easiest method of all is to divide the plants, when they are large enough, into two or more portions. Those with fibrous roots like the Pyrethrum are propagated most easily in this way. It is possible to lay the plant on the ground and to chop it up into suitable sizes by means of a sharp spade. A better method is to insert two forks back to back into the centre of the clump, and then, by forcing the handles apart, gently, but firmly, cause it to break into two pieces.

In the case of very large clumps that have been growing for several years the outer portions (being younger than the centre part) should be retained and the central (or original plant) thrown away.

This is done in the autumn, the clumps are lifted with as much soil attached to the roots as possible, and, after division, the selected portions should be replanted immediately. Some plants like *Chrysanthemum maximum*, should be divided in this way every two or three years, and Michaelmas Daisies every year. Other plants, like Lupins, are not easy to propagate in this way, and, in fact, are better left in their permanent positions for a much longer period of years. There are plants also, like Paeonies and the Japanese anemones, which hate disturbance, and are best left alone for as long as possible.

Cuttings.—There is yet another method of propagation which should be mentioned, and that it the taking of cuttings. Young side shoots, often with roots already attached to them, may be severed from their parent plants in the autumn, and transplanted into a specially prepared bed, or green cuttings of such perennials as Scabious may be severed from the plants early in the summer and planted out to " strike " in a sandy compost in a frame.

TIPS FOR PERENNIALS

Some plants will need special treatment – for instance, the Scabious likes a good covering of lime put over it before the winter sets in. Other plants, like the Delphinium, often have fine coal ashes put round them towards the end of the autumn, in order to keep the stems from rotting off and the slugs at bay.

Never allow the flowers to seed, and the cutting off of the flower heads regularly, in the case of varieties that flower early, often means a second crop of bloom.

Stake the taller varieties early enough if you want to ensure straight stems. This staking may be simply the use of a bamboo or two, placed firmly in the centre or at the sides of the clump so as to keep the stems upright. Pea-sticks are often used, especially in the herbaceous border, as advised for annuals.

The use of strawy manure, lawn-mowings or vegetable compost as a mulch is recommended, especially for perennials like Helenium, Phlox, and Trollius, which show the effects of dry periods very quickly.

When planted out for cut-flower purposes, all that need be done is to see, in the first place, that the plants have plenty of room for development ; this means that the rows may have to be 18 inches apart, and the plants a foot apart in the rows. Continuous hoeing will have to be carried out throughout the summer, to keep down weeds and to preserve a mulch.

TYPES AND VARIETIES

There are hundreds of herbaceous plants, and I can only attempt to give quite a brief list. In order to make it easier for readers to plan out borders, I have tried to classify those I have chosen in their various colours.

ORANGE AND YELLOWS

Name	Soil	Height	Propagation	Time of Flowering	Position
Alstroemeria	Light	2 ft.	*Seeds and division*	July	Sunny
Bocconia	Moist	5 ,,	*Division*	July	,,
Centaurea	Average	3–5 ,,	,,	June–July	,,
Coreopsis	,,	2 ,,	*Seeds*	July–Aug.	,,
Doronicum	,,	2 ,,	*Division*	April	Sunny or shady
Gaillardia	,,	3 ,,	*Seeds and division*	Aug.	Sunny
Geum	,,	2 ,,	*Seeds*	May–Aug.	,,
Helenium	,,	4 ,,	*Division*	July, Aug., Sept.	Sunny or semi-shade
Helianthemum	,,	¾ ,,	*Seeds and cuttings*	June	,,
Helianthus	Light	6 ,,	*Seeds and division*	Sept.–Oct.	,,
Oenothera	Average	2 ,,	*Division*	June–July	Sunny
Rudbeckia	,,	4–6 ,,	,,	August	Sunny or shady
Solidago	,,	4 ,,	,,	Sept.	Semi-shady
Thermopsis	,,	2 ,,	,,	June–July	Sunny
Verbascum	,,	5 ,,	,,	June–July	,,

BLUES

Name	Soil	Height	Propagation	Time of Flowering	Position
Aconitum	Average	4 ft.	*Division*	July–Aug.	Sunny or shady
Anchusa	,,	4 ,,	,, *and root cuttings*	June–July	Sunny
Delphinium	,,	5 ,,	*Seeds and division*	June–July	,,
Echinops	,,	3 ,,	*Division*	Aug.	,,
Erigeron	,,	1½ ,,	,,	June–Aug.	,,
Eryngium	,,	3 ,,	,,	July–Aug.	,,
Iris	,,	1½ ,,	*Division*	June–Aug.	Semi-shade
Mertensia	,,	1 ,,	,,	June–Aug.	Sunny
Nepeta	,,	1 ,,	*Division and cuttings*	June–July	,,
Salvia azurea	,,	2 ,,	*Division*	July–Aug.	,,

BLUES—continued

Name	Soil	Height	Propagation	Time of Flowering	Position
Scabious	Average	2½ ft.	Division	July–Aug.	Sunny
Veronica	,,	1 ,,	,,	April–May	,,
Vinca	,,	1 ,,	,,	May	Shady

RED

Name	Soil	Height	Propagation	Time of Flowering	Position
Dielytra	Average	2 ft.	Division	May–June	Semi-shady
Geum	,,	2 ,,	Seeds	May–Aug.	,,
Lychnis chalcedonia	,,	2 ,,	Seeds and division	July–Aug.	Sunny
Monarda	,,	2 ,,	Division	June and July	,,
Poppy oriental	,,	3 ,,	Seeds and division	May–June	,,

WHITE

Name	Soil	Height	Propagation	Time of Flowering	Position
Achillea white pearl	Average	2 ft.	Division	June–July	Sunny or semi-shady
Anemone Japonica	,,	4 ,,	,,	September	Shady
Gypsophila	,,	3 ,,	Seeds, grafting	July	Sunny
Helleborus	Heavy, rich	1½ ,,	Division	December	Semi-shady
Lilies	Average	3 ,,	Bulbs	June	Sunny or semi-shady
Phlox	Moist	4 ,,	Division and cuttings	Aug.–Sept.	Semi-shady

MAUVE AND PURPLE

Name	Soil	Height	Propagation	Time of Flowering	Position
Betonica	Average	2 ft.	Division	July–Aug.	Sunny
Galega	,,	4 ,,	,,	May–June	Sunny or shady
Stachys	,,	1 ,,	,,	May–June	,,
Campanula	,,	2½ ,,	,,	May–June	,,
Centaurea dealbata	,,	3 ,,	,,	June–Aug.	,,

PINK

Name	Soil	Height	Propagation	Time of Flowering	Position
Armeria	Light	½ ft.	*Division*	June	Sunny
Phlox	Moist	4 ,,	*Cuttings*	Aug.–Sept.	Semi-shady
Potentilla	Average	2 ,,	*Division*	June–July	Sunny
Sedum spectabile	Moist	1 ,,	,,	Aug.–Sept.	Semi-shady
Sidalcea	Average	1 ,,	,,	July–Aug.	Sunny

MIXED COLOURS

Name	Soil	Height	Propagation	Time of Flowering	Position
Aquilegia	Average	3 ft.	*Seeds and division*	April to July	Semi-shady
Campanula	,,	2–4 ,,	,, ,,	June–July	Sunny or semi-shady
Foxglove	,,	4 ,,	*Seeds*	June–July	Semi-shady
Hollyhocks	,,	10 ,,	,,	July–Sept.	Sunny
Lupins	,,	3 ,,	*Seeds and division*	May–June	,,
Paeony	Heavy, rich	2 ,,	*Division*	May–June	Sunny or semi-shady
Phlox	,, ,,	2 ,,	*Division and cuttings*	July–Aug.	,, ,,
Pyrethrum	Average	2 ,,	*Division*	May–June	Sunny
Thalictrum	,,	2–3 ,,	,,	June–July	,,

THE HERBACEOUS BORDER.

We have already discussed the way the ground should be prepared and the types of plants we can grow, and how they should be looked after, and so all we have to do now is to discuss methods of planting and good colour schemes.

In the first place aim at having the border looking as natural as possible, and so do not plant in rows. Try to have five or six plants in a group if possible, and in a small border three plants will do. These groups will be irregular in shape, some of them actually merging into the taller groups behind. I like to think of them as drifts – some of the groups drifting into, and even past, another set of plants of a different type planted behind them. It you have these drifts irregularly shaped they can sweep round about each other and prevent that dreadful artificial look which most of us abhor.

Do not make it a rule to have all the largest plants at the back and all the dwarf ones in the front. Keep to this idea as a general rule, but occasionally bring taller plants to the front so as to break up the " view " and prevent monotony. As a matter of fact this allows for a new " view-point " as you walk along the border.

It is a good plan to see that the earlier flowering plants are not placed in the front of the border, otherwise directly they have finished blooming this part is apt to look bare and unsightly. If, on the other hand, these plants are towards the centre of the border, it is possible to plant groups that bloom in September in front of them, so that they hide the fading stems of their earlier blossoming brethren. For this reason do not plant all the early blossoming varieties at one end of the border and those that flower later on at the other end. Try and distribute the blossoming period over the border as a whole, so as to have a bright effect all through it during the spring, summer, and early autumn.

BORDERS OF ONE COLOUR

Some people are particularly fond of one particular colour, and so like to have a blue border, a yellow border, and so on.

This is quite possible, and, if you are really keen on this, you can find out a larger number of perennials in the particular colours you require than those given in my simple list.

I know of a famous garden near Bournemouth that has nothing but white flowers in it. You can extend this idea, if you like, into having borders of one or two colours only. For instance, a blue and grey border is rather fascinating, and, if you like bright colours, why not try a border of yellows, oranges, and reds alone ?

THE PERIOD BORDER

If you have a big garden, you may want to plant out one or two borders to flower during particular months of the year. It is not usual to aim at much more than having a spring border and an autumn border. The latter will consist entirely of various varieties of Michaelmas Daisies, with perhaps some Chrysanthemums. It is perhaps rather nice to have a border of this kind to which you can go for inspiration during the duller months of the year. If, for instance, you are always away on holiday for the whole of August, you may want to miss out the plants that bloom during that month.

ASPECT BORDERS

Some parts of your garden will be sunny, others will perforce be shady. By using the plants that like shade you can have quite a pleasing border in such a position. Even in the general border there may be the sunnier and shadier portions, and care should be taken to plant these up with varieties that thrive best under such conditions.

NARROW BORDERS

In a small garden it is often impossible to have borders 6 feet or even 12 feet wide that are normally recommended for herbaceous borders. In this case it is quite convenient to use plants that are not too tall. There are plenty of attractive flowering plants of this character, both feathery and solid. I am thinking of such plants as Heuchera, *Salvia virgata nemorosa*, Bergamot, Blue Flax, Flag Iris, Montbretia, Phlox, the perennial Cornflower (Centaurea) and so on. There are other plants that do quite well as edgings. The Pinks, Lambs' Tongues (Stachys), Thrift (Armeria), various Veronicas, Violas, and even our old friend London Pride.

THE GENERAL HERBACEOUS BORDER

In this border you will plan out such a scheme as I have tried to demonstrate in the diagram so that you have all colours, all shapes, all sizes, grouped together in a fascinating manner. You will arrange that the border looks bright from, say, May until October by using plants of varying heights, blossoming at different times.

Take some care with regard to the colour ; it is not a good plan to have puce pinks fighting with the reds. Other than this, most colours blend fairly well with one another in the open. There is far more danger of hideous combinations in ladies' clothing than there is in the border in the garden.

If in your drifts you can arrange that one colour, say the blue, drifts into a deeper coloured blue and finally merges into another group of plants, taller and of another type of blue, so much the better. These drifts of colour planned in this way are very effective. You want great splashes of colour and not little " spots " here and there.

There are some plants that have more scent than others, and it is quite a good plan to include these. Scent in a garden is practically a necessity, and the Paeony, Monarda, and lemon-scented Verbenas are typical examples of those which add a pleasant perfume to their surroundings.

Backgrounds.—It is not a bad plan to have some background to one's herbaceous border. Most flowering plants look well against green, and, actually, a border planted with a lawn as a background is quite a good idea. Another plan is to have a background of an evergreen hedge – the Yew is often used for this purpose, but Lonicera or Cupressus will do as well. A fence of cordon fruit trees can be used, especially if space is restricted, while flowering shrubs and Rose pillars are quite allowable also.

These should not be planted to give shade to the border,

and so they will be normally on the north side.   Taller
specimens that are quite suitable are flowering Crabs,
Laburnums, and Prunus, while small trees with pleasant
foliage tints are, for example, the Maple, Berberis, Dogwood,
and Euonymus. Of course, there is no need for these to be
in a straight line.

Supports – staking.—In the case of the bushy types of
flowers, pea-sticks should be used. These should be placed in
and around each clump of flowers to allow the stems and foliage
to grow up among them ; thus the supports are hidden and yet
provide exactly what is needed, further, the natural shape
of the plant is ensured. Staking must begin as early as May.
Individual bamboos or stakes may be used for the flower stems
of the taller varieties such as delphiniums, and these should
reach nearly but not quite to the blossoms. Ties should be
made in two or more places to keep the stems at the right angle.

Management.—In the spring, as the young shoots start to
grow, care has to be taken to protect them from ravenous
insects like slugs. Use the bran and Paris-green bait recommended, and hoe the land regularly.

As the warmer weather starts, mulching with strawy manure
or lawn-mowings will be carried out. The lighter soils will
need this perhaps more than the heavier soils, and some plants
more than others.

As the plants grow they will need to be staked, and we
have already discussed this earlier on.

Continue the hoeing throughout the summer, and, should
it be difficult to get in between some groups, a small hand
fork can be used here.

Re-mulching may be necessary from time to time, and in
very dry weather the border can be flooded one evening a
week. Even a nice overhead syringing is useful to freshen up
a border, but this should be done in the evening hours also.

Go over the border regularly and remove the dying and
dead bloom. This will not only improve the look of the border,
but will enable the plants to flower more freely.

As they die down the stems of the plants should be cut with
a sharp knife to within 3 inches of the ground, and when

autumn comes the dead leaves and rubbish may be cleared away so that it assumes a neat appearance. Should this cutting down of the stems mean it is difficult to see where the clumps are, a little bamboo stick, or sticks, may be pushed into the ground to mark the positions.

After frosty periods it may be necessary to go over the border and firm some plants in. Aquilegias have a nasty habit of rising out of the ground, as do Geums.

BULBS IN THE BORDER

It is possible to get very beautiful spring shows by the use of bulbs. With these you not only have a very large choice of variety, but of colour as well. You have the opportunity, also of keeping up the flowering period for a very long time. There is no reason at all, for instance, why your early show of flowers should not commence towards the beginning of March and continue right on until the beginning of June. (*See* the author's book *A.B.C. of Bulbs and Corms.*)

It is very wasteful to consider bulbs as annuals. Too many amateurs plant them, allow them to flower, and then dig the bulbs up and throw them away. In many soils bulbs will increase, and if you manure the ground well before you plant them, and are careful to remove just the flower head before it goes to seed, the bulb will be grateful, and will build up a little bulblet at the side of it. To get this increase of bulbs the main thing is to allow the plant to grow naturally. Make certain that all the food in the leaves is passed back to the bulb – you can do this by not cutting off the foliage until it has turned brown and died away. The little bulblets can be severed from their parents and planted out in another position, and they themselves, in a year or two's time, will grow into full-sized bulbs and flower well.

There is no need to leave the bulbs in the place in which they were flowering right until the time of dying down if you wish to put other plants in their place. A good plan is to dig them up and heel them in in an odd part of the garden, and allow the leaves to pass back their food undisturbed.

Again, many bulbs, like Daffodils, are quite happy when

planted out in grass, and will go on growing there for years undisturbed. They will increase all the time, and for quite a small capital you can have a 100 per cent interest of beauty for many years.

DAFFODILS

This is perhaps one of the largest group of bulbous flowers, classified as Narcissi.

Those who are interested in this family should consult The Royal Horticultural Society's *Classified List of Daffodils*.

Planting.—Most types of Daffodils like a warm, well-drained soil, with the exception, perhaps, of the Poeticus group, which like a heavier soil. The planting should be done early in the autumn, the larger bulbs being planted deeper than the smaller ones. It is quite a good plan to plant bu bs at a depth equal to 3 times their own width.

Varieties

There are a very large number of varieties in each main section, but the following, which I have chosen at random, do very well in an ordinary garden :

Barrii conspicuous ; Emperor ; Empress ; Horace ; Sir Watkin ; White Lady ; Madame de Graaff ; Lady Margaret Boscowan ; Seagull ; King Alfred ; Beersheba ; St. Ives ; Adjutant ; Bonfire ; Horace Cheerfulness.

TULIPS

As in Daffodils, there are various divisions of Tulip varieties. For instance, there are the single earlies, the cottage Tulips, the Darwins for later on, and so on. In each division there are a very large number of varieties. For those who are keen on Tulips, the Royal Horticultural Society have a *Tulip Nomenclature Report*.

Planting.—Tulips do not, like Daffodils, do well in grass, but they can, on the other hand, be left in cultivated borders of the garden, undisturbed, for a number of years. On the whole, they do best on the heavier soils, and they seem to like lime. Many amateurs make the mistake of not planting Tulip bulbs deep enough, and if it is desired to be free from

Taking a cutting of a delphinium; this is a very effective
method of propagating a good variety.

A lovely bed of gentians in the Hocker Edge Gardens. The flowers are sky or royal blue.

Tulip Fire, a dreaded disease, planting at 9 inches deep is advisable.

Planting should be done early in the autumn, and the final lifting up and drying of the bulbs, if this is desired, should not be done until the middle of July. To get the best results from Tulips, the ground should be well dug and manured.

Varieties

Again it is impossible to give lists of varieties and descriptions, but I will mention a few, again taken at random, that I know will do well under ordinary garden conditions.

SINGLE EARLIES :
   Couleur Cardinal ; Cottage Maid ; Keizer's Kroon ; Prince of Austria ; Vermilion Brilliant.

COTTAGE TULIPS :
   Ellen Willmott ; Inglescombe Yellow Inglescombe Pink John Ruskin ; Orange King ; Rose Beauty.

DARWIN TULIPS :
   City of Haarlem ; Clara Butt ; Farncombe Sanders ; Pride of Haarlem ; Princess Elizabeth ; Bartigon ; William Copeland.

HYACINTHS

Hyacinths are divided up into various sections, the principle of these being the Roman and Dutch. They are grown a lot in pots for indoors, and they are perhaps the most suitable of all bulbs for this purpose. They can, however, be grown out of doors, and whole beds of these, of different colours, are very fascinating indeed. They are usually planted in a hole made 2–3 inches deep and 6 inches apart. On the whole they like a light soil rather than a heavy one.

The following are quite good varieties for out of doors :

BLUE :
   King of the Blues and Grand Maitre.

PINKS AND REDS :
   Gertrude ; Lady Derby ; Marconi.

WHITES :
   L'Innocence.

YELLOW :
   Prince Henry.
   C

CROCUS

These are much used as edgings for borders or for planting in grass, where they flower and look so natural. They are useful in a rockery, too, for spring colour. They should be planted 2 inches deep, and at least 2 inches apart.

Some good varieties are Golden Yellow, *Purpurea Grandiflora*, a deep purple, and Queen of the Blues, Kathleen Parlow, pure white, Amethyst, soft lavender, La Majesteuse, white striped lilac.

CHIONODOXA

This charming little flower, known as the Glory of the Snow, should be planted in clumps of at least 6 or more, allowing each bulb $1\frac{1}{2}$ inches each way. Plant them 2 inches deep, and they will flower freely and give a regular sheaf of blue very early in the Spring.

Two good varieties are Gigantea and Sardensis, which is dwarfer, the flower having a small white eye.

IRIS

I have heard Iris described as " the poor man's Orchid " and certainly they are quite cheap to grow. They are usually planted 3 inches deep, and about 5 inches apart. They are beautiful as border flowers, and as cut flowers they can hardly be surpassed. The Dutch Iris flower towards the end of May, the Spanish Iris towards the beginning of June, and the English Iris late in June.

The following are the varieties I would recommend you to grow :

DUTCH IRIS :
   Imperator (27 in.), large, brilliant blue.
   Wedgwood (24 in.), pale blue.
   The First (22 in.), dark, purply blue.
   Van Everdingen (24 in.), cream and canary yellow.

SPANISH IRIS :
   Cajanus (26 in.), large flower, bright canary yellow.
   Queen Wilhelmina (20 in.), pure white.
   King of Blues (20 in.), rich deep blue.
   Reconnaissance (18 in.), bronzy maroon.

ENGLISH IRIS :
Prince of Wales (18 in.), dark blue.
Mont Blanc (22 in.), pure white.
Blue Celeste (22 in.), sky blue.

MUSCARI (*GRAPE HYACINTHS*)

These only grow about 8 inches high, and can be grown in the border, rockery, or in grass. They prefer slight shade. It is usual to plant them in clumps 3 inches deep. The best varieties are Heavenly Blue and Plumosum.

SCILLA

These are planted in a similar way to Muscari and are very early flowering. Plant most varieties 2 inches deep, but Campanulata and nutans 3 inches deep. These two latter do well under trees and in borders. The ordinary Scilla is siberica, and this has bright blue flowers which come out at the same time as the Snowdrop.

WINTER ACONITES

These flower in February, and grow well in shady and moist situations. They look well under trees, and do well in grassland. The variety Cilicica grows 4 inches high, and the variety Hyemalis 3 inches high. Both bear yellow flowers.

SNOWDROPS

These are charming when planted in grass, or even in a border. Plant the bulbs 3 inches deep. The Giant Single Snowdrop grows 9 inches to 12 inches high ; its real name being *Galanthus Elwesii*. The family name for snowdrop is *Galanthus*, and *G. nivalis* is the ordinary variety which grows 6 inches high. You can either have a double or a single type.

CHAPTER V

SHRUBS

Most gardens will have some shrubs and the following points are dealt with :—

1. The planning of the shrubbery.
2. How the border should be prepared and manured.
3. Pruning is always a difficult problem, but it is made more simple here.
4. Lists are given of the best shrubs for varying needs.
5. It is necessary to remove the seed pods directly the flowers have faded.

IT is very difficult in a short chapter to say much about shrubs, but it should be possible to persuade readers that there are large numbers of beautiful flowering shrubs to be had, and that these should be used whenever possible in place of the commonplace, cheap evergreens. Shrubs have their uses, as they can be grown for different purposes. For instance, they make a good background for a herbaceous border ; they provide shelter, and they give large splashes of colour to a height often unattainable by the herbaceous plant.

There is such a large selection of hardy flowering shrubs to-day that there should be enough varieties to suit practically all soils and gardens.

Planning the Shrub Border.—Plant in groups or drifts much in the same way as suggested in the chapter on herbaceous borders. Even in narrow borders avoid having only two rows of shrubs by planting some of the smaller growing varieties in groups of 3 or 4, with an occasional large or tall shrub to give height and variation. Shrub borders always look sparsely planted if the back shrub is placed directly behind the one in the front row.

Try not to plant close together shrubs bearing flowers of colours which obviously clash. Try to arrange that the period of blooming is spread right the way through the border – for instance, don't have one end of the border in a blaze in the spring, and then looking dull for the rest of the year, while the other end is only at its best in the autumn. Distribute the flowering periods evenly throughout, if possible. Even in quite small borders try to see that you have some colour for most of the months of the year. There are to-day many beautiful shrubs that have brilliantly coloured leaves throughout the autumn and winter, or that bear scarlet, yellow, and orange berries and fruits.

Give thought to the height to which the various shrubs will grow, and the space of ground they will take up when fully grown. Remember that some shrubs will creep along the ground, while others will stand up straight like soldiers on sentry go.

You can arrange to fill up the spaces between your shrubs in the first few years by sowing annuals, by planting out wallflowers and the like, or by putting in one or two herbaceous plants as a temporary measure.

In order to get height in the shrubbery, it is possible to use flowering trees like the Prunus, the Mountain Ash or the Laburnum, and some people like to have pillars of Rambler Roses instead.

Preparation of the border.—Be sure to bastard trench the ground all over, digging in at the same time a liberal dressing of well-rotted farmyard manure, deep down, and incorporate into the top 9 inches of soil rotted leaves or other vegetable mould. If the soil is heavy, try to lighten it by adding strawy material and sand ; and, if sandy, well-rotted organic material to help conserve the moisture. Remember that it is possible to plant shrubs to suit either kind of soil. Deep digging, and generous manuring will do much to ensure that the shrubs grow away freely and so get established early. Whatever is done, care must be taken to see that all the perennial weeds are eliminated during this initial cultivation.

Lime.—Many shrubs will appreciate a dressing of lime from time to time, but the Azaleas, Rhododendrons, Heaths, and Kalmias (peat-loving plants) should never have lime given to them in any form.

Manuring.—Every year it may be necessary to give the shrubs a mulching of dung early in May. If they are growing too fast, this may be withheld. The lighter soils will appreciate a dressing of 2 ozs. of sulphate of potash per square yard every year, in addition to a similar quantity of superphosphate. The dung can be lightly forked in in the autumn, taking care not to damage the roots, but the artificials will be hoed in after they are applied.

General cultivation.—Keep the ground where the shrubs are being grown free from weeds all the year. See that the trees are planted firmly in the first place, and then keep them firm by any staking necessary. When staking, do not tie the stake directly to the stem of the shrub or the latter may easily be injured, but wrap a piece of sacking round the stem. Use tarred string when tying, and be sure to untie in the August and October of every year, and tie up again.

Planting.—Deciduous shrubs can be transplanted any time from September to May. October and November are usually preferable, but February and March are quite suitable for the general run. The months of April and May are suitable for evergreen shrubs such as the Hollies and Rhododendrons.

Dig a hole sufficiently large to take all the roots of the shrub without having to bend them back. Prune the damaged roots with a sharp knife in such a way that the cut faces the ground. Do not plant any deeper than the soil mark seen on the stem. Plant when the soil is in a nice friable condition, and not during wet periods or frost. Late planting often means that the shrubs have great difficulty in living through a hot summer. In this case, regular soakings with water will have to be carried out during the drought.

Pruning.—It is necessary to realise that pruning should only be done if it is necessary. Do not prune, then, unless you have to, and be quite sure you are doing the right thing at the right time.

In the first place, there is the simple pruning, which can be carried out every winter. This consists of cutting out the dead or dying branches, the removal of very weak wood and a thinning out where the branches are obviously overcrowded.

A good general rule is that shrubs should be pruned just after the flowers fade.

There are, for instance, shrubs that flower early in the year (many of them on walls), on wood made the previous summer. These obviously should be pruned after flowering, and this leaves a full season in which further flowering branches can be produced. The following are typical examples of shrubs of this character : Flowering Currants, Forsythias, *Prunus triloba*, and the following Spiraeas : *S. arguta*, *S. prunifolia*, *S. canecens*, and *S. Thunbergii*.

There are large numbers of evergreen shrubs that are merely pruned by having the awkward and straggling shoots shortened back so as to make a more shapely bush. Examples are the Rhododendrons, Choisya, *Buddleia globosa*, and several of the Berberis'.

Some shrubs have to be thinned back hard if they are too tall, and the lower and shorter branches may, of course then be left unpruned. The Deutzias, the Weigelas, the Snowball-tree or Guelder Roses are examples of this.

Most people are fond of Lilacs, and these are apt to grow tall very quickly. To keep them small a percentage of the branches may be cut back in June, the weak shoots being pruned back hard also. Be sure to remove all the growths coming up directly from the roots (these are known as suckers), as these will rob the bush and will make cultivation difficult.

Then there are the shrubs which flower on the young wood made that year. These, as I said before, are cut back during the early spring, some, like the *Buddleia variabilis*, being pruned back really hard.

Other examples of similar treatment, though perhaps not quite so drastic, are Colutea, the Honeysuckles, *Ceanothus azureus*, *C. Gloire de Versailles*, etc., *Jasminum officinale*, and so on.

Whatever pruning is done, be sure to use a sharp knife or a very sharp pair of secateurs, and large wounds certainly should be cleaned up and made smooth, only to be painted over afterwards with thick white lead paint.

TRAINING WALL SHRUBS

Cut out all crossing branches (shown in black)

Buddleia variabilis pruned hard

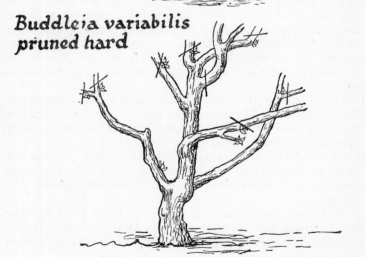

SNOWBERRY

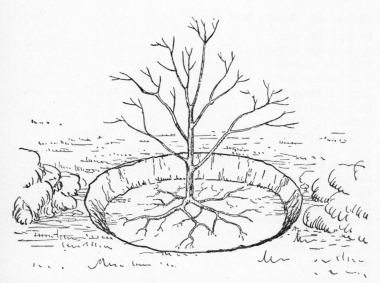

Spread out roots of shrub when planting

Tidying.—There are shrubs, like the Azaleas and Rhododendrons, which tend to form seeds directly the flowers have faded. Make it a practice to remove all faded flowers immediately they are seen ; in this way you will not only improve the appearance of the shrubbery, but you will help the bushes materially.

HARDY SHRUBS FOR VARIOUS NEEDS

It is obviously impossible to give a complete list of all the shrubs one could grow. All that can be attempted is to mention, in the first place, a number of shrubs that are easy to grow and will give plenty of colour.

Flowering Shrubs and Trees

Berberis Darwinii	*April*	Yellow	8 ft.
Berberis stenophylla	*May*	Yellow	8 ft.
Buddleia globosa	*June*	Orange	10 ft.
Buddleia variabilis	*July*	Mauve	10 ft.
Cistus in variety	*June-Aug.*	White and Pink	2–5 ft.
Crataegus Oxyacantha (Scarlet Thorn)	*May-June*	Red	15 ft.
Cytisus in variety	*May*	White, Yellow, Red	6 ft.
Deutzia gracilis	*June*	White	3 ft.
Deutzia Kalmiaflora	*June*	Pink	4 ft.
Diervilla	*May-June*	Pink	5 ft.
Escallonia macrantha	*June-Nov.*	Pink	5 ft.
Forsythia spectabilis	*March*	Yellow	8 ft.
Genista hispanica	*May-June*	Yellow	3 ft.
Hamamelis mollis	*January*	Yellow	10 ft.
Kerria japonica	*April*	Yellow	6 ft.
Lilac (*see* Syringa)			
Olearia Haastii	*June*	White	5 ft.
Philadelphus	*June-July*	White	2–8 ft.
Rhododendron	*May*	White, Red, Mauve	2–10 ft.
Ribes sanguineum	*April*	Pink	7 ft.

Rosemary	*April-May*	Mauve	5 ft.
Spiraea : Anthony Waterer	*June-Sept.*	Pink	2 ft.
Spiraea arguta	*April-May*	White	8 ft.
Spiraea confusa	*May*	White	8 ft.
Syringa (Lilac)	*May-June*	White, Purple	12 ft.
Ulex europaeus	*April-May*	Yellow	5 ft.
Viburnum opulus	*June*	White	9 ft.
Viburnum Tinus	*Dec.-March*	White	8 ft.

Autumn Tinted Shrubs and Trees

Acer japonicum
Berberis aggregata Pratii
Berberis Thunbergii
Berberis Wilsonae

Crataegus prunifolia
Rhus typhina
Spiraea Thunbergii
Viburnum Lantana

Berried and Fruiting Shrubs

Berberis aggregata
Berberis gagnepainii
Berberis polyantha
Berberis verruculosa
Colutea arborescens
Cotoneaster all varieties
Cydonia Maulei
Pyracantha

Pyrus baccata
Pyrus Malus
Rosa Moyesii
Sambucus
Skimmia japonica
Symphoricarpus
Viburnum Lantana

Catkin-Bearing Shrubs

Alnus glutinosa
Betula nigra
Garrya elliptica

Populus tremulus
Salix Caprea

Coloured Stems and Bark

Betula alba verrucosa
Cornus alba sibirica
Kerria japonica

Rubus biflorus
Salix vitellina
Salix vitellina britzensis

Lime-Hating Shrubs

Andromeda
Azalea
Erica
Kalmia

Pernettya
Rhododendron
Vaccinium

Shrubs for Shade

Berberis aquifolium (Mahonia)
Euonymus japonica
Leycesteria formosa

Ruscus aculeatus
Symphoricarpus
Vinca

Shrubs for Walls

SOUTH

Actinidia chinensis
Aristolochia sipho
Bignonia capriolata
Ceanothus dentatus
Ceanothus Gloire de Versailles
Clematis
Eccremocarpus scaber

Jasminum primulinum
Jasminum revolutum
Magnolia grandiflora
Solanum crispum
Solanum jasminoides
Veronica Hulkeana
Vitis heterophylla

WEST

Bignonia capreolata
Ceanothus rigidus
Chimonanthus fragrans
Clematis

Cydonia japonica
Forsythia suspensa
Pyracantha angustifolia
Rambler Roses

EAST

Cotoneaster Simonsii
Cotoneaster horizontalis
Garrya elliptica
Hedera (Ivy)

Jasminum nudiflorum
Pyracantha
Vitis inconstans Veitchii
   (Ampelopsis)

NORTH

Cotoneaster horizontalis
Cotoneaster Simonsii
Garrya elliptica

Hedera
Jasminum nudiflorum
Polygonum baldschuanicum

CHAPTER VI

ROSES

We need beauty and scent in our garden and roses will give us these.

1. Can roses be grown on all soils ?
2. Should we plant them in the autumn or in the spring ?
3. Some people tell us to cut our roses hard back and others to leave them alone. Which is right ?
4. Are ramblers and climbing roses different ?
5. What are meant by the terms disbudding and suckering ?
6. Can you give us a list of the best varieties to grow ?

MOST people will want to grow a few Roses in their garden. After all, the Rose is the national emblem of England, and we learn that the houses of Lancaster and York chose red and white Roses as their symbols many years ago. Even in times of war the interest in Roses has not abated, and history relates how head gardeners to foreign royalties were allowed to travel to England and other countries in search of new Roses.

It was really the Empress Josephine of France who initiated the great boom in Roses, and whose head gardener was allowed to travel anywhere – even through enemy country – when on " Rose " duty."

SOIL

It is really astonishing in how many different and varied soils Roses seem to grow satisfactorily. The very light sands and sharp gravels do not suit them well, however, unless they are properly prepared. It is difficult, also, to grow the best blooms on chalky soils.

Roses will grow quite well in boggy soils, providing they are well drained. Perhaps the best soil is a rich heavy loam, which must be well drained and be well away from tall or overhanging trees.

Should your soil not be ideal, you can improve it in various ways. First of all, in the autumn the land should be trenched to a depth of 2 feet, and the soil left rough in ridge form. The frosts and dry winds will act on this and pulverise it, so that early in the spring it can be levelled and prepared for planting. During the trenching process, well-rotted farmyard manure should be added at the rate of one good barrow-load to every 8 square feet, and during the final preparation give 4 ozs. of steamed bone flour and 2 ozs. of sulphate of potash per square yard. Lastly, just before the Roses are ready to put in, hydrated lime can be applied on the surface, if the ground is acid and had not been limed recently. A good dressing would be 8 ozs. to the square yard.

Sandy soils and gravels should have, in addition to the dung, a liberal dressing of rotted leaves or chopped-up turves added, and incorporated in the top 9 inches or so. Further, after the Roses are in position, the ground should be mulched with dung, so as to hold the moisture.

If you are planting over chalk, you will have to excavate and remove the chalk so that you can have at least 18 inches of soil – 2 feet would be preferable.

See that the roots of the roses, when planted, never come into contact with fresh manure ; to prevent it, be sure that the dung is buried low down.

MANURES

These have already been discussed in the paragraph dealing with the soil. It is generally accepted that, in the lighter soils at any rate, cow and pig manure should be used for the bottom layer, while well-decayed stable manure is incorporated in the top layer of soil. Bone meal, or steamed bone flour, is much recommended also, up to $\frac{1}{2}$ lb. per square yard being used. Potash will be necessary, especially on the lighter soils, and sulphate of potash can be used at 1 to 2 ozs. per square yard as necessary. Wood ashes are useful if there are plenty available. remember that these contain a very low percentage of potash, however. Every year it is usual to give a mulching of dung in May, and this not only acts as a plant food, but is useful in dry years to prevent the moisture in the soil from evaporating

PLANTING

Roses can be planted at any time from the third week in October until the middle of March. It will much depend on your soil, and when you are able to prepare it, which time of the year will really be preferable. Actually the period before December is advisable, but is not always possible. Should the weather be inclement, or there be very heavy frosts about, by all means delay planting until March, or even April.

Whatever you do, do not plant on a wet day, when the soil is sticky. Even if the weather is quite suitable, it is not a bad plan to have under cover some fine soil with which you can fill in part of the hole at planting-time. This dry soil should be used for covering the roots, and the wetter soil can be placed on top.

When the trees arrive from the nursery, open the package, and, unless the weather is frosty, heel the plants in immediately. Some people prefer to stand the roots in water for a few hours first of all. What is important, is to see that they do not get exposed to the wind or sun, and so get dried up. Should the ground be too hard for the heeling-in process, cover the roots with a damp sack and keep them under cover. Remove all the leaves and any seed pods you see, and, before the bushes are put into the hole you have prepared for them, see that the roots are pruned. The long ones may be trimmed back, and the damaged ones cut to a healthy part, with a sharp knife.

When making the hole, see that it is large enough for the roots to be spread out evenly from the centre, and deep enough so that the base of the plant, where it was originally budded, is at least an inch below the level of the soil. Place the plant in the hole, separate out the roots and put them in their right position, and then fill in with some of the dry soil you may have put by. Whatever you do, cover your soil in small amounts at a time. Get someone to hold the bush and to lift it up and down gently while you are putting the soil into position ; in this way it will get all round the roots evenly. When you have added an inch of soil, you must tread down firmly, and every inch of soil you add must be followed by firm treading with a heavy boot. Finally, rake over the surface of the ground so as to leave a little loose soil at the top.

If you plant early, the severe frosts that follow may easily damage the plants ; further, the thaw which follows may lift the bushes out of position. It is a good plan, then to give newly planted roses some protection, and straw does this quite well. You can either just put straw loosely around the plants or you can tie one of the bottle straw envelopes round the base. When the thaw sets in, be sure to go over the beds and tread round every plant. After such treading, hoe the beds and rake the top of the soil.

Standard Roses must be staked at planting. See that the stake comes right into the head, and then tie them securely at the top. Unless you do this, the roots never have a chance of growing, because they are being rocked about in the soil. The heads, also, are apt to be damaged unless they are securely tied into position.

Normally the bushes will need to be planted 2 feet apart, but strong growers, like Hugh Dickson and Frau Karl Druschki, will need $2\frac{1}{2}$ feet. When planting a bed do not plant the outside row any closer than 18 inches from the edge of the bed, though in the case of the Dwarf Polyantha type, 12 inches from the edge may do. It is becoming fashionable to plant Roses much closer than this, as people seem to have a horror of seeing soil in between. If this is your choice, you can plant the H.T.s as close as 15 inches, and the strong varieties that I have mentioned 18 inches apart.

Whatever you do, see that the Roses are labelled directly after planting, and a good permanent label is well worth having. There are metal labels on the market, at the moment, already printed with the name of the variety, and that do not come very expensive.

PRUNING

Most newcomers to gardening seem to regard Rose pruning as something extremely difficult, and yet actually it is comparatively simple.

Roses are pruned every year in order that the bush may

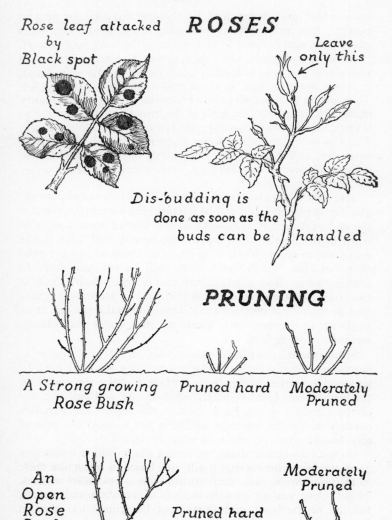

ROSES

Rose leaf attacked by Black spot

Leave only this

Dis-budding is done as soon as the buds can be handled

PRUNING

A Strong growing Rose Bush

Pruned hard

Moderately Pruned

An Open Rose Bush

Pruned hard

Moderately Pruned

grow wider and wider, and the blooms may be larger and better. You must aim at producing fresh, healthy growths every year, and in doing so you will keep the bush really dwarf.

As a general guide, one can say that if a bush is growing vigorously you need not cut it hard, but if, on the other hand, it is not growing well, it needs to be cut very hard indeed. Then, again, there seems to be a connection between the quality of the bloom and the strength of the growth that bears it. So if you cut hard you get a strong growth and good blooms as well. There is something also in the place from which the growth emanates, and it seems that, providing, of course, you do not cut down below the budded part, the lower you cut the stronger the resultant branch.

The newly planted tree.—This will not be pruned immediately after planting, but will be left until the normal time–either the end of March in the south or the first or second week in April in the north. The bush must be cut well back in the first year, in order to help it to establish itself and to get good branches also. Each shoot, then, will be cut well down to within two or three good, plump, easily recognisable buds at the base. Be sure and cut to a bud, and an outward-growing bud at that – this means to say, that you make the cut at an angle of 45 degrees, with secateurs, just above this plump, outward-growing bud.

Subsequent pruning.—After this, it is not quite so necessary to be so severe. The general idea is to cut back to six good eyes (i.e. buds), being certain to keep the centre of the bush open. Remove all the weak shoots, and cut, say, one of the stronger shoots hard back to the base. The varieties coming under the headings of H.P.s are usually not pruned any harder than to seven or eight buds.

Do not be worried about the strong shoots which sometimes grow up from the variety itself, and learn to recognise these from the growths that come up from the roots called suckers. These strong variety growths do help to maintain and prolong the life of the bush, and should not be pruned too hard in consequence.

Ramblers.—By ramblers we intend to include the Wichuraianas, the Climbing Polyanthas, and the Multifloras. These, when newly planted, should be pruned back to seven or eight eyes, and the weak growths cut out altogether. It is true that by pruning in this way you sacrifice bloom for the first season, but you do, in consequence, get good strong growths that will blossom profusely the following year.

In the following seasons prune back the growth immediately after flowering, making certain to cut out the shoots that have bloomed. The new growths made that season are then tied up in their place.

Climbing H.T.s.—These include the climbing types of the Pernetianas, the Teas, and the Noisettes. These must be pruned in quite a different manner from the ramblers. In the first place they are pruned at the end of March or at the beginning of April, and in the second place they must not be pruned too hard or else they lose their climbing habits and revert to the bush type. It is usual to cut back two or three of the strongest growths by one-third of their length, and to cut back the weak and the unripe shoots to four or six eyes. Once the trees are established you want to encourage lateral growths, as it is these that flower profusely. This is done by training the main shoots in a horizontal position, or, if you are growing them up posts, to wind them round like a screw thread. Whatever you do, do not tie them up vertically like you do ramblers.

Standards.—These trees may be pruned in the same way as bush plants, but it is usual to study the shape of the head very carefully in so doing.

Weeping Standards.—Keep the shape of the head in perfect symmetry, remove the older shoots as necessary, and see that the branches are evenly placed. Always prune weeping standards hard, the first March after planting.

Dwarf Polyantha.—If you are using these for bedding, you can cut them quite hard every year. Normally all that is done is to cut away the old flower stems every March, and to thin out the old wood.

GENERAL CULTIVATION

Keep the beds hoed throughout the summer. See that the

bushes are mulched before the hot weather sets in, and water. by giving a good soaking, if you really feel the soil is too dry.

Whatever you do, never mulch Roses with dung in the late autumn. This only keeps the bed wet and cold. If you must get some protection, use, as I have already suggested, plain straw. Cut off all the bloom directly it starts to fade. Never allow seed-pods to form. If you do not want flowers for decoration inside, there is no need why you should ruin the bushes by leaving them on the plant to seed. If you make up your mind to cut Roses with nice long stems during the months of June and July, you can ensure getting good bloom during the month of September.

Disbudding.—If you are growing varieties that will produce good firm bloom, disbud them so as to only leave one flower bud to swell and develop on a shoot. Do this disbudding early, and do not leave it until the colour is showing. The best time to do this is when the buds are smaller than peas.

Suckering.—Most Roses are budded on to a type of briar root, and beginners should realise that the briar often tries to assert itself. It may, then, suddenly send up a shoot from the roots, which can be distinguished from the cultivated variety by its wild " look." If you are in doubt as to whether the shoot you are examining is a sucker or not, trace it down to the point from which it emanates. If this is below the point at which the rose bush was budded, it is obviously a wild briar, and should be cut out to the base.

PESTS AND DISEASES

These are dealt with in Chapter XV, but it is well to know that you must be on the look-out for green-fly all the time. Trees that are not pruned hard enough, trees that are too near a shrubbery or in the shade of bigger trees, and trees near the house usually suffer far worse than those in an open situation. In fact, Roses always do better when they are grown in a perfectly open place which gets all the sun and yet is not too wind-swept.

Look out also for caterpillars, and keep an eye open for the mildew and the dreaded black spot.

Varieties

There are a very large number of varieties, and it is practically impossible to make a choice. I am, however, being entirely selfish in making this list, as I am choosing those which I like and have found to grow satisfactorily. If you want further details study the author's work *Roses*.

Reds

Covent Garden (H.T.). Bright-red. Strong Growing. Very Floriferous.

Ena Harknes (H.T.). A rich, glowing red. Very popular.

Etoile de Hollande (H.T.). A bright dark red. Petals large and of good substance. Foliage dark bronze green.

General McArthur (H.T.). Crimson. Blooms carried on strong stalks. Foliage glossy green ; nearly mildew-proof. Heavily perfumed.

Hadley (H.T.). Crimson, shaded black. Long pointed bud on stiff stalk. Foliage dark green. Very sweetly scented.

McGredy's Scarlet (H.T.). Long bud, strong growth. Foliage attractive, dark green. Can produce large, exhibition blooms.

Hugh Dickson (H.P.). Crimson. Good foliage. Strong grower. The blooms are large and do not fade. Good autumn bloomer.

Crimson Glory (H.T.). Deep velvety crimson. Free flowering and bushy. Colour does not fade.

Blush Roses

Admiration (H.T.). A most delicate pearly cream-pink.

Madam Butterfly (H.T.). Salmon flesh, delicately flushed with golden pink at centre. A perfect bud on a stiff stalk. Delightfully fragrant. Does well everywhere.

Ophelia (H.T.). Salmon flesh, with yellow at base of petal. Well-shaped bloom borne on stiff stem. Very fragrant. Can have exquisite blooms in September.

Lady Sylvia (H.T.). Flesh pink, yellow base. Long buds, well shaped. Upright growth. Perfumed.

Madam Abel Chatenay (H.T.). Rose pink with silver reflex. Flowers freely ; every bloom a good shape. Seldom makes a well-shaped plant.

Orange and Apricot

Mrs. G. A. Van Rossem (H.T.). Deep coppery orange. Large well-shaped blooms. Stiff stems, bearing dark bronze green foliage. Fragrant.

Mrs. Sam McGreedy (H.T.). Scarlet coppery orange. Good-shaped flower. Bronze green foliage. Spectacular and scented.

Lady Forteviot (Pernetiana).   Deep yellow, the inside of the petal being rich apricot.   Long pointed buds on good stiff stems.   Foliage deep glossy green.   Should be disbudded.   Sweet, fruity fragrance.

Emma Wright (H.T.).   Orange.   Pointed and shapely bud.   Dark green glossy foliage.   Ideal in habit of growth.   Very free flowering.

Carmine Pink

Shot Silk (H.T.).   A cherry pink overshot with orange.   A well-shaped rose.   Foliage bright glossy green.   Delightfully fragrant. Makes a compact and bushy tree.

Betty Uprichard (H.T.).   A delicate rose pink and glowing carmine. Rather flat blooms on long straight stems.   Blooms not really full enough.   Not quite the ideal bedder, as it throws up such tall shoots.   Excellent for cutting.

Mrs. A. R. Barraclough (H.T.).   Rose pink, heavy fringed with carmine.   Large well-formed blooms on long stiff stems.   Straggling in habit, slightly fragrant.

Golden Yellows

Christine (Pernetiana).   Golden yellow.   Blooms shapely though small.   Foliage dark green, glossy, and practically mildew-proof. Very fine as a standard.   Flowers continuously.

McGredy's Yellow (H.T.).   Pale yellow.   Very bright, attractive blooms.   Good stiff stems.   Dark green foliage.   Mildew resistant.

Golden Emblem (Pernetiana).   Golden yellow.   Not quite such a good bedder as Golden Gleam.   Gives better individual bloom. Strong grower.   Dark, glossy green foliage.   Subject to black spot.

The Rev. Page Roberts (H.T.).   Fawny yellow.   A full bloom, with petals of good substance ; the colour deepens as the rose expands. Foliage, mildew resistant.   Growth sturdy and compact.

Spek's Yellow.   Bright golden yellow.   Bloom large.   Foliage dark green, glossy, stout, and large.   Growth bushy and compact.

Soft Yellow

Peace.   Large blooms, light yellow petals edged pink.

Barbara Richards (H.T.).   Maize yellow, flushed rose.   Blooms large and borne in profusion.   Disbud for exhibition.   Distinctly scented.

White

Abol (H.T.).   Fine, full, bold flowers.   Exceptionally fragrant.

Frau Karl Druschki (H.P.).   A good grower.   Must be disbudded. Foliage bright and glossy.

Marcia Stanhope (H.T.).   Perfectly shaped.   Lemon tinge at centre. Tremendous blooms.   Foliage pale green.   Fragrance reminiscent of Verbena.

Clear Pink

Dame Edith Helen (H.T.). Large bloom on stiff stalk. Of exhibition quality. Foliage light green and leathery. Exceptionally fragrant.

Picture (H.T.). Clear lovely rose pink. Shape absolutely ideal. Very free flowering.

Mrs. H. Bowles (H.T.). Rose pink and carmine. Exceptionally good. Slightly liable to mildew. Fragrant.

The Doctor. A very fine, pure clear pink rose. Much to be recommended.

Copper Pink

Lady Pirrie (H.T.). Blooms freely. Perfect-shaped buds. Distinctly fragrant.

Los Angeles (H.T.). Good-shaped bloom. Holds its colour splendidly. Distinctly perfumed. Suspectible to black spot and to dying back.

Flame

Mme Edouard Herriot (Austrian Hybrid). Brick terra cotta ; the colour is so vivid that it may kill all other colour near it. Excellent as a standard.

President Herbert Hoover. A lovely rose of brilliant colours, beautifully blended.

Cream

Clarice Goodacre. A very finely shaped rose of good substance.

McGredy's Ivory (H.T.). Large perfect rose, borne on strong stem. Ideal for exhibition.

Various Shades

Portadown Fragrance (H.T.). An orange salmon pink, shaded with orange scarlet. Bears large flowers on long stems. Foliage bronze green. One of the most deliciously scented roses I know.

Ramblers.

The following are very popular ramblers :

Paul's Scarlet Climber	Vivid scarlet
American Pillar	Deep pink
Dorothy Perkins	Double Pink
Emily Gray	Golden yellow
Dr. Van Fleet	Flesh pink
Albéric Barbier	Creamy yellow
Excelsa	Crimson
Lady Gay	Cherry Pink
Sanders	White

Climbers

Many of the varieties that can be bought as bush Roses can be bought as climbers also. For instance, one might mention Madam Butterfly, Madame Edouard Herriot, Ophelia, Madam Abel Chatenay, Caroline Testout, Golden Emblem, Marechal Niel, and so on. This latter is the best of all climbing Roses for the green-house.

There are others like :—

Lady Waterlow	Salmon, blush carmine edge
Zephirin Drouhin	Deep silvery pink
Romance	Shell pink
William Alan Richardson	Apricot yellow

which can be bought as climbers only.

Polyantha Roses

Gloria Mundi	Brilliant orange
Ideal	Dark scarlet
Paul Crampel	Flaming orange scarlet
Karen Poulsen	Bright currant red
Else Poulsen	Rose pink
Coral Cluster	Coral pink

These are all Dwarf Polyantha Roses, and are excellent for bedding, doing well in town or country gardens, and in most soils.

CHAPTER VII

THE ROCK GARDEN

*A fashionable form of gardening and a very fascinating one.
I want to tell you about it.*

1. The site. How it should be prepared.
2. The kind of rock materials you should get.
3. What kind of soil to use between the rocks.
4. How the rock garden should be built. (A very important point this.)
5. How to look after your rock garden when it is made.
6. A list of plants and where they are best grown.

THERE is a far greater interest being taken to-day in rock gardens and alpine plants than in the past years. Most people seem to want to have a rock garden of some sort, even if it be quite small. It is naturally impossible in such a short chapter as this, and in a book of this character, to do more than give general ideas and schemes.

Those who are keen on making a large rock garden should study books devoted wholly to this subject and call in experts to help them. (*See* the author's book *The A.B.C. of Rock Gardens and Pools.*)

THE SITE

A great deal depends on the position and shape of the ground, but a sunny site should be chosen, as nearly all alpine plants are used to unrestricted light. Secondly the site should be in a place where the rock garden can be made a separate feature. Even a belt of shrubs, planted on purpose, is better as a division than having no separation at all.

Never plan a rock garden near Elms or Sycamores, or, in fact, near any large trees, as these send out their roots tremendous distances, and so rob the rock plants of food and moisture.

If the site chosen has a slight slope, so much the better, as it is much easier then to place the rocks naturally and to produce most pleasing effects. Should the ground not be variable in contour, then an attempt must be made to break up the outline by forming mounds of earth and by putting the stone into suitable positions. Another thing that can be done is to make the path below the natural level of the soil ; thus one has to look up to the garden.

It is not advisable to make a rock garden in a low-lying place. Such a position is apt to be damp, and, unless it is drained very thoroughly, will give the owner a lot of trouble.

In the small garden do not attempt anything too elaborate. See that your rocks are natural by all means, and try to give height by planting an evergreen shrub or two at one point or another. In the same way it is better to have the highest point at one end and a point not quite so high at the other. The intervening space can be naturally undulating, but not too symmetrical.

There should be no difficulty in the choice or number of plants, as most of the finest specimens grow no larger than an area which can be covered with a 3-inch flower-pot even when fully grown. There should, then, be no reason why a large number of different types and varieties should not be grown in even the smallest rock garden. Choose plants, in this case, of a neat-growing habit, and you can have, as it were, a rock garden in miniature.

On a small rockery the trees and shrubs that are used must be small themselves, or the whole of the proportion is lost.

The large rock garden should be planned in a way that resembles Nature at her best. Note the outcropping on the Derbyshire hills and moors and in the gorges of Somerset, and you will see how the rocks ought to be placed in position. A winding path can traverse the garden, while it goes up the gorge and down into the little valley. Bold masses here and there can swell out, while secondary valleys are arranged as seem expedient.

During all this, care is taken to see that there are pockets and crevices facing in all directions, so there may be grown plants that like sun, that like shade, and so on. It is often possible to have steps of unhewn stone or a path composed of crazy paving, in both of which special plants will grow in the crevices.

SUITABLE ROCK MATERIALS

It is not everyone who can afford to buy rock brought from long distances. There is, for instance, some beautiful weathered limestone, which can be obtained from Derbyshire and other counties of the northern midlands. I know of some beautiful rock gardens made of stone from the Cotswolds. Those who live in Kent may like the Kentish rag, while sandstones from Surrey and Sussex are much admired by some people. Granite is sometimes used, though on the whole the harder stones of this character do not absorb moisture, and so, in consequence, do not encourage plants to cling to them.

Fairly " soft " stone on the whole is advisable, but not such stone that is easily damaged and that flakes in frosty weather. Use natural stone if possible in every case. Do not fall into the error of using such stone as white " marble," such as you often find, unfortunately, in front gardens. In the same way, concrete and " brick-bats " are by no means natural or beautiful.

The stones should be if possible at least 2 feet in length, and of about the same breadth. Larger stones will be used in the more extensive rock gardens, while the smaller pieces such as I have outlined will be useful for the rockeries of smaller gardens.

SOILS

You will probably have to use the soil already in the garden as a basis for all the pockets and the general mass used in making up the mounds and undulations. It is well worth while, on the other hand, importing or making up special pockets for the plants that need definite types of soil. It may be that your soil is too heavy or too damp. Perchance it contains far too little fibre, and so needs organic material added to it. Study the plants you are going to grow. Read about them, and find out their habits and needs. In this way you will be able to produce the right " mixture " for individual cases.

BUILDING THE ROCK GARDEN

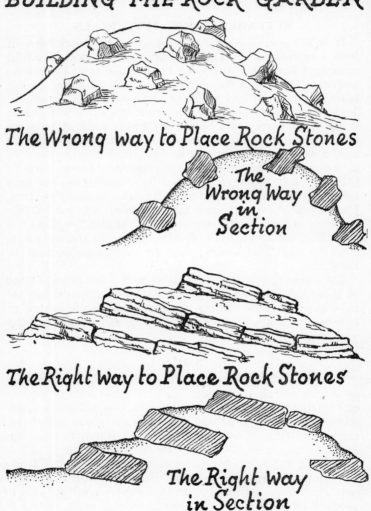

The Wrong way to Place Rock Stones

The Wrong Way in Section

The Right way to Place Rock Stones

The Right way in Section

SECTIONS of GOOD ROCK WORK

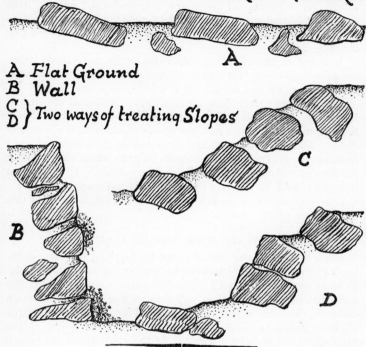

A. Flat Ground
B. Wall
C.
D. } Two ways of treating Slopes

A

C

B

D

Winter Protection for a Delicate Rock Plant

A sheet of glass supported
on Wire stays.

The pockets may contain only 18 inches of soil, but below there will be a good root run. Quite a good general mixture would be 8 parts of ordinary garden soil, mixed with ½ part of coarse sand and ½ part of rock chippings. To this may be added leaf mould if the soil is of a heavy clayey character.

Just before the planting, other materials may have to be incorporated – peat for some plants, more sand for others, and addition of leaf mould for a third group, and so on.

Do not forget that some alpines like a good deal of crushed limestone or granite. The granite will suit those that dislike lime in any form – such as *Campanula alpestris* and *Saponaria lutea*. Many of the smaller Androsaces like more than a quarter of the compost to consist of grit, while the stronger Saxifrages will do quite well in ordinary loam. The Gentians like peat, and so do the Primulas and Lithospermums.

It is impossible to go into further details in a book of this character.

BUILDING THE ROCK GARDEN

Always start at the lowest point by bedding the base rocks in the ground. They should be put in sufficiently deeply, at least two-thirds of rock buried to make them look just like a natural outcrop, and they will thus incline towards the main body of soil in which they rest. This tilting backwards slightly, helps to guide the rain down to the roots of the plants and not to take it away. As the other rocks are placed into position they may have a tilt either to the right or to the left. Whatever tilt is given to the lower stones the higher ones should follow the same sequence – at any rate for a good distance. In this way the idea of stratification is shown simply.

As the stones are put into position, suitable soil may be placed behind them and rammed tightly to keep them in position. Do not forget the pockets, which may be as large as 3 feet square even if these large ones have smaller rocks peeping through. As I have said before, do make it look natural, and for this reason do not build pinnacle-like effects.

There is no reason why grass should not form part of your rock garden scheme – in fact stones outcropping from grass look both natural and fascinating.

Even in a small rock garden see that certain stones have a flat surface, to act as stepping stones for getting about from place to place.

The photographs and the drawings will perhaps explain the ideas even better than words.

As a last word of warning, whatever you do, do not stick your stones into the ground so that they look rather like the almonds in a trifle.

PLANTING ROCK PLANTS

Once the rock garden is made, most people want to see it furnished and carpeted at the earliest possible moment. There are several plants that will do this quickly, but because they are strong growing they are apt to smother our weaker and choicer plants in consequence. Be sure, then, not to overdo the strong growers, and, once you have planted them, see that you cut them back and keep them within bounds. I have known too many rock gardens start off with a choice selection of plants only to end up a year or two later just a mass of one or two of the rampant types.

The following are quick growing, and should be watched carefully : Iberis, Aubretia, Cerastium, Arabis, and *Alyssum saxatile*.

Planting can be done at any time in the autumn and spring, providing the ground is fit to work. As the rock garden is often at its best late in the spring, autumn planting is on the whole preferable.

The next point to consider is the likes and dislikes of the plants you are going to grow. Many of the Primulas like moisture – for instance, *Primula Bulleyana* – and so should be planted in the lower positions, and near water if you have a small pool. The Sempervivums and Sedums would soon rot away if they were planted in such a position. The members of the Dianthus family like the sun, while the Oxalis like shade.

Do not, then, put the plants in anywhere, but see that they are where they would like to grow.

Plant firmly. Make a hole with a trowel, put the plant into position so that it is at the right level, and make the soil all round it very firm. See that there is no hollow beneath it, and so press down all round the base of the roots. There is a great danger, when planting between clefts of rocks, of looseness of soil at the base. In this case it is better to ram the soil into position first of all, making certain to see that it is sufficiently open by putting some gritty material in with the compost. Do not plant too deeply so as to bury the plants, but, on the other hand, see that they are not out of the soil and left " high and dry."

After planting, see that the groups are labelled.

GENERAL CULTIVATION

During the year weed regularly. This usually means going over the garden about once a fortnight, stirring the soil with a little hand fork, and removing the weeds by hand. Such regular attention which can only take half an hour or so in small gardens, saves hours of labour later on.

Directly the groups of plants have flowered, they will need attending to, and all the dead flowers and stems should be cut off. The stronger growing types should be cut back to prevent them spoiling other plants – and, in fact, spoiling themselves.

Early in February the Aubretias and Mossy Saxifrages which may appear to be nearly dead should have the straggling growths removed from the brown patches carefully picked off. A little sifted soil may then be given as a top dressing, being forked in lightly here and there.

Many of the early flowering types have their blooms damaged by birds when they are in the bud stage, and these will need protection by little twiggy pieces of wood – these being pushed in around the plants, with strands of black cotton stretched in between them.

Some plants are apt to die during the winter, not so much because of the frost, but because of the damp. These should be covered with a small piece of glass before the winter starts.

Bulbs in Bowls, having been under a heap of sand outside for 9 weeks. They are now ready to bring indoors.

This is the Eremurus, a lovely tall plant for the
Herbaceous Border.

Many of the Androsaces, and the less hardy Sempervivums, have to be treated in this way.

CONIFERS

If you want to get the Lilliputian effect in your rock garden there is nothing that helps more than the planting of the conifers that are in themselves so perfect in shape and yet that never grow to any size. Buy the conifers that keep small, as they will then be always in keeping with your alpine plants.

The following are suitable varieties :

Cupressus obtusa var caespitosa. Produce moss-like dense tuffets. Rounded growth.

Cupressus plumosa aurea compacta. Golden ; miniature cone-shaped.

Juniperus communis compressa. Small and column-like ; neat.

Picea Albertiana conica. Pyramidal in shape. Grows very slowly. Likes moist soil and a sheltered position.

Taxus baccata pygmaea. Very dwarf. Beautiful green.

Taxus compacta. Slow growing and compact.

Thuya occidcntalis Ellwangeriana Aurea. Golden pyramidal bush.

Thuya plicata aurea Rogersii. Pryamidal form. Gold and bronze foliage.

Ulex nanus. Dwarf gorse, flowers September.

BULBS

Many of the dwarfer growing bulbous plants are very suitable for the rock garden. They will grow in light soil, and should be planted in depth according to the size of the bulb. Types and varieties can be obtained which flower at different periods of the year.

Here are a few examples :

Spring-flowering bulbs : Allium in variety ; Anemone in variety ; Chionodoxa and Crocus, several species ; Fritillaria in variety ; *Iris, reticulata, histrioides,* and *Warleyensis;* Muscari ; Scilla in variety ; many dwarf Tulips.

Summer - flowering bulbs : *Allium pulchellum* ; *Oxalis floribunda* ; *Tritonia crocata,* etc.

Autumn - flowering bulbs : Crocus, various varieties ;

D

Cyclamen africanum ; *Cyclamen europaeum, C. neapolitanum* ; *Scilla autumnalis.*

Winter-flowering bulbs : Anemone, various varieties ; Crocus, various varieties ; Galanthus in variety ; *Iris alata, I. Persica, I. reticulata,* and *I. stylosa.*

LIST OF ROCK PLANTS PARTIAL TO PARTICULAR PLACES OR CONDITIONS

(The lists are, perforce, short.)

SHADE-LOVING PLANTS :

Androsace oliosa ; *Arenaria balearica* ; *Cyananthus lobatus* ; Primulas in variety ; Ramondia ; Ferns and Aconites.

PLANTS FOR HALF SHADE :

Androsace arachnoidea ; *Aquilegia caerulea* ; *Aster alpinus* ; *Campanula pulla* ; *Epigaea repens* ; *Erodium chamaedryoides* ; Mertensia in variety ; Primulas in variety ; the mossy Saxifrages ; *Viola pedata.*

PLANTS THAT LOVE MOISTURE :

Mimulus ; Lysimachia ; Parnassia ; Trillium.

ROCK PLANTS DISLIKING DAMP :

(These should always be covered with a piece of glass a few inches above them in winter) : Androsace ; *Artemisia lanata* ; *Asperula suberosa* ; *Campanula hirsuta* ; the tufted Dianthus ; *Helichrysum frigidum* ; *Hypericum Coris* and *tomentosum* ; *Lychnis alpina* ; *Papaver alpinum.*

ROCK PLANTS FOR WALLS :

Saponaria ocymoides ; *Alyssum saxatile* ; Aethionema Warley Rose ; *Dianthus caesius* ; Iberis Snowflake ; *Campanula portenschlagiana* ; *Corydalis lutea* ; Linaria ; Erinus ; and Aubrietias.

CRAZY-PAVING PLANTS :

Achillea tomentosa ; *Alyssum montanum* ; *Antennaria tomentosa* ; *Dianthus deltoides* ; *Erinus alpinus* ; *Mentha Requieni* ; *Thymus lanuginosus, T. serpyllum* and T. Annie Hall ; *Sedum Lydium* ; *Cotula squalida.*

ROCK PLANTS FOR SUNNY PLACES :

Practically all the rock plants like sunny positions best.

CHAPTER VIII

LAWNS

Is there a garden without a lawn ? Yes, there are gardens with grass patches full of weeds. To have a lawn we must :—

1. Be careful about the preparation of the soil.
2. Sow the right seed, not just any grass seed.
3. Cultivate in the right way.
4. Get rid of excess worms, and the pests and diseases.
5. Apply the right fertilisers regularly and so help to get rid of the weeds.
6. Cut regularly and at the right time.

THERE is something very English about a lawn, and those of you who have lived in the East will know what a welcome sight it is to see the beautiful green swards in the gardens of our colleges, country mansions, and even in quite small cottage gardens.

You may want to make a small lawn or even a tennis court. You may be going to have grass paths or well cut and turfed banks. Whatever you are going to do in this direction, you will have to give the same care and thought to laying them down as you would to any other part of your garden.

There are two ways of making a lawn – one by seeding, and the other by turfing. There is actually another method, and that is by planting out little portions of the creeping grasses, but this is seldom done in this country. I propose, therefore, to confine your attention to the two methods only.

PREPARATION OF THE SOIL

Lawns seem to grow best on a medium loam, and so you should aim at producing a soil as near to this character as possible. With heavy clay soils it may be necessary to add sand, well-decomposed farmyard manure, rotted leaves, or even finely ground peat. With sandy soils it is a help to dig in some moisture-holding material, in order to prevent, if possible, the soil drying out too much during the summer.

There is no need to dig very deeply, especially if the soil is already of the right character. You want to aim at making the top 4 or 5 inches in a perfect condition. If you are digging in organic matter, you may dig to the depth of 6 inches.

Be sure the land is well drained (*see* Chapter I). It is most annoying, especially if you want to use the lawn for games, to find that it is impossible to play on owing to it being sodden after rain.

It will probably be necessary to level the ground, and here care should be taken to see that the subsoil is not brought to the surface. I have been into gardens where in order to get a level surface the top soil from one end of the proposed lawn has been wheeled to the other end. The result, of course, is that you get a double depth of good soil on one side, and only subsoil left at the other. Though it seems a good deal of extra work, the only thing to do in this case is to take away the top soil as stated in the diagram, *see* page 102, placing it in a mound nearby. The subsoil is then dug up and put in its new position and the topsoil from the nearby mound is replaced. In this way, you see, you get the level you require, and yet the whole surface is covered with good soil.

So very often with new houses, the builder has very kindly put a good deal of subsoil, that he dug up when preparing the foundations, all over the soil you want to use. In order to be more helpful, also, he has very often included with this stones, lime, and other kinds of rubbish. This unwanted material must be removed.

Having got your levels right, the next thing to do is to decide whether the land is really clean enough to sow the seed or not. If you are satisfied that you are not going to get an inordinate crop of weeds, you could sow immediately, but, if not satisfied, fallowing to eradicate the weeds is desirable.

This process is described on the opposite page.

SEED SOWING

Seeds can be sown either in the spring or in the autumn. My experience in the north midlands tells me that the spring is probably better there, while in the south-east, at any rate, autumn sowing is usually preferable. The severe winters in the north-west, and the very heavy rains experienced during the winter, never give the young grasses much chance. In the south-east we often get a dry May and June so that spring sowing often means poor germination and poor growth.

If you are sowing in the spring the land should be dug in the autumn, the manures incorporated – the leaf mould, the sand, or whatever you are going to use – and the land left rough. In this case the land is forked over 4 inches deep in the spring, and allowed to lie bare for a period of three weeks to a month. During this time weeds will, of course, grow, and so, before sowing the seed, they may be hoed down and raked off. Actually "fallowing" as mentioned before is not a bad plan, leave the land bare all the first summer, so as to be able to hoe continuously and eradicate all the weeds in consequence. If your lawn preparation commences in the spring, with digging and levelling, you will not mind, I hope, not sowing the seed until late August or early September. Whatever you do, do not miss the opportunity of getting rid of both annual and perennial weeds at the start. I have seen too many lawns ruined through careless preparation, and on too many occasions I have had to advise that the so-called lawn be dug in that the whole process might be started all over again.

The kind of lawn I want you to have is one that consists of fine grasses and of nothing else. The lawns that are full of clover and moss, the swards that are spoiled by daisies and plantains, should not be for you.

Lawns will do well in all kinds of places, and under all kinds of conditions, if you lay them down properly at the start.

If your land is stony, you may be very worried about it, and think that you have got to remove every stone before you start. Stones do no harm unless there are a superabundance

MAKING A LAWN

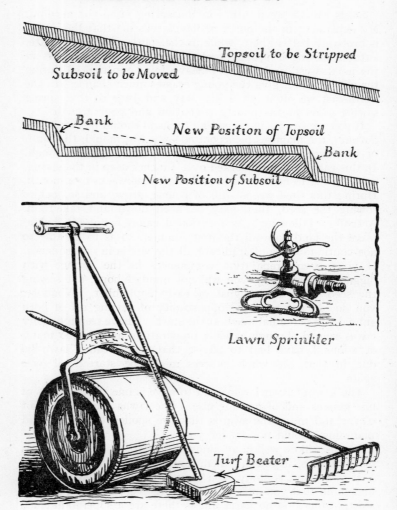

Topsoil to be Stripped

Subsoil to be Moved

Bank

New Position of Topsoil

Bank

New Position of Subsoil

Lawn Sprinkler

Turf Beater

of them. When digging, should this be so, you can bury large numbers of them, and they will thus ensure good drainage.

Do not attempt to sow the seed until the surface has been raked down into a very fine condition. It has been suggested that the soil is never in the right condition unless every particle is as small as a grain of wheat. In order to get it into this condition you may have to wait for the right kind of weather. Do not attempt to make this final preparation until the soil is workable.

You want to get the land firm, and so you will roll when the surface is dry. Alternate rolling and raking will enable you to do the final levelling. Then, just before you are ready to sow, roll again, and rake to produce a fine loose surface.

The seed.—I have tried all the way through the book to impress upon readers that it is worth while buying good seed, and of the right varieties also. This is just as important in the case of lawns. Do not just buy " lawn seed," but be aware of the fact that lawn grasses have names just like other seeds. Many of the cheaper lawn seed mixtures contain a good deal of rye grass, and this never makes the perfect sward. It is safe to say that your lawn will be down for years, and so if you can get it right at the start by using the right seed you will never regret it.

Do not go from one extreme to another and because I have suggested that you want to know the names of the seeds do not believe that it is necessary to have a very complicated mixture. It is possible to produce a lawn by sowing one kind of seed only, and, if you want to try this, it is advisable to use Agrostis tenuis. This is a poor starter and often disappointing in the early stages ; it is more suitable for the heavier and medium soils than for light sands.

A very simple mixture, which has done well in many gardens, consists of :—

> 25 per cent Agrostis tenuis
> 75 per cent Chewing's Fescue

Increase the proportion of Fescue and reduce the amount of

Agrostis (known commonly as the Brown Top Bent) should the soil be light.

Another popular prescription, which some people think is an improvement, is :—

> 5 parts Chewing's Fescue
> 2 parts Creeping Red Fescue
> 3 parts New Zealand Bent

The disadvantage of the Agrostis family is that the lawn may look " benty " during a dry summer. The lawn in this case looks brown, and seems covered with very fine strings.

A prescription which also omits the bents is :—

> 25 per cent Fine-leaved Sheep's Fescue
> 50 per cent Chewing's Fescue
> 25 per cent Sea-washed Fescue

As a general rule people prefer to use the Agrostis mixture, as it does make for a quicker lawn and one which smothers out weeds more effectively.

If you have cleaned the soil thoroughly, and are determined to sow the right seed, get a guarantee that the seed mixture is not weedy. It is most disheartening, having cleaned the land, to find you have inadvertently sown weeds thereon again. Conversely to sow seed of high purity on unclean land is the height of folly.

The process of sowing.—Sow evenly – this is really very important. Divide the seed up into equal lots, and see that the right amount of seed covers the exact amount of ground it is required to. Sowing is made easier if the seed is mixed with a larger bulk of sand or sifted soil.

Careful people mark off the whole lawn into square-yard plots, by strings stretched from one end of the plot to the other, a yard apart, both down and across.

Sow on a still dry day, and when the surface is in a good friable condition. This may be any time from the middle of March to the end of April. After the even distribution of seed, rake the land over lightly. It is possible to sift some light soil over, as a top dressing, first of all. In applying soil to cover seeds, care should be taken, as very little is required. Anyway, the final operation will be a light rolling. This will only be done when the surface is dry.

Amount of seed.—Some gardeners advise 1½ oz. of seed to a square yard, and this is not far wrong when using the last two formulæ mentioned. When an Agrostis mixture alone such as the Agrostis tenuis, 5 lb. of seed is sufficient for 100 square yards – this is 1 oz. to the square yard.

Birds.—Birds can sweep down on to the newly sown lawn and gobble up all the seeds. It does not matter if they only have a few of the seeds, but they can easily overdo it ! You can arrange to cover the lawn with fruit-tree netting, strung up on bamboos, or black cotton may be threaded from twiggy sticks in a criss-cross manner, all over the surface. There is a product called " Horticule " which is poured on to the seeds before they are sown, and so prevents them from being eaten.

Time to cut.—Do not be in too great a hurry to mow the newly laid lawn. You may drag the young grasses up by the roots and spoil everything. In the same way it is a bad plan to wander all over the lawn when the young grass is growing. Wait until it is at least 2 inches high and then scythe it over.

It is often difficult in a small garden to get your lawns scythed, and so the only thing you can do is to set the blades of your mower high and run it over the lawn once. If you can roll it over a few days beforehand, so much the better. Even the next four or five cuts should be made with the blades in this position, and then you may lower them and now quite short.

I know small-garden owners who have been patient enough to go over their new lawns with a pair of shears in the early stages, and this is quite a good plan.

Weeding and Manuring.—Look out for weeds the whole time, and pull them out immediately they are seen. It is not a good plan to put on artificial manures at this early stage. On the lighter soils a top dressing may be given with some finely ground peat, as this not only helps rooting, but acts as a " moisture holder." New Zealand Brown-top sometimes

D*

damps off in the seedling stage, and requires quick-acting nitrogen to help it through.

LAYING A LAWN WITH TURF

This is a far more expensive method, and, unless good turves are obtained, free from weeds, it is not to be advised. It has the advantage, perhaps, of ensuring that a good lawn results far more quickly, but needs far greater " expertness " in the laying.

The turves usually arrive rolled up in lengths a yard long, a foot broad, and $1\frac{1}{2}$ inches thick. It is preferable to lay them down in January, as the turves will not knit with the soil underneath should the weather be dry afterwards. This does not mean to say that you should lay them down during a wet period.

Put the turf down directly it arrives (it should not be stacked for days – much damage is done this way), if the weather is suitable, on the level soil prepared. The preparation will be exactly the same as in the case of sowing seed. Once they have been laid down, beat them into position, one area at a time, by means of a turf beater. Never overbeat – rather get the soil level first (*see* page 102). When the whole area has been covered, pass a heavy roller over to consolidate it. If there are any spaces between the sods, and these should be very small, fill them in with equal parts of fine leaf mould and sand. Then roll the whole lawn over again.

THE CARE OF LAWNS

Having made your lawn, it is obviously necessary to look after it with care. Some readers will have lawns that were made many years ago, and will want to know how to maintain them.

The operations necessary for the production of the perfect lawn are as follows : (1) regular cutting ; (2) rolling ; (3) intelligent feeding ; (4) spiking ; (5) raking ; (6) the elimination of an over-production of worms ; (7) the control of pests and diseases.

Regular cutting.—Whatever you do, never let a lawn go to seed. Cut it at least once a week as soon as the warm weather starts in the spring, and in the full flush of the summer, after a feed and after a rainfall, it may be necessary even to cut twice a week. When the grass is established, the knives can be kept low and the grass very short. Should the weather turn dry, it is not a bad plan to leave off the grass-box so as to allow the cut blades of grass to lie on the lawn and act as a mulch.

Do not cut during frosty weather, but if the winter is mild you may have to start cutting early in March.

When motor mowers are reasonable in price, many garden owners will indulge in one, and when they do there is every likelihood of the grass being cut more regularly. The only danger of the motor mower is the drip that sometimes takes place of oil and petrol and so kills out some of the grasses. See that this does not happen.

Rolling.—Much of the rolling will be done throughout the winter when the soil is sufficiently moist. Rolling does help to level a lawn and to compact it. It also, when used in the spring, at any rate, encourages the young grasses to tiller out. Never roll a lawn when it is covered with wormcasts. Either brush these off with a besom, or give the worm treatment before rolling commences.

A certain amount of rolling can, and will, be done in the spring and summer. It is not much use running a roller over, though, when the ground is dry. Rolling is made all the more easy if you have got a counterbalanced handle ; if you have got to take the weight of the machine as well as keeping the handle up, with a heavy roller it is by no means easy.

With lawns on heavy soils be careful not to overdo the rolling when the ground is sodden. It is better to wait until the spring in cases of this kind.

Regular rolling, backwards and forwards in long straight lines, is to be preferred to the unmethodical meanderings that some people seem to prefer.

Intelligent feeding.—The experiments that have been carried out in the U.S.A., and at the Board of Greenkeeping Research Station in Yorkshire, have tended to show that to produce the perfect sward acidity is necessary. It is undoubtedly an advantage to have the surface layer of soil in a lawn acid. This seems to prevent the invasion of both worms and weeds. When this is present in old lawns the condition should be preserved at all costs. If the condition is absent, it is better to induce it by using such things as powdered peat, sterilised compost, and sharp sand.

For this reason, as the last paragraph in this chapter suggests, lime should be withheld.

Do not be tempted to try and induce soil acidity by the addition of too heavy dressings of sulphate of ammonia. This must be regarded, first and foremost, as the valuable nitrogenous fertiliser, and, secondly, as the weed destroyer.

The use of sulphate of iron and sulphate of ammonia together seems to give better weed control than when sulphate of ammonia is used alone. The action is said to be a burning one rather than due to the extra acidity so induced.

There is no need, then, to go on using either of these two chemicals if all the weeds and mosses have been eradicated.

It seems to be very important to give top dressings of weed-free compost from time to time. In the case of the lighter soils a more peaty compost, and for heavy soils a more sandy compost. Do not think of the compost purely as a carrier for the fertilisers.

Sulphate of iron is used not only to eradicate mosses, but because it has a tendency to improve and darken the colour of grasses. It will keep down such weeds as mouse-ear chickweed also. Used calcined sulphate of iron.

One would advise lawn owners to use a mixture of 3 parts sulphate of ammonia and 1 part calcined sulphate of iron, applied at the rate of 2 ozs. per square yard. The first application should be put on at Easter, and another similar dressing at Whitsun. Keep these artificials perfectly dry before they are applied, and crush up any lumps that may be present into a fine condition before using. It is most essential to apply this mixture evenly at the rate desired.

It is difficult to advise about phosphatic or potassic fertilisers, as if you use these they tend to encourage the clovers. In certain soils, and after a few years, it may be necessary to add these.

As a general guide, give, then, a dressing of 1 oz. super-phosphate and ½ oz. of sulphate of potash every three years in addition to the sulphate of ammonia and sulphate of iron.

Two methods can be recommended. The first one is to throw the chemicals well up into the air and allow them to fall down evenly as a dust. If it is only applied at knee height, a too heavy dressing is likely to fall on one patch, leaving, in consequence, another part of the lawn untreated. The too heavily dressed part will be burnt and the other part neglected in consequence. The second method, recommended for small gardens, is to plot out the area into one-square-yard plots, then place 2 ozs. sulphate of ammonia (or the mixture) into a large cocoa tin with a perforated lid, and distribute this amount evenly over the square. Naturally this method is tedious, but there is no doubt that it is fool-proof, especially where there are flower-beds or rose-beds near by.

Not only, then, are you feeding, but you are eliminating weeds also. The acidity produced will discourage the clovers as well.

Though the author has himself used such a dressing for many years without scorching taking place, there have been cases where, through carelessness, damage had been done. If you fear this will take place, reduce the dressing to 1 oz. per square yard, and increase the number of applications.

Lawn sands consist almost entirely of sand and the two chemicals that have been mentioned. The sand makes the artificials easier to apply, helps to open up heavy soils, and prevents undue scorching. There are lawns on clay soil, in districts with a high rainfall, where the use of coke breeze or charcoal is recommended. In this case the 2 ozs. of the mixture already recommended is added to 6 ozs. of coke breeze, the whole being put on to the plotted square yard.

In addition to pure artificials, it may be necessary from time to time to give a top dressing of finely ground peat compost for sandy lawns, and for " clays " a sandy, leafy compost contain-ing a little charcoal. If these composts can be sterilised by heat – that is, bringing them up to a temperature of 210 degrees F. – they are then not only weed-seed free, but also freed from insect pests and fungus diseases. A sterilised top-dressing not only improves the physical condition of the lawn, but nitrogen is given at the same time.

Spiking.—A certain number of worms in a lawn are of value, as they tend to aerate it, and, by the wormcasts they throw up, provide a simple top-dressing. Acid lawns never encourage worms, and so artificial spiking may have to be carried out. To-day there is a kind of spiked roller available, which, in the case of large lawns, can be run over in a simple manner from time to time. With small lawns a long, fine-tined fork is used, and this is pushed in as deeply as possible all over the lawn every three years.

Raking.—When the lawn is composed largely of the stoloniferous grasses (the creeping bents), raking is all the more important, and should be done before Easter. It is a good plan to commence this about the beginning of March – in the south, at any rate. Raking not only disturbs the dead stolons, but removes unwanted mosses. The most suitable rake for this purpose is the Springbok, which may be bought in varying sizes.

The elimination of unnecessary worms.—In the spring, if there are an overabundance of wormcasts, one of the following remedies should be applied :—

(1) Copper sulphate. Dissolve 1 lb. of this in 50 gallons of water, and give the lawn a good soaking. In careless hands this may do damage.

(2) Mercuric chloride. Dissolve 3 ozs. in 50 gallons of water, and soak the land as above.

Both these are poisonous, and mercuric chloride is corrosive, and will burn metal vessels.

(3) Mowrah meal. This, perhaps, is the safest of the three, and should be applied at 8 ozs. to the square yard. If this is done just before a rain, you will have no need to trouble further ; if in a dry period, the mowrah meal will have to be watered in.

The worms will rise to the surface in their hundreds, or even thousands, and can be swept off.

Control of pests and diseases.—Lawns are often troubled by leather-jackets, the grub of the crane-fly, known to most of us as daddy-longlegs. This pest is particularly bad in the south of Britain and on the sandier soils. The turf will be found to be dying in irregular patches, because the roots of the grasses have been eaten away. If the turf is lifted in these places, a tough-skinned grub will be found, about $1-1\frac{1}{2}$ inches long when fully grown, and of an earthy colour.

There is no known way, at the moment, of keeping the female fly from laying her eggs in the lawn, but the grub may be exterminated by watering with a 64 per cent emulsion of orthodichlorobenzene ; $\frac{1}{8}$ pint of this is diluted into 7 gallons of water, and this is sufficient for 200 square yards of lawn. This is a discovery of the Board of Greenkeeping Research – who state that even better results are achieved when Jeyes fluid is added. The disease which does most damage on lawns is " Fusarium patch " caused by *Fusarium nivale*. A small patch appears on the lawn about the size of a penny, and if examined carefully is found to consist of dying or dead bleached grass. The trouble can spread in further patches somewhat the shape of a Rugby football. Sometimes large areas of grass are killed.

To make certain that this is the cause of the trouble, cover the patch with a bottomless seed box, and place a piece of glass on the top. In a day or so a pink or white growth may appear, and this indicates " Fusarium " trouble. Such patches must be removed bodily and burnt.

The improvement of neglected lawns.—In the case of a lawn which has been badly neglected for years, it may be necessary to take out some of the largest weeds bodily. There are special instruments, which can be filled with arsenical poison, and have at the end of them a needlelike point ; this is pushed into the centre of the weed, and when a lever is depressed the poison is injected into the plant by releasing a spring. This enables the liquid to flow down the needle. This is simpler than trying to remove deep-rooted weeds by hand.

If, when doing the latter, you leave portions of the root in the lawn, they have a nasty habit of growing again. The more shallow-rooted weeds, like daisies, can, however, be removed *in toto* if desired.

It is no use removing such weeds without replacing them with something else. A good plan is to fill the hole in with a light compost, and then to sow suitable lawn seeds on the surface.

Should moss be very bad and, after raking, the lawn looks very bare, it would be a good thing for the lawn if the whole of it is top-dressed with light soil into which lawn seed has been mixed beforehand.

Apart, perhaps, from these two special operations, the usual applications of sulphate of ammonia and calcined sulphate of iron will be put on at regular intervals. It is surprising how such applications, and the regular attention of rolling and mowing, will improve the lawn out of recognition in a very short time.

Lime.—Lime is dangerous to use, as it makes for weediness and susceptibility to disease. In years of drought, however, limed lawns often remain green much longer. Do not be tempted to put lime on more often than every five years at the most, in the autumn.

CHAPTER IX

VEGETABLES

Rotations — Potatoes and Roots

Most people want to grow a few vegetables and so we discuss :—

1. The difference between permanent crops, catch crops and annual crops.
2. The necessity of crop rotation and how to carry it out.
3. What kinds of potatoes to grow and how to get them early.
4. How root crops need special soil preparation and which are easy to grow.
5. The most delicious vegetable known as Salsify.
6. The best varieties to grow in each case

THE vegetable garden should be planned, just as much as any other part of the garden. It should have sufficient paths in it so that manure, etc., can be wheeled about in barrows, if necessary, and so that cabbage stalks and other rubbish may be taken away. There is no need for it to be all paths, and in small gardens one path at the side would be sufficient.

Whatever the size of the vegetable garden may be, some system for the rotation of crops should be thought out. Some people, of course, do not want to grow all kinds of vegetables, but want to restrict the number to two or three. If this is the case, then the rotational scheme will be a very simple one. What must be aimed at is to see that the ground is fully occupied for most of the year, and that no part of the garden is wasted. In a garden of this kind, the crops that are grown may be divided into three groups.

PERMANENT CROPS

Common examples are herbs, like thyme and sage, rhubarb,

113

seakale, asparagus, and globe artichokes, while spinach beet or perpetual spinach may be included in this class also.

CATCH CROPS

Crops that only occupy the ground for a short space of time and do not form part of the rotational scheme. For instance, you can grow shallots along the ridges of celery trenches ; radish can be sown in between rows of peas when these are first put in. Apart from this, it is possible to grow a catch crop during the period between the harvesting of one crop and the sowing of another. After an early crop of peas, which come off, say, at the end of July, you may not want to use the ground again until August or early September for autumn-sown onions. You have, therefore, got a month or two in which to produce a quick-growing catch crop.

Common catch crops are mustard and cress, radishes, French beans, early turnips, stump-rooted carrots, and dwarf peas.

ANNUAL CROPS

Most vegetables fall into this category. Some crops take less than twelve months to mature, while others take the whole or more than this period.

DOUBLE CROPPING

Keen gardeners can often save a week or two by planting or sowing one crop in between the rows of another before the original one is harvested. Some writers advise, for instance, the planting of Brussels sprouts or savoys between rows of early potatoes, but this we shall never find a good plan as the brassicæ always suffer. It is possible, on the other hand, to plant marrows in between rows of early peas, as the marrows like the shade of the peas for a start, and then, when the peas come out, the marrows get all the sun they want. Leeks can be planted in between peas in the same way. French beans may be sown in between rows of cabbages, and, as the French beans require the room, the cabbage, of course, may be cut and used. Keen cultivators will be able to work out other and perhaps better schemes for saving time and space. Be careful not to overdo the idea or neither crop will benefit. Some crops, however, actually prefer to grow near others, for instance, Tomatoes do well when trained up Sweet Corn. Lettuces do well in between Peas.

" MANURIAL CROPPING "

As manures play such an important part in arranging the rotation, it is as well to mention one or two points to be borne in mind. The root crops – the beet, carrots, and parsnips, etc. – will not grow to advantage in ground that has been freshly manured, as this causes them to " fork," and so makes the roots useless. The cabbage family likes well-manured land, and can do with a good dressing of nitrogen. Peas and beans, because of the nodular growths on their roots, can extract nitrogen out of the air, and so after they have cropped, if the roots are left behind, nitrogen is left also. Potatoes, because of their particular method of growth, and because of the way they are cultivated, act as a good " cleaning crop." Potatoes are well manured, and so leave the soil in a high state of fertility. On the other hand it is not usual to lime potatoes, and so the land may be slightly acid. Cabbages and peas like lime. Root crops like plenty of phosphates, while peas and beans like potash. The only reason these likes and dislikes have been mentioned is to help readers to realise what rotational cropping may mean.

ROTATION OF CROPS

If one is asked for a simple definition of the words " rotation of crops," one is tempted to say that rotational cropping is a system by which vegetables of the same *character* do not follow one another on the same piece of ground year after year. You can classify vegetables in all kinds of ways : the botanist will do so by means of natural orders ; the chemist might do so by means of the manures they particularly desire ; the gardener can do so by studying their root systems – deep-rooting crops *versus* shallow-rooting crops ; crops that tend to

FOUR COURSE ROTATION

	Year 1	Year 2	Year 3	Year 4
Plot 1	A	B	C	D
Plot 2	B	C	D	A
Plot 3	C	D	A	B
Plot 4	D	A	B	C

THREE COURSE ROTATION

	Year 1	Year 2	Year 3
Plot 1	Potatoes	Roots	Cabbages
Plot 2	Roots	Cabbages	Potatoes
Plot 3	Cabbages	Potatoes	Roots

POTATO CLAMP

A Type of Four Course Rotation.

A	B	C	D
Potatoes Celery Leeks	Carrots Parsnips Beet Salsify etc.	Peas Beans Onions Shallots	Cabbage Savoy Cauliflower Broccoli Sprouts Turnips
PERMANENT CROPS HERBS ASPARAGUS RHUBARB			

A Three Course Rotation

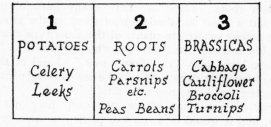

1	2	3
POTATOES Celery Leeks	ROOTS Carrots Parsnips etc. Peas Beans	BRASSICAS Cabbage Cauliflower Broccoli Turnips

TYPES OF CARROT

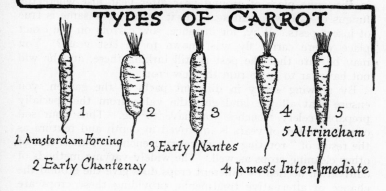

1. Amsterdam Forcing

2 Early Chantenay

3 Early Nantes

4 James's Inter-mediate

5 Altrincham

clean the land well or to leave it rather dirty. The pathologist might put crops into groups according to the diseases and pests which attack them. You can, then, classify vegetables in various ways, and it is as well to look at the matter very broadly.

It would be foolish to attempt to lay down a hard-and-fast rule as to the way that rotational cropping should be carried out. Likewise, no one could say that unless you carried out such a system your vegetable garden would be a failure. It is for the reasons that follow that this system is advised, and it would doubtless be foolish to neglect adopting some simple scheme.

REASONS FOR ROTATIONS

It is said that plants give off what are known as " toxins " from their roots. These are not usually harmful to other plants, but a great accumulation of them in the ground can prevent perfect growth to plants of the same type that follow them. For instance, land can get what is known as " strawberry sick " and also " cauliflower sick." Land in this condition will not grow strawberries in the one case and cauliflowers in the other – at least, not successfully.

Fungus diseases that attack one crop may not attack another, and it would be foolish to plant the same type crop in the same piece of ground year after year just where the fungus disease was waiting to do it harm. The same is true of insect pests. Why, for instance, sow carrots on the exact place where carrot fly was known to be last year ? You may be sure that the pest is still lurking there, and he will not have far to go to ruin the new crop.

By growing celery in different parts of the garden, you ensure that all the land gets the value from the specially prepared celery trenches you have to dig. Thus your soil over a number of years is improved in depth and texture as the result of " rotating " your celery trenches. This is true of other cleaning crops as well. The widely varying methods of cultivation needed by different crops does give the ground the chance of alternative treatments, providing these crops are grown in different parts of the vegetable plot year after year. By moving the crops about, you do not allow the soil to deteriorate in the way it might if it got the same treatment year after year.

Then there is the old story about some plants requiring one particular food out of the soil while other plants may require another. Thus to rotate your crops, what one plant does not use up is taken up by the crop that follows. But we mustn't make too much of this idea, as it should be possible, with intelligent manuring, to make up these so-called deficiencies.

Other advantages that might be mentioned are that it gives a gardener something definite to work on. It ensures that lime is regularly applied, as, if it has to be put on for the cabbages and the peas, and these move round from year to year, the whole of the ground gets limed in its turn. You do get the chance, also, of green manuring. Some crops are harvested early and allow for this, so, in your rotation, green manuring " rotates " also.

It is not easy to plan out a rotation to suit the individual needs of every reader, but there are two simple ones known as the three-course and the four-course.

THREE-COURSE ROTATION

In this scheme the vegetable land is divided up—mentally, at least—into three plots : (1) for the roots ; (2) for the cabbage family ; and (3) for potatoes. Plot 1, then, has potatoes growing on it the first year, roots growing on it the second year, and the cabbage family growing on it the third year. The simple plan below will explain the idea, also see pages 116 and 117.

	Year 1	Year 2	Year 3
Plot 1 . .	Potatoes	Roots	Cabbages
Plot 2 . .	Roots	Cabbages	Potatoes
Plot 3 . .	Cabbages	Potatoes	Roots

In this way we have endeavoured to group together the crops that need similar treatment and have the same kind of requirements. We try and see, also, that deep-rooting crops alternate with shallow-rooting vegetables. As far as possible we arrange that " families " are kept together. For this reason we put turnips in with the cabbage family, as they are closely related and get the same diseases and pests – notably club root.

A three-course rotation is simple to use, but it is not very easy to fit in all crops. Growers are apt to wonder where to put such things as celery and leeks, for instance, but these can be used as dividing lines between the areas if necessary – and so can runner beans or peas, if desired. In some ways, then, the four-course rotation has its advantages.

THE FOUR-COURSE ROTATION

Here the land is divided up into four equal plots, and the vegetables are grouped into four sections also. Group A would be potatoes, Group B the pulse family, (i.e. the peas and beans), and in this group for convenience sake we can include our celery, leeks, onions, and shallots. Group C can be the root crops (i.e. carrots, parsnips, beetroot, and unusual vegetables like salsify, scorzonera), and Group D the cabbage family (i.e. Brussels sprouts, savoys, cauliflowers, turnips and swedes, kale, and kohlrabi) ; in this section, also, may be included spinach.

The crops that we have left out are either the permanent crops that must have a place all to themselves, so that they needn't be disturbed, plants like artichokes that grow very tall and so need growing at one end of the garden. Dwarf friends, like parsley and chives, which make excellent edgings, and catch crops, like radish and lettuce, that can be grown almost anywhere, fitting in as they do where convenient.

See plan on top of page 117.

See to it that you use the rotational system to its fullest advantage. It will help you to rotate your systems of manuring, your systems of cultivation, and will save you time and labour in the long run. Not only this, but many have found that rotations do save money.

TUBEROUS CROPS

Quite a small group really, but a very important one. There are only two that we need worry about – the potato and the Jerusalem artichoke.

POTATOES

Perhaps this is the most important crop in the garden, and you can hardly find an allotment in England that does not have at least a row or two of this vegetable on it.

Soil.—Nearly all soils are suitable for potatoes, though clays and peaty soils produce tubers which are commonly called " soapy." The best preparation for potatoes is to bastard trench the land, or even ridge dig it in the autumn. If ridging is done, the rows should run north and south. It is seldom that you can get gardeners to apply the manure in the autumn, though this is the best time to do it, except perhaps on light soils in warm situations. As soon as possible after the beginning of March, the soil should be forked over to bring it down to a fine tilth.

The Seed.—Be sure and buy your " seed " from Scotland or Ireland, or even Wales. Such seed always give heavier crops, and you can purchase Scotch or Irish seed from your local merchant, who will give you the necessary guarantee. Do not try and save your own seed or buy it from neighbours. The seed tubers should weigh about $2\frac{1}{2}$ ozs., and should be about the size of a hen's egg. If you have to have large tubers, these should be planted directly they are cut. It is a bad practice to cut some time before putting them in the ground. When cutting a tuber in two, be sure to see that each portion has at least one " eye."

Sprouting.—Potatoes do best if they are sprouted in trays before being put into the ground. A potato has two ends, and these are known as the rose end and the heel. The " rose " is the end that has the most " eyes," and will be found always to be at the opposite end to the part that was attached to the root.

Stand the tubers rose-end upwards in a shallow wooden tray (you can buy them specially made for the purpose, or you can soon knock them together yourself). A potato tray is normally 2 ft. 6 ins. long, 1 ft. 6 ins. wide, and 3½ ins. deep, and has corner posts standing 3 in. above the sides. This allows the trays to be stood one above the other while the sprouting process is going on. Put the trays anywhere where they will be free from frost, and where there will be plenty of light. Air should circulate freely amongst them as well. Some time afterwards shoots will grow, and, if too many arise from the same tuber, they can all be rubbed out except one or two. A good " sprit " should be stout, strong, and dark green, and not longer than two inches. Spritting ensures the potatoes being several weeks earlier than if they were left unsprouted. Heavier crops result as well.

General cultivation.—It is difficult to dictate about distances between the rows and distances between the plants themselves. Roughly speaking the " very earlies " on a south border should be planted with the rows eighteen inches apart and the tubers 1 foot apart in the rows. Normally, the distances advised are: first earlies, 1 ft. 9 ins. by 1 ft.; second earlies, 2 ft. 3 ins. by 1 ft. 3 ins. and main crops 2 ft. 6 ins. by 1 ft. 6 ins. You can alter the distances to suit varieties and to suit soils, and these distances are merely put here to guide you. Never plant deeper than four inches, any extra depth required is done by earthing up. Drills for planting are drawn out with a Canterbury hoe, and the " seed " is placed carefully into position, so as to avoid injuring the " sprits." A handful of grass mowings may be put over each potato. This prevents them from becoming scabby. The soil is then drawn over, leaving a very slight ridge to mark the row.

In some districts it is possible to plant in the middle of March, but north of the Potteries the second week in April is perhaps more usual. When the plants are about eight inches high, the soil should be brought up to them, again with a Canterbury hoe, making a ridge five or six inches high. This encourages the plant to throw tubers. Keep hoeing in between the rows, to keep down weeds and to keep the soil loose. The constant stirring of soil where potatoes are grown is one of the most important operations. Further earthing up may be practised in a few weeks' time to bring the soil up yet another inch.

Manuring.—In addition to the dressing of dung or compost, which should be at the rate of 1 good barrowload to 10 square yards, or one ton to a ten-rod plot, the following artificials should be applied, per square yard : $\frac{1}{2}$ oz. sulphate of ammonia, $\frac{1}{2}$ oz. sulphate of potash, 1 oz. superphosphate, or 3 ozs of Cornish Fish may be used instead. With early potatoes it is usually useless to give artificials, as they are out of the ground before the plants can make use of the plant foods.

Storing.—Early potatoes can be dug up as soon as they are fit to use. The main crops should be left in the ground until the haulm has died down. They should then be lifted carefully and stored. A shed or cellar is quite suitable, but they can be kept in " burys " or " clamps." This consists in choosing a convenient piece of ground on the dry side, putting down a 3-inch layer of straw – putting the potatoes in a mound on the straw, and then covering over with straw and, finally, soil. To ventilate the clamp a twist of straw is arranged to " peep out " at the top. *See* page 116.

Pests and diseases.—Unfortunately there are large numbers of these which space does not admit our describing. The commonest is the blight (*Phytophthora infestans*), which can be controlled by spraying with Bordeaux – *see* Chapter XV. Common Scab (*Actinomyces scabies*) is seen on the tuber in little scabby spots. If plenty of lawn mowings or grass cuttings are put into the drills at planting time, this prevents the disease.

Varieties

EARLIES :
Arran Crest ; Ninety Fold ; May Queen ; Duke of York ; Home Guard ; Doone Early ; Arran Pilot.

SECOND EARLIES :
Arran Comrade ; Great Scott ; Dunbar Cavalier ; Dunbar Rover.

MAIN CROPS :
Majestic ; Arran Chief ; Arran Banner ; Kerr's Pink ; King Edward ; Arran Cairn ; Dunbar Standard.

SPECIAL NOTE

If you own land that is subject to wart disease remember
there is no known cure for this. You are bound by law to
grow what are known as immune varieties. Among those
I have mentioned, the following are immune : Ally, Arran
Comrade, Great Scott, King George, Kerr's Pink, Majestic,
Arran Pilot, Gladstone, Arran Crest.

JERUSALEM ARTICHOKE

One of the most easily grown vegetables in the garden. It
will grow practically anywhere, though you cannot expect large
tubers of good quality if you plant them in an odd neglected
corner.

Planting.—The tubers are planted any time from February
to the beginning of April, the rows being 2 ft. 6 ins. apart, and
the tubers 12 inches in the rows. They grow to a height of
6 feet or more, and will provide quite a good screen at
the bottom of the garden. See that the tubers are put about
6 inches deep in the ground.

Manuring.—*See* Potatoes.

General cultivation.—Hoe along the rows from time to
time, to keep down weeds and to provide a mulch, but do
not earth up.

Lifting.—Directly the tops have died down, the roots may
be lifted and stored in sand. On the other hand, they can be
left in the ground, as they are not affected by frost, and so can
be used as desired. Be sure and dig up every single tuber, as
if even the smallest one is left in it will grow next year.

Varieties

Grow the **White Skinned** and not the Purple Skinned.

ROOT CROPS

All root-crops need well-prepared soil, but they much dislike
fresh manure. If you want to get a good, clean, straight root,
then you must not manure with dung. When fresh manure
is used, the roots always fork. Be very careful not to damage

the roots while hoeing, as otherwise they may go to seed. In fact anything that checks growth – excessive drought, too much rain, attempts at transplanting – all have the same effect. Root crops need phosphates and potash, and little nitrogen.

BEETROOT

You should aim to grow beet that are not too coarse, and that, on cutting, are free from white rings. The root should be crimson right the way through. Beet bleed very easily, and should not be damaged either during cultivation or lifting.

Soil.—The best soil for beet is probably one of a light and sandy nature, though good roots can be grown in clays, providing they are well worked.

Seed sowing.—The seed should be sown at the end of April or at the beginning of May, though in heavy clay soils sowing should be deferred a fortnight. The drills should be 12 inches apart, 2 inches deep, and the plants should be thinned out finally to 8 inches apart. It is usual to thin beetroot at two periods – first of all, when they are a few inches high, to 4 inches apart, and then, when they are at first fit to use, to 8 inches apart.

Cultivation.—Hoe continuously between the rows. Should any part of the row fail, it is possible to transplant, especially if the weather is showery or if plenty of watering can be given.

Manuring.—On light land salt may be given, at the rate of 2 ozs. per square yard, when the plants are half grown. A good artificial mixture, which should be applied a week or ten days before sowing the seed, is 1 part sulphate of ammonia, 2 parts sulphate of potash, 4 parts superphosphate. These are well mixed together and applied at the rate of 4 ozs. to the square yard, or use an organic fertiliser like Fish Manure at the same rate.

Storing.—Lift carefully, and store in a clamp in the same way as potatoes, or in dry earth or sand in a shed. The beet must be dug up before the winter frosts, and this usually means the middle of October. The roots will usually keep in good condition until the following June.

Varieties

ROUND :
  Empire Globe (the colour when cut through is an even bright blood red) ; **Model Globe** (a good early variety).

LONG :
  Cheltenham Green Top ; Bell's Non-bleeding Red.

TANKARD :
  Obelisk. A ½ long and ½ round variety.

CARROTS

As in potatoes, there are early varieties and main crops, but further than this, there are round-rooted types, intermediate types, and some which have long red roots. Seedsmen often divide them into 5 groups, viz. : (*a*) Forcing, (*b*) Shorthorn, (*c*) Guerande, (*d*) Intermediate, and (*e*) the Long. *See* page 117.

Soil.—Carrots do best on a deep sandy loam. If you have heavy soil, then you should grow the short- or stump-rooted varieties.

The earliest carrots can be produced by sowing towards the middle of March on a specially prepared warm dry border. Do not sow if the soil is wet and cold, but wait for warmer weather. The drills should be 6 inches apart. When the plants are up, they should be thinned out to 2 inches apart. Another sowing may be made at the beginning of April.

Seed sowing.—Under ordinary cultivation, drills are made about ¾ inch deep and 12 to 18 inches apart, according to the variety. For private gardens the intermediate varieties are most useful, and for mid-season work and for main crops the long reds.

Cultivation.—As soon as the seedlings are large enough to handle, they are thinned out with a draw hoe to 3 inches apart, the final thinning being done by hand, either to 4 inches or 6 inches apart, according to the variety. The thinnings should not be left about, but should be taken away and burnt so as to help prevent carrot fly attacks. Immediately after thinning, draw the soil up to the row and fill the spaces up where the roots have been removed. Continue hoeing throughout the summer.

Manuring.—For early varieties 1 oz. of fish manure per square yard will do, though if growth is not quick enough, waterings with liquid manure may be given at fortnightly intervals as well. For main crops use the same artificials as recommended for beetroot.

Storing.—Carrot roots should be lifted and stored as for beetroot.

Pests and diseases.—The Carrot Fly is the most common, and preventive methods should be used, as previously outlined. In addition, burn all the roots that have been attacked and naphthalene the rows well after thinning. *See* Chapter XV.

Varieties

SHORTHORNS :
Improved Early Nantes ; New Model.

INTERMEDIATE :
James's Scarlet Intermediate.

MAINCROP – HALF LONG :
Autumn King ; Chantenay.

LONGS :
Long Red ; Long Red Surrey ; Altrincham Selected.

PARSNIPS

The parsnip is perhaps the easiest of all the root vegetables to grow. It is curious that, although it is so easy, it should be so unpopular on the table. Perhaps it is a case of " familiarity breeding contempt."

Soil.—The parsnip will do in any type of soil provided it is not too stony. To grow well-shaped roots, quite a good plan is to bore a hole 3 feet deep, and 3 inches in diameter at the top. Fill this up with friable sifted soil, and sow two or three seeds on the top. Thin out to one plant when the seedlings grow.

Seed sowing.—Parsnips can be sown at the end of February or the beginning of March, provided the ground is dry enough. Parsnip seeds should be sown thickly, as only about half of them will germinate. The rows should be 18 inches apart, and 1 inch deep. When the seedlings are an inch or so high, thin them to 8 inches apart.

Cultivation.—Hoe continuously, to keep down weeds and to ensure a dust mulch.

Storing.—There is no need to store parsnips ; they can be left in the ground until they are required. In fact parsnips always taste better after they have had some frost on them. If you are in a district which normally has hard winters, it is a good plan to dig some of them up and store them. It is very annoying to know you have got parsnips in the ground but, because the soil is frozen, you cannot dig them.

Pests and Diseases.—The Celery Fly : Will attack parsnip leaves and may do some harm (for remedy *see* p. 233). Canker : This is bad in some soils, but at present there is no known cure.

Varieties

Improved Hollow Crown   The Student   Tender and True ; Turnip Rooted – a roundish sort.

TURNIPS

Do not forget that turnips should really be grown with the cabbage family, because they belong to it and are liable to the same pests and diseases.

Soil.—They are not very particular as to soil, though a sandy loam is said to grow them better than heavier soils. They are very difficult to grow on shallow soils over chalk, as these do not retain moisture easily. Roots on droughty soils seem to be more readily attacked by the turnip flea beetle and run to seed easily.

Seed sowing.—Turnips may be sown during the early part of March in a sheltered spot, providing the ground is dry enough to get down to a fine tilth. Such sowing is usually done broadcast, and thinning is done roughly to 4 inches apart when the plants are large enough to handle. Early White Milan is used in this connection. Later sowings are made in drills 12 inches apart, the turnips being thinned to 6 inches apart in the rows.

The main late-summer supply is obtained by sowing in May, preferably in a shady situation, while seed for autumn and winter crops is sown from the middle of July to the end

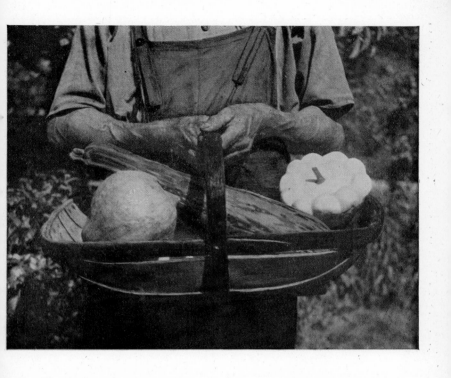

A basket full of marrows and squashes.   The left-hand one
is a Hubbard's Squash ;   the centre one a Long Green ;   the
third a Custard Marrow.

Pinching off the tops of broad beans helps to prevent attacks of Black Fly and causes earlier cropping.

of August. The drills for winter turnips are 18 inches apart, the first thinning being to 6 inches, and the final thinning being to a foot, for the roots that are being left to stand throughout the winter.

Some people like turnip-tops as a green vegetable, and, if so, sowings are made early in September in rows 2 feet apart. No thinning is carried out.

Cultivation.—Hoe the ground regularly ; constant stirring not only helps the crops to grow, for the reasons I have previously given, but raises a " dust " disliked by the flea beetles.

Manuring.—Keep the ground rich in organic materials ; this will help to retain the moisture and prevent bolting. As the turnip is often grown as a catch crop, the manuring given to the previous vegetable will often suffice. The artificials recommended for beetroot may be given, but do not forget that the turnip is a lime lover. A top dressing of lime at 4 ozs. per square yard just before sowing the seed will help matters considerably.

Storing.—In normal winters the roots may stand outdoors. But in districts subject to sharp frosts the roots will be spoiled. In this case they should be lifted and clamped as for potatoes.

Pests and diseases.—The Turnip Flea Beetle : This attacks the leaves, gradually eating them away. A dusting with Derris is quite a good control. Destroy also such weeds as shepherd's purse and charlock, as these are alternative hosts. Turnip Gall Weevil : A maggot will be found inside the gall on the root, and people often confuse this with club root. The control is difficult. Club Root : *see* Chapter XV.

Varieties

FRAME

Early Long White Frame – has a blunt nose and minute tap-root, being very tender ; **Jersey Navet**
These varieties can be sown in frames early in February if a hot-bed has been prepared.

SUMMER :

Early Snowball ; Early White Stone ; Golden Ball ; Jersey Lily – the epicure variety.
In this case the seed is sown outside from March onwards.

E

WINTER :
   Chirk Castle ; Veitch's Red Globe – a quick growing yet hardy
sort ; **Manchester Market.**

SALSIFY

A very delicious vegetable that is not grown enough by
amateur gardeners. It is often known popularly as the
vegetable oyster.

Soil.—Possibly the best soil for salsify is a deep, well-worked
light loam. It will grow quite well in a heavy soil, especially
if ridged in the autumn.

Seed sowing.—The seed should not be sown until April,
the drills being 12 inches apart and 1 inch deep. Directly the
seedlings can be handled, they should be thinned out to
4 inches apart, and finally to 8 inches apart.

Cultivation.—Hoe continuously, to keep the surface soil
crumbly.

Manuring.—No dung should be dug in when the land is
prepared, but salsify will grow best if it follows a well-manured
crop. The organic fertilisers recommended for root crops
should be applied 14 days or so before sowing the seed.

Storing.—It is usual to leave this root crop in the ground
and to dig it up as required. They can be dug up, and stored
in moist sand in a shed, but, if this is done, they must be
handled with care as they bleed easily.

Pests and diseases. This crop is practically free from
pests and diseases.

Varieties
Mammoth Sandwich Island.

CHAPTER X

VEGETABLES

Brassicaes — Peas and Beans

Here we discuss how to grow the members of the cabbage family as well as peas and beans.

1. What is the brassicæ family ?
2. How can I get Broccoli (the winter cauliflower) to live through the winter ?
3. My Brussels Sprouts never give me heavy crops of *firm* sprouts. How can I ensure this ?
4. Is there really a vegetable called Colewort ?
5. How can I stop my peas from being taken by birds and mice ?
6. I can't get poles for my runner beans. What can I use instead ?

THE BRASSICÆ FAMILY

THE Brassicæ family includes practically all the green crops that are grown for the table. Green vegetables are so essential to health that it should be every gardener's wish to supply some sort of green vegetable for every day of the year.

All members of the brassicæ family are subject to club root, and this is one of the reasons why it is necessary to see that a rotation of crops is carried out. Lime will not only prevent the land getting too acid, but will act as a deterrent against this disease. Lime, then, should always be applied before planting out the members of this family.

Nitrogen is a necessary factor in the successful cultivation of all such crops, and in addition to the farmyard manure other nitrogenous manures will be given.

BORECOLE OR KALE

This is a hardy winter vegetable which can be cut, and cut again. It is certainly a vegetable to grow in hard winters, as frost seems to improve the quality.

Soil.—Kales will grow in practically any soil, though perhaps the heavier soils suit them best.

131

Seeds.—Seeds are sown at the beginning of April, in a seed-bed, and, if the young plants grow too thickly, they are thinned out when two inches high.

Cultivation.—The plants can be put out during June and July, either between other crops or in rows on their own. The distance apart depends on the variety, the smaller types needing 2 ft. by 2 ft., and the taller varieties 3 ft. by 2 ft. 6 ins. There will be little need to do much cultivation between this crop directly the winter sets in.

Manuring.—Do not manure too heavily, or else the plants are apt to grow soft and luxuriant, and so be damaged by frosts and cold winds. No dung need be given, but a complete organic fertiliser like fish may be used at 3–4 ounces to the square yard.

Pests and diseases.—*See* Chapter XV.

Varieties

There are a very large number of varieties and, in fact, types of kale. You can have tall or dwarf ones, curly ones, and those that heart, and special ones like the **Portugal Cabbage** or **Chou de Burghley.** The **Cottager's Kale** is hardy and prolific ; **A1** is densely curled and compact ; while there is a **Green-Curled Dwarf** and a **Green-Curled Tall. Asparagus Kale** has distinctive long, thin shoots. **Hungry Gap Kale,** sown June for cropping May–June following year.

BROCCOLI

This is, of course, the winter cauliflower. It is not perhaps quite so tender as its prototype, but it is very useful to have a nice supply of such " cauliflowers " throughout the winter.

Soil.—Broccoli seems to prefer a heavy loam. It is very important to see that the soil is firm, as rich loose soil only produces loose open hearts. On light land it will be necessary to add farmyard manure, and then to firm the ground down afterwards, before the plants are put in.

Seed sowing.—The seed is sown in shallow drills, 9 inches apart, on a specially prepared, friable bed. If you wish to cut good heads in the autumn, sow at the end of March.

Winter varieties should be sown at the end of April or the beginning of May, while for the varieties that will be cut in May and early June the following year, the seed should be put in in the middle of May. Never let broccoli plants get thin and leggy, so thin out the seedlings early in their growth. It is not a bad plan to take out the best plants, so that they can be transplanted into another seed-bed 3 inches apart. At any rate keep the seed-bed and the transplanted bed free from weeds.

Cultivation.—It is convenient to use broccoli as a crop to follow potatoes, dwarf beans or peas. The ground has then been well manured and yet had time to settle down and to be firm. Put the plants out at 2 ft. 6 ins. between the rows, and 2 ft. in the rows. If possible do this on a showery day, and, if not, water the plants in.

As the plants get ready to cut, if you wish to keep the curds perfectly white, bend one of the leaves over the top, breaking it if necessary to keep it in position.

In hard winters it is a good plan to heel the plants over to the north. A spadeful of soil may be taken out on the north side of the plant, so that the plant may more easily be bent over. What injures the curd is not so much the frost itself, but the alternate frost and thaw. Heeling over helps to prevent this. *See* page 141.

Manuring.—Do not give fresh manure unless absolutely necessary. It is far better to manure the previous crop more heavily than you would normally do, in order to leave the ground enough for broccoli. Apply 3 ozs. of fish manure to the square yard before planting.

Pests and diseases.—*See* Chapter XV.

Varieties

Broccoli varieties may be divided into three divisions:

FIRST DIVISION :
    Veitch's Self Protecting. Cuts in October and November.
    Extra Early Roscoff. Cuts late November.
    Winter Mammoth. Cuts in November and December.
    New Year. Cuts December and January.

SECOND DIVISION :
Early Feltham.   Cuts Mid-January and early February.
Mid Feltham.   Cuts in March and April.
Snow's Winter White.   Cuts in April.

THIRD DIVISION :
Late Feltham.   Cuts in May.
Late Queen.   Cuts end of May and early June.
Clucas June.   Cuts June.

SPROUTING BROCCOLI

This can be grown in the same way as broccoli, only it does not produce a white curd, but a large number of green leaves and tender flowering stems.   These are cut off before the flowers open, while they are yet immature, and are very delicious.

Varieties

For Christmas work, **Christmas Extra Early Purple** is useful   for March, **Early Purple Sprouting**, and for April, **Late Purple Sprouting**.

A novelty comparatively recently introduced is the **Nine Star Perennial**, which produces large numbers of small cauliflowers on one stem.

BRUSSELS SPROUTS

With care it should be possible to pick Brussels sprouts from September until March.   To grow them well there are five points to be borne in mind : (1) They need a long season of growth ; (2) They need plenty of room for development – most amateurs plant them too close ; (3) They must be heavily manured ; (4) Firm ground is an absolute necessity ; (5) Deep cultivation.

It is rather difficult to get a combination of all these things. For instance, if you manure heavily and cultivate deeply, then it is difficult to ensure that the ground is firm.

Soil.—They are not particular as to soil, though they usually crop more heavily on the clays than on the sand.

Seed sowing.—To obtain succession it is a good plan to sow batches of seed at various periods of the year.   The first sowing can be made in August, the plants being in a sheltered border, planted 3 inches apart, throughout the winter. Another sowing can be made in a frame early in February, or sowings can be made outside during March. The seed-bed should consist of light, rich soil, and be in a sheltered position. When the seedlings are fit to handle (this refers to the spring sowings) they should be transplanted into further seed-beds at 3 inches square. It is not a bad plan to pick out the largest plants the first time, and then to go over the original bed again a fortnight later, and pick out the largest of those that are left, and so on. Successive batches of plants can be obtained in this way from one sowing.

Cultivation.—The sturdy plants that you have by now produced are planted out at least 2½ feet square during May, or perhaps even early June. Some of the taller and more prolific varieties actually need 3 feet square. Plant during a showery period, or water the plants in. If you wish, because you think the ground looks bare, you may grow catch crops in between the sprout rows.

Whatever you do, see that the ground is firm before planting. Loose open sprouts only result from similar soil.

When the sprouts are fit to gather, it is better to cut them off, leaving a very short stalk on the main stem. In this way further sprouts are encouraged, and this lengthens the season.

Hoeing will be necessary to keep down weeds and to provide the dust mulch.

As the main leaves turn yellow, they may be removed with a knife, but it is a bad plan to cut off the large leaves while they are still green.

The head should not be removed until the end of February, as this helps the plant in sprout formation and does give protection to the plant as a whole.

Manuring.—Brussels sprouts are always very " hungry," and you should dig in a heavy dressing of farmyard manure or compost, deeply, when you are preparing the ground. Market gardeners use up to 30 tons per acre for this crop. In addition to this, a fortnight or so before putting the plants out, sprinkle fish manure or meat bone meal over the soil at 3 ozs. to the square yard.   Do not forget a dressing of lime at 5 ozs. per square yard.

Pests and Diseases.—*See* Chapter XV.

Varieties

Evesham Special	*Medium height*	Large firm sprouts
Timperley Champion	*Tall variety*	A good keeper
Cambridge Early No. 1	*Large size*	Solid sprouts
Clucas Favourite	*Tall*	Studded with solid sprouts

DWARF STRAINS :

Dwarf Gem	*under* 18 *ins. high*	Small solid sprouts
Darlington	*under* 18 *ins. high*	For light soils

FAIRLY STRONG STRAINS :

Evesham Special	24 *ins. high*	Large firm sprouts
Harrison's XXX	24 *ins. high*	Heavy cropper

TALL VARIETIES :

Ormskirk Giant	3 *ft. high*	Solid sprouts
Cambridge Late No. 5	3 *ft. high*	Heavy cropper, good flavour
Timperley Champion	3 *ft. high*	Good for the North

Special Note.

Whatever you do, do take notice of the five points mentioned in the first paragraph, especially the one about plenty of room for development.   You cannot give Brussels sprouts too much room.

CABBAGE

There are cabbages for the summer, cabbages for the spring, and nice firm-hearted ones for the winter. You ought to be able to get a supply of good cabbages all the year round. For this reason, it is proposed to divide cabbages up into three groups, and then, by different sowings, and using suitable varieties, we shall arrange to have a continuous supply.

Soil.—Providing you can work the soil deeply, and add organic manure, cabbages will grow well on almost any land. If they do prefer one soil more than another, this is a moist, retentive loam.

Seed Sowing.—

SPRING CABBAGE : This is usually sown in the month of July, or, perhaps, in the south-west, in the month of August.

Rake the ground down to a fine tilth, and sow the seed thinly in drills 9 inches apart and $\frac{1}{2}$ inch deep. Thin sowing makes it possible for you to leave the plants in the seed-bed until they have to be put out in September. Of course, sturdier plants do result if you transplant them when they are fit to handle into another prepared bed.

SUMMER CABBAGE : Summer cabbage, sown in March, and, if you like, at fortnightly intervals afterwards, can provide plants which may be planted directly there is any vacant land.

WINTER CABBAGE : This is sown in April or May, though in the north they are often sown in March with the summer varieties.

GENERAL NOTE

The method of sowing and planting for summer and winter cabbage are the same as for spring cabbage.

Cultivation.—The spring cabbages (as they are fairly small, and will be cut early) can be planted 18 inches between the rows and 12 inches between the plants. If you have a big variety, like Durham Early, it will need 18 inches by 18 inches. The summer cabbages can be planted 2 feet between the rows and 18 inches in the rows, while some of the large drumhead winter cabbages may need 2 feet square.

The ground should be limed, if it is at all acid, using 5 ozs. of hydrated lime to the square yard. Constant hoeing should be done between the rows. The stalks should be removed from the ground as soon as possible after the cabbages are cut, put on the compost heap after being bashed up with the back of an axe or a chopping block. If this is impossible, Adco Accelerator will help to rot them down.

Manuring.—The cabbage, like the Brussels sprout, is a gross feeder, and, except in the case of the spring cabbage, the ground should be well manured. In addition to the dung, apply 3 ozs. of fish manure or meat and bone meal. In very light soils it is possible to give sulphate of potash at 2 ozs. the square yard. In the case of the September planted spring cabbage, basic slag may be used instead of superphosphate, especially on heavy land ; 4 ozs. to the square yard should do.

E*

Varieties

SPRING CABBAGES :

Clucas First Early. 218. One of the best early cabbages in cultivation.

Myatt's Early Offenham. Firm hearts, few outside leaves.

Durham Early. Dark green ; a large cabbage.

Wheeler's Imperial. Noted for its flavour.

SUMMER CABBAGES :

Primo. Early, dwarf and compact, " cut " in July and August.

Glory. Large, firm, round heads.

Winningstadt. Conical, pointed heads.

Simpson's Long Standing. Will keep well hearted for a long time without splitting.

The Swift. Compact, pointed heart.

WINTER CABBAGES:

Early Paragon Drumhead. Drum-like heart.

Christmas Drumhead. Drum-like heart.

RED PICKLING CABBAGE

This can be sown the first week in August in exactly the same way as for any other kind of cabbage. The manuring and cultivation are similar also.

Varieties

Danish Stonehead. Early, good-sized firm hearts.

Lydiate. Red drumhead ; large and late.

Ruby Red. The earliest for spring sowing.

COLEWORTS

Coleworts are delicious little winter cabbages. They are usually sown in the spring and summer for autumn and winter cutting. Treat as for cabbages, except that they can be planted out 18 inches between the rows and 1 foot between the plants.

Varieties

Hardy Green. Large hearts, which are very hardy.

Rosette. Have rosette-shaped heads ; used in the winter.

KOHLRABI

This may be said to be a cross between a turnip and a

cabbage. A large turnip-like stem is produced above the ground, with leaves growing all round it. The side leaves gradually fall off, and the " roots " are used any time throughout the winter. Kohlrabi is perfectly hardy, and is an excellent crop to grow in dry years.

The seed is sown outdoors, where the plants are to grow, at any time from the beginning of April until the end of June. The seedlings are thinned out to 9 inches apart, and these can be transplanted if necessary. Manure as for cabbages.

Varieties

Early Vienna Purple. Small and delicious.
Early Vienna White. Small and delicious.

There is also a large green and large purple type.

SAVOYS

The savoy has deeply crinkled leaves, being extremely hardy, and is used throughout the winter. Frost does not spoil the plants, but actually improves the flavour.

Soil.—They prefer heavy, deeply cultivated, rich land, and may follow crops like potatoes and peas that have been " well done."

Seed sowing.—The seed is usually sown in three batches ; in the first place in the middle of March, secondly at the beginning of April, and a final sowing at the end of April. The seedlings are thinned out early, the drills being 8 inches apart. Keep the rows clean and free from weeds.

Cultivation.—The plants are put out into their permanent position during June and July, and on showery days if possible. The smallest varieties need only have 17 inches between the rows and 15 inches in the rows. The larger varieties need planting 2 feet square.

Manuring.—After the previous crop has been cleared, it is quite a good plan to cover the ground with calcium cyanamide at 4 ozs. to the square yard. This will kill the weeds, and provides a form of nitrogen which savoys seem to like. Fork in, previous to this application, $\frac{3}{4}$ oz. sulphate of potash and 3 ozs. of a good fish manure per square yard.

Varieties

LARGE TYPES :
Best-of-all. Large, early ; ready late in October.
Latest-of-all. Rich dark green, compact, intensely curled.

SMALL TYPES :
Dwarf Ulm. Very early.
Belle Ville. Deep colour, beautifully curled.

To get a succession of solid heads good varieties are :—

Ormskirk Early. Cuts in October.
Ormskirk Medium. Cuts from November to February.
Ormskirk Late. Cuts from January to the end of March.
Ormskirk Extra Late. Cuts March-Early April.

THE PULSE FAMILY

This is a very large family of pod-bearing vegetables, all of which have on their roots nodules containing bacteria which live in harmony with the plant. These are able to make use of nitrogen from the atmosphere, and if the roots are left in the ground when the crop is cleared much nitrogenous plant food is left behind.

It should not be thought that because this family can extract nitrogen from the air that they should not be given any nitrogenous manure, especially in the early stages.

Lime should always be applied on any but calcareous soils at the rate of a quarter of a pound per square yard before sowing the seed.

PEAS

There are all kinds of peas to be grown, not only tall and dwarf varieties – those that are early or late – but special types, like sugar peas or asparagus peas.

Soil.—Peas will grow on most soils, though those that are light and sandy seem to suit them best. The later varieties prefer a retentive loam that has been well drained.

Seed sowing.—Prepare the ground for peas in the autumn by digging it and leaving it rough. In this way it will " fall down " to a fine tilth in the spring. Drills are then drawn out 5 inches wide, and 2 to 3 inches deep, the distance apart

A Good Way to Keep Birds off the Peas

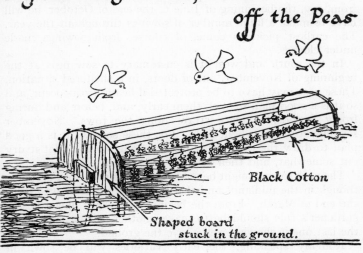

Black Cotton

Shaped board stuck in the ground.

Protect Broccoli in Winter

N

by Heeling Plants Over to the North

between the rows being equal to the height of the variety sown.

If the grower desires to provide a succession of green peas from, say, the beginning of June to the end of October, he will have to make a large number of sowings throughout the year. The earliest pickings come, of course, from sowings made under cloches.

In the south and west it is customary to sow peas at the beginning of November, out of doors, in a sheltered situation. These peas may have to be protected if heavy frosts occur, and so it is a good plan to stick them early, and, before and during frosty periods, to place straw along the rows. November sowings do best on light soils. For these sowings it is a good plan to draw the drill out in the morning, so as to let it dry out somewhat, and then sow the seed in the afternoon.

The next sowing might be made at the beginning of February, though in the midlands and the north it is safest to wait until the end of March. From the beginning of April onwards, the gardener's rule should be to make another sowing as soon as the last one is showing well above the ground.

Roughly speaking, the early varieties will be sown in November, February, and March, and, of course, again if necessary in June. The second earlies are sown in April, and the main crop in May.

General Cultivation.—You cannot grow good peas unless you are prepared to keep the ground stirred regularly. Moisture is absolutely essential, and apart from cultivation, mulchings should be given. Lawn-mowings, leaves, can be placed along the rows early in June. If watering has to be carried out, it should not be done on the row itself, but in small trenches on either side of the row. The ground should be soaked and not just damped.

All peas should be " sticked " if this is at all possible, though the dwarf 18-inch types will grow quite well without support. Place the pea sticks in position 6 inches away from the peas, and 1 foot away from one another. They should be put in at an angle of 45 degrees ; the angle on one side being opposite to the angle on the other. In this way the sticks can support one another. Small twiggy pieces of stick can be inserted in the ground near the peas so as to encourage the plants to climb upwards.

Pick peas regularly, as one pod left on to ripen and to go to " seed " will immediately reduce the cropping powers of that plant. Regular picking helps materially towards heavy cropping.

Manuring.—The dung or compost should be dug in in the autumn rather than in the spring, as fresh manure tends to send the pea all to leaf. Just before planting, fork in 5 ozs. of meat and bone meal or fish manure ; potash may be given in addition. Directly the plants are through, ½ oz. nitrate of soda may be applied per yard run.

Varieties

It is very difficult to make a selection from the large number of varieties of peas offered by seedsmen. I would, however, draw your attention to the following, which I have found crop heavily :—

DWARF EARLIES :
   Kelvedon Wonder. 1½ feet. Wrinkle seeded.
   Meteor. 1½ feet. Earliest Pea. Good for sowing in autumn.
   Little Marvel. 18 inches. Best flavoured early pea.
   Laxton's Superb. 2½ feet. Good for sowing in autumn or January.

EARLY MAIN CROP :
   The Lincoln. 2 feet. Compact grower, heavy cropper.
   Giant Stride. 2½ feet. Very large pods.
   Miracle. 4 feet. Bears pods right to the top.

MAIN CROPS :
   Onward. 2½ ft. Resistant to Mildew. Good flavour, heavy cropper.
   Telegraph. Suitable for autumn sowing.
   Lord Chancellor. 3 feet. Excellent flavour.
   Quite Content. 6 feet. Large pods, Good Marrowfat.

LATE VARIETIES :
   Gladstone. 4 feet. One of the latest and best.
   Autocrat. 3 feet. Blunt-ended pods.
   Alderman. 5 feet. Heavy cropper, long podded.

General Remarks

To keep away mice and birds, it is a good plan to soak the peas in a mixture of paraffin and red lead for a couple of hours before sowing. This liquid should be at about the consistency of cream. To get earlier peas, it is possible to pinch out the growing points, but if this is done the plants will not grow so tall.

BROAD BEANS

The broad bean is one the hardiest of the podded vegetables, and can be sown in the autumn with safety in most districts.

Soil.—It is not particular as to soil, and will grow well almost anywhere. It does like deep, moist soil, however.

Seed sowing.—The first sowing is done in November, the rows being 2 ft. 6 ins. apart. A drill is made 3 inches deep, 6 inches or so wide, and a double row of beans put in 6 inches apart. Double rows are usually preferred to single rows, and, as the beans will not be prevented from cropping heavily, a heavier yield is obtained from the same area of ground when compared to single rows.

To obtain succession, it is possible to sow outdoors again at the beginning of February, and again early in March. Some people like to raise the plants in a frame, from seed sown at the beginning of December. The plants thus raised are put out early in March. When sowing beans outside it is a good plan to sow a dozen or so extra beans in a group at the end of the row, and these may be planted out into the row when they are 3 inches high, should any blanks occur.

General cultivation.—When the plants are 3 or 4 inches high the soil should be drawn up to them during hoeing. After this, regular surface cultivation is carried out. Keep a look-out for the black fly, and, to prevent this damaging the crop, the growing point may be pinched out directly the first blossom has set (*see* Colour plate facing page 129) (for further control of this pest *see* Chapter XV).

Manuring.—*See* Peas.

Varieties

Aquadulce. Very early ; enormous pods.
Extra Early Giant Windsor. An early 4-seeded bean.
Early White-Eyed Windsor. Probably the earliest Windsor bean.
Seville Mammoth Long Pod. A large-podded variety.
The **Long Pods** are usually sown early, and the **Windsors** in March.

DWARF BEANS

Dwarf beans are given all kinds of names, sometimes being called kidney beans and sometimes French beans. There are, however, climbing French beans, and these are often grown under glass. You cannot sow dwarf beans until the ground is really warm. Actually they need a temperature of 60 degrees F. before they will germinate properly.

Soil.—A light soil suits them better than a heavy one. Clays and heavy loams should, then, be " lightened " with any material available.

Seed sowing.—It is impossible to sow the seed outside much earlier than April, and it is often the first week in May before the soil is ready in many gardens. The drills are 2 inches deep, 4 inches wide, and from 2 to 3 feet apart, depending on the variety. The beans themselves are put into the rows by hand, in a " staggered " formation, so that the plants when they grow are 6 inches apart. A dozen or more beans are then planted at the end of the row, and any gaps that arise may be planted up with ease.

To get earlier beans than this, you can sow in February in boxes or pots under glass. About the middle of March, the plants should be hardened off, and planted out during the last week of April.

Seed can also be sown in frames, 2 inches apart, early in April, and these will be ready to put out the second week in May. When sowing in frames be sure to protect them from frost at night-time ; remember they are very soft and can be cut down easily.

Cultivation.—It is customary to sow French beans in between another crop, like spring cabbage or autumn-sown lettuce. The advantage being that the established crop gives some protection to the young beans when they come through. The original crop is cleared by the time the beans require the room, and so space and time are saved.

Directly the previous crop is out of the way, the ground is forked over between the rows, and, after this, all that is necessary to do is to hoe regularly.

SUPPORTS for RUNNER BEANS

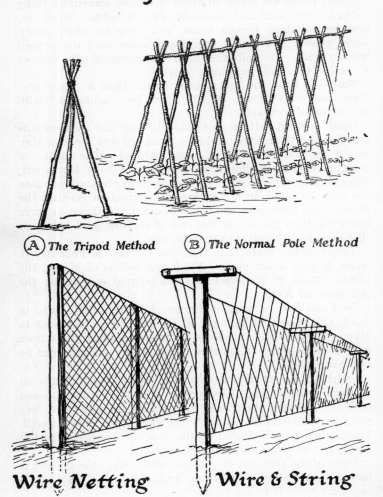

(A) The Tripod Method   (B) The Normal Pole Method

Wire Netting   Wire & String

Whatever you do, keep picking all the time. Do not be tempted to leave the pods on until they are old and stringy.

Manuring.—They will be sown on ground that has been well treated before, and all they should require is a dressing of lime. Broadcast a good fish manure or meat and bone meal where the rows are to be, 10 days or so before making out the drills. Do not forget that, if growth is slow when the protected crop has disappeared, you can give ½ oz. Chilean potash nitrate per yard run also, to help matters.

Varieties

The Prince. Heavy cropper; early; outstanding.
Feltham Prolific. Very dwarf; quick in growth.
The Wonder. Long pods; heavy cropper; early.
Black Wonder. Heavy cropper; early.

RUNNER BEANS

Most garden owners like to grow a few runner beans, and, as they look quite decorative, they are often grown as a division between the vegetable garden and flower garden. Or they are sown at the end of the garden – to screen off the refuse heaps or to clamber up the fence.

Soil.—As in the case of all members of this family a light loam is preferable to a heavy clay. Undrained clays are a real danger.

Seed sowing.—Runner beans are less hardy than dwarf beans, and it is impossible to sow the seed any earlier than the beginning of May. If necessary another sowing may be made in June. Runner beans can be grown up poles, string, wire netting, or on the flat, the trailing growths being cut back with a sickle to keep the plants bushy. Some people grow them in rows, while others put three poles into the ground to form a triangle and the beans climb up these. These groups may be at the four corners of the garden, or put anywhere else convenient.

If you are growing the beans up some structure and in rows, you will need to have these about 6 feet apart. Most people sow double rows, these being 3 inches deep and 9 inches apart.

The seed is put 9 inches apart in each drill, on the staggered or alternate method. If poles are used, these are put in a foot apart between the two drills, and on each side. The poles cross at the top about 6 inches, and a series of poles are now laid on the top where the sticks cross, and all are lashed tightly together. This makes a very firm structure. If you are growing on the flat, the rows are just sown 3½ to 4 feet apart, the seeds being sown 8 inches apart in the rows.

Cultivation.—When the seeds start to grow, the soil should be stirred along the rows, or when the plants are 3 or 4 inches high ; when hoeing, a little soil is drawn up to them.

Beans grown on the flat are cut back regularly with a sickle. In dry seasons it is a good plan to syringe the plants either early in the morning or at night time. This helps the flowers to set, and keeps the pods fresh. Be sure and pick the plants over regularly, and do not miss any that are fit to use.

Manuring.—Deep cultivation and quite heavy manuring with dung or other organic material is very advisable. In addition to the dung, add a good fish manure or meat and bone meal of 3–4 ozs. per square yard. This may be raked into the ground a week prior to sowing the seed. Lime will be needed, also, on the surface of the ground, using about 3 ozs. per square yard.

Varieties

Emperor. Long pods, fine quality.
Princeps. Early and dwarf ; heavy cropping.
Czar. White flowers ; broad pods.
East Anglian Champion. Stringless ; much liked by cooks.

CHAPTER XI

VEGETABLES

Celery — Onions — Asparagus — Leeks — Marrows

Deep rooted vegetables improve the soil, as special preparation has to be made for them. I try and answer in this chapter some of the many queries I have had put to me in lectures.

1. Can I raise celery plants free from disease ?
2. What is self-bleaching celery ?
3. I want to grow big onions for exhibition. How do I do this ?
4. Is Asparagus easy to grow ?
5. I want to grow spinach that will not go to seed in a hot summer.
6. Can marrows be grown on the flat ?

I HAVE grouped these vegetables together largely because they all need deep cultivation. The only exception, perhaps, is spinach, and this may be regarded as a catch crop.

Celery, leeks, and onions do need well-prepared ground, and asparagus and rhubarb are, of course, permanent crops. If you include spinach beet and seakale spinach, you will then have two more crops that will remain in the ground for over a year.

CELERY

Most people like celery either as a salad or as a cooked vegetable. There are many types that can be grown, such as the self-bleaching, the pink, red, and white. I am often told that celery is a nuisance because the plants have to be raised in a greenhouse in slight heat. This is not quite true, as many thousands of celery seedlings are raised in frames, and what the market grower can do, you ought to be able to do also.

It must be a popular vegetable with the masses, as there are over 7,000 acres of it grown in this country alone.

Soil.—Celery soil should be deep. If there is plenty of organic matter present, so much the better, and, curiously enough, acid soils grow celery better than those that have a lime content. It should be possible for these plants to obtain water throughout the season, and so soil with a fairly high water table is useful.

Seed sowing.—It is best to prepare a hot-bed in a frame, and this is done by using horse manure, placing it a foot deep, and covering this with 4 inches of soil. Make certain that the soil used is sterilised, and this can be done by soaking it with a 2 per cent solution of formaldehyde at least a week beforehand – this is the mixture of 1 pint of formalin to 6 gallons of water. This should be watered on to the soil when it is in the frame; 4 gallons is usually sufficient for a frame 6 feet by 3 feet. If you can get garden soil with plenty of organic matter in it, this is preferable. Cover the soaked soil with sacks, and then, four days later, fork the soil over to release the fumes. Half an ounce of celery seed should sow a frame light of this size, though few amateurs will need anywhere near this amount of seed. If you choose to use your frame for raising other plants at the same time, you can raise your celery plants in a corner of the frame, or, if you prefer, sow the seed in boxes, which you sink into the frame at least to half their depth.

After sowing, cover the seed lightly with soil, pressing it down with a board, and watering it well. Shut the frame up immediately, and, if it is likely to be frosty, cover the frame up at night-time with an Archangel mat or old sacks. Directly the seedlings appear, a little air can be given in the day-time, and the amount of air given can be increased until by the middle of April the lights are taken off during the mild days, though it may be necessary to replace them at night. Directly the plants are 2 inches high they are pricked out 3 inches apart into a cold frame. Water them well and close the frame, and shade it until the young plants have rooted again. Be careful not to get them frozen either, and so cover the frame up at night.

If you want very early crops – that is, celery that you will use in August – you will have to make your first sowing late in February. For ordinary work the middle of March will do, and the seedlings produced in this case are usually transplanted in the rows 6 inches apart, though the plants are 3 inches in the rows. For very late crops delay sowing until the second week in April, pricking out the plants as before.

The general rules with regard to these seedlings are : (1) they must always receive plenty of water ; (2) they must never be frozen and receive any check at all ; (3) the soil they grow in should always be full of organic material, to allow of free root run ; and (4) be careful not to allow the celery fly to attack the young plants in the frame. It may be necessary to spray with nicotine even when they are seedlings.

General cultivation.—When lifting the plants from the frames, care should be taken to see that they are removed with as much root as possible ; for this reason either a trowel or a spade should be used.

The self-bleaching varieties of celery can be grown on the flat, and, to help these to blanch, it is a good plan to place straw round about them. Self-bleaching celery need not be planted further apart than 1 foot square, or at the *most* 18 inches, as the plants do not grow very tall.

Ordinary celery is grown in trenches, and these should be specially prepared. Dig down 18 inches, making a trench 18 inches wide. If you throw the soil thus excavated upon either side in equal proportions, you should end up by having two ridges of equal height. To allow for this it is usual to have at least 2 ft. 6 in. in between each trench. It is possible to have wider trenches than this, in order that two or three rows may be grown in the one " excavation." For every extra row you want to grow, you will have to dig a trench 6 inches wider. It is not a bad plan to stick to the single trench if you can. In the bottom of the trench, place a layer of rotted manure, at least 6 inches deep when trodden down, and cover this with about 5 inches of soil. You should now have a trench 8–10 inches deep – that is, if you measure from the top of the ridges on either side. You should see that these ridges are flat-topped, as along them you will be able to grow catch crops. If you make up your mind to prepare these trenches very early in the season, you can start growing your catch

Celery trenches showing intercrops

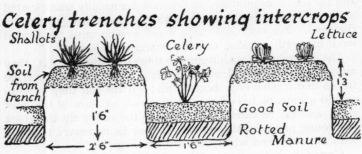

Shallots

Celery

Lettuce

Soil from trench

Good Soil

Rotted Manure

Soil from trench

1' 6"

2' 6"

1' 6"

1' 3"

Celery after first earthing up

OLD LEVEL
GROUND LEVEL

Tie while earthing

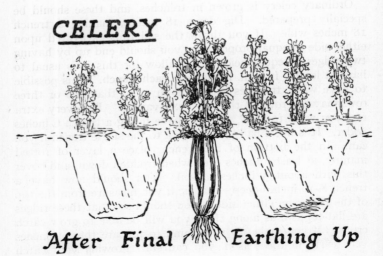

CELERY

After Final Earthing Up

crops **early** also. Shallots grown on the ridges is an idea which has not struck many people, though lettuces and French beans are often used.

See that each plant is set carefully, with its ball of soil still attached. After planting, firm the plant well, and then, having completed planting the trench, give it a thorough watering. Should you get very hot sunny weather the next few days, it is not a bad plan to cover the trench up with brown paper until the plants get established. You may have to water again three days later, and after this, unless it rains, a good flooding once a week will be advisable.

During the summer be sure and keep the rows free from weeds, and remove any side growths coming from the base. These are commonly referred to by gardeners as suckers.

Earthing up.—This is a special operation, and it consists of taking the soil from the ridges and bringing it up to the plants. The celery plant must be grasped firmly with one hand while the soil is put into position. You do not want soil to get in between the stems. For this reason it is usual to chop the earth up, and let it dry for an hour or two before it is worked into its new position. It is better to earth up in two operations – the first one when the plants are over a foot high. This may be during the middle of August. Another earthing may be done three weeks or so later, and the final earthing is usually completed in October. At this last earthing the whole of the stems are covered, the soil being brought right up to the top leaves. The ridges should now be smooth and steep, so that the rain is carried away quickly.

Just a few " don'ts." Do not allow any soil to get into the heart of the plant. If you are worried about this, always get one person to grip the plant with both hands while you do the soiling up. Do not soil up, at the first earthing, higher than, say, half-way up the stem. Never earth when the plants or the soil are wet.

There is no reason at all why celery should not keep in its trenches until the end of January or the middle of February following. To prevent early decay setting in, it is not a bad idea to cover the green tops with straw – firstly to prevent the rain getting down, and secondly to give a protection against hard frosts.

Manuring.—The digging of large quantities of dung into the bottom of the trench has already been mentioned. After this, manure water is perhaps the most convenient method of feeding. This may be either liquid farmyard manure, or liquid from cow, sheep, or even fowl manure, prepared in a tub. The method is to hang an old sack containing the manure in a tub full of water. Most people now use a liquid manure, which is bought in bottles and is then diluted. " Liquinure " is a well-known brand which is produced from an organic origin. This should be put on from, say, July 15th, four times at fortnightly intervals.

Varieties

WHITE :

White Perfection. Large-sized heads, very firm and solid.
Darragh's White. Resistant to Septoria blight.
Blundell's White. Blanches quickly, tall.

PINK :

Clayworth Prize Pink. Large, early ; excellent quality.
Clucas Winter Pink. Late, heavy ; blanches nearly white.
Resistant Pink. Somewhat resistant to blight.

RED :

Covent Garden Red. Large, tall ; solid.
Standard Bearer. Large, firm head ; good flavour.

SELF-BLEACHING :

Doré. Dwarf ; pure white.

LEEKS

Leeks are always thought of as a speciality for Welshmen, but if you live in the northern counties of England you will known there are a large number of Leek Societies which encourage the growing of giant leeks. They always grow best when they have plenty of moisture, but this must not be stagnant water. Well-drained land, then, is necessary, but there should be plenty of organic material present, not only as a plant food, but for its moisture-retaining properties.

Soil.—Leeks will grow well on most soils, providing they are deeply worked. They will not grow to perfection on the very light sands, or on the badly drained clays, for the reasons given above.

The seed is sown about the middle of March in the south, often outside, but north of the midlands, usually in frames. If sown in the open, the drills are 18 inches apart, and if in frames, 9 inches apart. When the seedlings are fit to move, they are transplanted to 8 inches apart in such a way as to leave the remaining plants at that distance in the original bed. The seedlings are usually left in this bed until they are 6 to 9 inches high.

General cultivation.—The ground where the leeks are to be grown in the ordinary way should be deeply dug and well-manured, the manure being put well down. After this drills can be made, 12 inches apart and 6 inches deep, and the leeks planted in these at 8-inch distances. Another method is to make holes with a dibber about 9 inches deep, at the above distances apart, the leeks being dropped into the bottom of the hole. The holes are not filled in, but the plants soon get a fresh hold and grow away.

If you want to produce large leeks, trenches should be dug out a spade's width, in the same way as for celery. The trenches are 2 feet apart. Manure is dug into the bottom of the trench, and at the end of this operation the trench should be 6 inches deep. In this the leeks are planted 12 inches apart. As the plant grows, the trenches are filled in gradually, in order to blanch the stem. Further earthing up is done right up to the base of the leaves as necessary.

Try and do the transplanting during a showery period, or water the trenches or drills well afterwards. Regular waterings are useful, especially in dry weather, and liquid manure can be given from time to time.

Keep the ground hoed all the time, and if the leaves tend to droop on to the soil they may be shortened back.

Manuring.—Without a doubt the main requirement of the leek is to have plenty of organic manure. Nitrogen is also important, and this can be given either as poultry manure or as guano, say 1 oz. to the square yard. Artificials, which may be given in addition to this, are 1 oz. of superphosphate, and $\frac{1}{2}$ oz.

of sulphate of potash per yard run. When the leeks have been established for about one month, give a dressing of " Liquinure " per yard run in addition.

Storing.—Leeks can be left in the ground right up to the end of February, but, if it is necessary to clear the ground for other crops, they can be stored for a month heeled in – in sand or soil.

Varieties

London.   An early ; suitable for the South only.
Walton Mammoth.   Large and early.
Giant Musselburgh.   A good all-round variety.
Prizetaker.   Stems long and thick ; one of the Lyon type.

ONIONS

The onion is grown for salads, and for use, also, as a vegetable to be boiled, roasted or fried. It is much liked as a vegetable, not only because it is high in food value, but because of its piquancy and for its rich vitamin content.

Soil.—Onions seem to prefer a sandy loam, but, whatever happens, they must have a very deep root run.

Seed sowing.—Seed can be sown at three different periods : (1) August, either to provide salad or spring onions early the following year or to produce fair-sized bulbs the following summer. Different varieties are chosen for the two purposes. (2) March, out of doors ; this sowing provides for the bulk of the ordinary bulbs that we use for cooking. (3) January, these are sown in boxes under glass and produce the giant onions, the seedlings being pricked out 2 inches square, when they are an inch or so high, into further boxes containing sandy compost. As in the case of leeks, some growers prick them out into 3-inch pots, and plant them out from these.

When the seed is sown outside, care should be taken to see that the surface is dry and friable. It is necessary to have firm soil, and for this reason some men attach pieces of wood to their boots, a foot or more square, so as to tread the ground down evenly. Be careful not to do this if the soil is in any way sticky. The seed is sown in rows about 12 inches apart, the plants being thinned out either 4 inches apart or 6 inches, according to the variety. The drills must be shallow.

In the case of spring onions, no thinning is done, the plants being pulled in the spring *en masse*. The autumn-sown varieties that you are hoping to use " bulbed up " can be transplanted in the spring, say 15 inches between the rows, and 9 inches between the plants.

Sets.—It is possible instead of sowing seed to buy what are known as sets, which are planted in a similar way to shallots, in rows 15 inches apart, and 6 inches in the rows. Unfortunately some of these go to seed, but, if the flowering head is cut away directly it is seen, a fair-sized bulb results. This method is recommended for growers in the north of England. It is a way of ensuring onion fly control and usually you get well ripened bulbs as a result.

General cultivation.—When the seed is sown outside, directly the rows can be seen hoeing should start. If they are to be thinned, as in the case of the March sowings, this will be done when the plants are 2 inches high – first of all by means of a hoe, and finally by hand. It is usually after this thinning that the first attack of onion fly occurs. When hoeing, never drive this tool in deeply, and draw the soil away from the rows rather than up to them.

Those that are raised in moderate heat under glass (55 degrees F.) are planted out in April, and if they are long and lanky some of the top can be cut off as well as a portion of the root. It is most important to keep the ground clean in any form of onion growing.

Depending on the district, it may be necessary to bend the tops of the onions towards the end of August, in order to help the bulbs to ripen off properly. Final ripening off is done by lifting the bulbs on to the surface of the ground, or laying them down on an ash path.

Manuring.—A good rule to remember is that onions should not have any organic manure within the top 6 inches of soil. For this reason the ground where they are to grow is often trenched to the depth of 2 feet, and quantities up to 5 cwt. of dung or compost per square pole are then incorporated

Making
an
Onion Rope

Planting Asparagus on Light Land

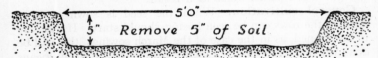

5'0"

5" Remove 5" of Soil

Good Soil trenched 3 spits
                and manured well

Place Plants on mounds

Remove more soil to make mounds
Cover Crowns 6" Deep

Path
1'6"
wide

deeply. This preparation is usually done in the autumn. In March the bed can be forked over, and, in order to add a certain amount of potash and to help provide a seed-bed, wood ashes are spread over the surface at the rate of, say, $\frac{1}{2}$ lb. to the square yard – these are raked in, 1 oz. of sulphate of potash per square yard is usually given in addition. Poultry manure is good if applied dry, at the rate of 3 ozs. per square yard, just before planting. Some people use soot, guano, or fish manure at about the same rate. Soot is usually put on with the wood ashes, but the artificials are put on ten days or so before planting or sowing. To give a " fillip " nitrate of soda, or Chilean potash nitrate, can be applied, at $\frac{1}{2}$ oz. per yard run, from time to time throughout the season.

Storing.—The large onions that you wish to keep throughout the winter are " ripened " on the ground, and then are cleaned, have the tops removed, and stored in a dry cool place. If you can " rope " them, and hang them up under the eaves of a shed, or on the inside walls of some building, they will keep quite well.

Varieties

(1) AUTUMN SOWING :

(*a*) For salad :
White Lisbon and **New Queen.**
(*b*) For early bulbs :
Giant Rocca and **Giant Zittau.**

(2) SPRING SOWING :
Bedfordshire Champion.
Rousham Park Hero. An excellent keeper.
Up-to-Date.
Reliance. Can be sown in autumn.

(3) SOWING UNDER GLASS :
Sutton's Selected Ailsa Craig.
Dickson's and Robinson's Premier.
Crossling's Selected.

PICKLING ONIONS

These can be produced quite easily if the seed is sown in April, broadcast over some well-prepared land. There is no need to thin or to apply special manures – in fact the soil should be rather poor. The crop is harvested when the onions are quite small.

Varieties

Paris Silver-skinned Pickling and **The Queen**.

ASPARAGUS

Asparagus is comparatively easy to produce.

Soil.—It does best in a deep rich loam, on the sandy side, but can be grown, of course, on most soils that have good drainage. On the light sands, a little trouble will have to be taken in preparing the beds, and a good deal of moisture-holding material incorporated.

Seed sowing.—It is quite possible to raise your own asparagus plants by sowing seed. Dig the ground deeply in the autumn, leaving it rough, and then get it down to a fine tilth in the spring. The seed is sown early in April, when the surface is dry, in drills a foot apart, and 1½ inches deep. It is a good plan to put the seeds in separately, 3 inches apart. Asparagus seeds are very slow to germinate, and, to help you recognise the rows much earlier than you normally would, it is a good plan to sow radish seeds in the rows at the same time. During the summer, see that the seed-bed is kept moist with watering, and the surface is kept loose by hoeing. At the end of the first year you should have nice young plants that can be put out into the permanent beds.

General cultivation.—The first thing you have to do is to prepare your asparagus bed. You will bastard trench it in the autumn to a depth of 2 feet, and you will dig in, say, 1 good barrow load of well rotted dung or vegetable compost to 10 square yards. If you can place this manure evenly distributed between both spits, so much the better. Should your soil be very heavy, and therefore liable to be badly drained, it is a good plan to have " ridge " beds, but normally you will plant on the flat.

There are so many ways of planning out the beds, and I only propose to mention one of them. A bed, 5 feet wide, on which

Storing apples in trays is a very simple way of keeping them. If each specimen can be wrapped in an oiled piece of tissue paper the fruits keep better. Note one tray is wrapped and the fourth one down unwrapped.

Sowing seed in a shallow drill. Note the line used to ensure that the rows are straight and the way the seed is being pushed out with the thumb.

you plant three rows 18 inches apart, the plants themselves being 18 inches apart also.

The one-year-old plants you have raised will now be put into these beds, early in April, 9 inches deep. It is usual to get out a trench 6 inches or so wide, into which a special light compost can be put. Where the plants are to be placed a little raised mound is arranged, 4 inches high, and this enables the roots of the asparagus to be spread out evenly and in the way they naturally grow. The trench is filled in after all the plants are put into position, and the rows are sprinkled with the artificial manure. *See* page 158.

During the season the beds will have to be kept free from weeds, by hoeing and weeding. During this time a sharp look-out should be kept for any plants that have failed to grow. If this is seen, the cause should be ascertained immediately, and, should the original plant be dead, a new one must be planted right away. If this is done in the summer, be sure and soak the ground well afterwards.

As the foliage starts to turn yellow in the autumn it should be cut down and burnt.

When the beds have been established for two years, it is necessary in the autumn to cover them with farmyard manure or compost to a depth of 2 inches. The loose litter from this is raked off again late the following February. As the soil may get removed from the beds during summer operations, it is customary to cover them with an inch or so of soil at the same time as the litter is removed.

Cutting.—You will not get much to cut before the fourth year, and this is why so many people choose to plant three-year-olds. Cutting should commence in April and continue till mid-June. Do not make the mistake of cutting everything that comes, as you must have some " grass " to manufacture plant foods to keep things going. The method of cutting is important also, as care must be taken not to damage the crowns. Cut, then, at about 4 inches below the surface only, and with a long knife. There are special asparagus knives made for the purpose.

Manuring.—Something has already been said about the

F

use of dung or compost, and heavy dressings *are* required at the beginning of things.   When the trenches are being prepared, apply superphosphate 1½ oz. to the square yard, and sulphate of potash ½ oz. to the square yard.   In the spring, when the plants start to grow, nitrate of soda is given at the rate of ½ oz. to the square yard, four times, say, every fortnight.

Every year a dressing of Kainit and superphosphate is given, in April, at 3 ozs. per square yard, in equal proportions.   Kainit is preferable to common salt, which is sometimes advised.

Varieties

There are both American and French varieties, but the following may be recommended :

> **Connover's Colossal.**   Very large and early.
> **Early Argenteuil.**   Early.
> **K.B.**   Large and vigorous, heavy cropping.
> **Mary Washington.**   A heavy cropper.

SPINACH

There are all kinds of plants that seem to be classified under the name of spinach.   It is proposed to describe the culture of some of these, giving them special headings.

The Annual Spinach.—This is sometimes referred to as the round-seeded spinach, but, of course, includes the prickly-seeded spinach as well.

Soil.—Spinach will grow on nearly all types of soil.   The main requirements seem to be sufficient moisture, available nitrogen, and well-worked land.   Under drought conditions it fails to grow, and goes to seed very quickly.

Seed sowing.—Here again we shall have to divide the instructions given into two parts : (1) summer spinach, and (2) the winter spinach.

Summer Spinach.—It is possible to sow this towards the beginning of March in a warm and sheltered position.   Every fourteen to twenty days afterwards another batch should be sown in order to provide continuity.   The drills should be a foot apart and 1 inch deep.   As soon as the seedlings are large enough to be used, it is usual to thin the plants to 6 inches apart. Thinnings are delicious when cooked. Because the seed is comparatively cheap, people will sow spinach too thickly, and then never thin rigorously enough.

If you soak the seed for a day before sowing, you will find that it will start into growth much more quickly.

Winter Spinach.—This should be sown from the first of August to mid-September at periods of fourteen to twenty days. Be sure and prepare the soil well, and in the case of heavy soils, or in districts with a high rainfall, it is better to ridge up the beds where the seed is to be sown. Normal beds are 5 feet wide, and this allows for ease in picking. The seed is sown in rows 9 inches apart, and is thinned as in the case of the summer spinach, only this time to only 4 inches apart.

General Cultivation.—Hoe the rows of spinach regularly, and mulch the rows should the weather be very dry. Lawn-mowings come in useful here.

The winter spinach usually has to be protected, and this can be done either by covering with frames and lights or by using straw, heather or bracken. Beginners often make the mistake of picking the winter crop too hard. Care should be taken not to remove more than a moderate proportion of leaves from each plant.

Manuring.—Dig deeply, incorporate plenty of dung or well rotted compost, remembering that you want ample root run and sufficient moisture-holding material present. Spinach should grow quickly, and should be given nitrogen. Watering with weak liquid manure* is useful, say, once a week, once the plants have started to grow.

Varieties

SUMMER:

    Monstrous Viroflay. Round-seeded, very large leaves.
    Reliance. Very large leaves, long standing.
    Bloomsdale Green. Very large, broad-leaved round spinach ; dark green.

WINTER:

    New Giant-Leaved Prickly. Very large ; dark green, thick leaves.

* Can now be obtained in bottles ready for dilution.

SPINACH BEET

Sometimes called Perpetual Spinach as it produces a continuous supply of large succulent leaves during hot summers.

Manuring.—As for Beetroot.

Seed sowing.—April – August. The rows should be 15 inches apart and the plants thinned to 8 inches apart.

General Cultivation.—As for other Spinach.

SEAKALE SPINACH

So called because the large white mid-ribs of the leaves can be cooked separately and served as Seakale, whilst the green part is dressed as spinach.

It is grown exactly as spinach beet above, except that the plants should be thinned to 12 inches apart, and not be sown in the autumn.

NEW ZEALAND SPINACH

This will not stand any frost, and so the seed has to be sown in boxes, at the end of March, under glass. When the plants are large enough to handle, they are potted up into 3-inch pots, and, after being hardened off, are planted out in the open at the end of May. Readers who have no glass-house may either raise the plants in frames or may sow the seed out of doors about the middle of May. As the plants scramble over the surface of the ground, and are very strong growing, they need 3 feet between the rows and 3 feet between the plants.

General cultivation.—There is little that can be done, as the plants will soon cover the ground with a " mat." Picking must be done regularly. Instead of picking off the leaves in the ordinary way, the growing points are pinched back so that the part used is about 2 inches long. The result of this pinching back is that new stems are sent out. The growing points are very tender and delicious. An excellent spinach for a dry summer as it does not go to seed.

RHUBARB

This must be considered a permanent crop, as it can easily

remain in its bed for eight years, providing it is well manured. It is much liked because it grows so well in town and city gardens.

Soil.—Choose if possible a deep rich loam, see that it is well drained, and then prepare it by digging deeply. It is not every garden that has this light soil, but readers will no doubt improve heavy clays by adding plenty of organic material.

Propagation is effected by the splitting up of the old stools, and " crowns " can be bought of various varieties. Should you wish to increase the stock of rhubarb you already have, it is quite easy to chop the stools into four or five pieces, each portion having at least one good bud, and this is best done in March.

General Cultivation.—When the bed is ready, rhubarb planting crowns should be put in firmly, 3 feet between the rows and 2 ft. 6 ins. between the plants.

All the time it is possible to get down between the rows, hoeing should be carried out. In the winter the ground between the rows is forked over, and each plant should be given a dressing of dung or well rotted compost.

Should flower stems appear, they should be removed immediately, as seeding only exhausts the plant.

Pulling.—Never gather any stalks the first season after planting. Even the second-year gathering should be sparsely done. Be careful not to tear the crown when pulling, and the best method of doing this is to turn the stalk slightly and then to pull downward and outward. Do not be tempted to go on gathering rhubarb after the middle of August. You must give the plants the chance to establishing themselves before the winter.

To get earlier rhubarb than one would naturally, it is possible to cover the bed or part of the bed with strawy manure.

Rhubarb forcing pots may be stood over the plants, dung being placed round about to provide the necessary heat. The rhubarb grows quite quickly inside the pots, and may be pulled when ready.

Manuring.—The regular waterings with liquid manure can be made throughout the summer. Every winter give the dung or compost as advised, and in addition 4 ozs. of a good fish manure per square yard. On light land 2 ozs. Kainit may be used as well to supply extra polish.

In the spring give 1 oz. nitrate of soda per square yard a week or two after growth has commenced.

Varieties

Timperley Early. The earliest rhubarb there is.
Hawkes Champagne. Early ; large and a fine quality.
Dawe's Challenge. Good colour ; forces well.
Glaskin's New Perpetual. One of the first to be pulled.
Linnaeus. A large second early.
Prince Albert. Early ; long and thick.

THE VEGETABLE MARROW

Most people like to grow two or three marrow plants, especially as they will do quite well planted on the rubbish heap. They do quite well on the flat in dry seasons, but in wet summers they are better grown on beds or ridges. North of, say, Manchester, they are often grown in frames, especially in smoky districts.

Seed sowing.—Seeds are usually sown in 3-inch pots filled with special compost of equal parts of chopped up loam and old manure. One seed is put into each pot, and, after watering, it can either be placed in a greenhouse, at a temperature of 50 to 55 degrees F., or can be plunged in soil over a hot-bed. The plants thus raised are gradually hardened off until they are ready to put out in the open the third week in May. Seed may be sown out of doors under continuous cloches in April, where the plants are to grow.

General cultivation.—When planting in large quantities, it is usual to set the young marrows in rows 4 feet apart, the plants being 3 feet apart in the rows. For this purpose the bush marrow is preferred to the trailing type. When trailers are used, they are often kept pinched back.

Keep up clean cultivation until the plants cover the ground. Mulching can be carried out with rotted leaves, spent hops, or grass-mowings about the beginning of June.

Manuring.—Be sure to incorporate plenty of organic

material where the marrows are to grow. When grown on the flat, 3 – 4 ozs. of a good fish fertiliser may be forked in per square yard a fortnight before planting.

Varieties

Clucas Roller. A long white ; trailing ; smooth ; no rib or neck.
Long Green Running. Striped ; long ; very prolific.
Bush-Shaped Green. Medium-sized fruits ; bright green.
Bush-Shaped White. Early ; prolific ; tender.
Rotherside Orange. Flattened globe-shaped fruits ; golden ; delicate flavour.

CHAPTER XII

VEGETABLES

Salads — Herbs — Unusual Vegetables — Frames and Cloches

It is here we become more " scientific " as we deal with cloches and frames.

1. Tomatoes can be grown out of doors.
2. Your own frame cucumbers will be delicious if you remember to remove the male flowers.
3. It is possible to have lettuces all the year round.
4. You may like to have plenty of herbs. Grow the right varieties.
5. The Dutch frame with a single piece of glass has much to recommend it.
6. Hot-beds are very useful for producing early crops.

TOMATOES

This vegetable is chiefly grown under glass, but there is not space in this book to describe glass-house work. In the south, however, it is quite possible to grow tomatoes out of doors, and in hot dry summers most people have heavy crops in the open.

Soil.—It is possible to grow tomatoes on both sands and clays. See that the drainage is perfect ; dig in the right amount, and the right kind, of manure, and dig deeply and consistently. Whatever cultivation you do, be sure that it is done in the autumn, so that the soil can become really friable by the spring.

Seed sowing.—It used to be the custom to raise tomato plants under glass, but the more modern method is to raise them under continuous cloches. The seed in the greenhouse is sown in boxes, placing each seed 1 inch square, (*see* page 170) but under cloches is sown in the soil outside. The seedlings when they come up are transferred into small pots, being careful not to hold them by the stem. Readers should have no difficulty in buying plants from reliable nurserymen if they have not their own cloches.

General cultivation.—It is usual to plant at the end of

May, and the plants themselves should then be sturdy and hard and about 8 inches high, but if you are planting under cloches such as the Tomato " T " you can plant in April and so get a flying start ! Do not plant out without cover until the weather seems warm and settled ; it is sometimes better in this case to wait until the middle of June ! Make a hole with a trowel sufficiently large to take the whole ball, and plant this so that it is about a quarter of an inch below the soil level. Soak the ground well afterwards.

As the plants grow, keep them to a single stem by removing the side growths which appear at the joints of the leaves, but be careful not to remove the flowers at the same time. (*See* page 170). It will be necessary to put a stake or bambo to each plant, tying it loosely to this with raffia. The plants should be 18 inches apart in the row, the rows being 2 ft. 6 in. apart. See that the rows run north and south.

Hoe regularly, and, in hot weather, mulch with any organic matter available. It is a good plan to stop the plants – that is, to remove the growing point during the second week of August, and as the bottom leaves turn yellow these can be removed. Do not be encouraged to remove all the leaves from your tomato plants, though a few removed here and there will help to ripen the fruit.

During the hot weather it may be necessary to give the rows a good soaking, say, once a week, in the late afternoon.

Pick all the fruit as it ripens, and if there is any fruit still hanging at the end of September, this may be gathered green on the trusses, and, if hung up, will ripen indoors.

Tomatoes do quite well when grown against south walls.

Manuring.—Dig in farmyard manure when preparing the land, but add as well 2 ozs. of sulphate of potash per square yard; $1\frac{1}{2}$ oz. of superphosphate and an equal quantity of bone meal should also be used. In dry years it may be necessary to give a little more nitrogen in the form of nitrate of soda at $\frac{1}{2}$ oz. to the square yard, say, in July, but in wet years a further dressing of sulphate of potash should be applied at 1 oz. per square yard late in June. After each truss of fruit is set give a feed with Liquinure – or some other complete tomato food.

F*

CUCUMBER Flowers

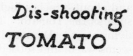

Dis-shooting TOMATO

Male

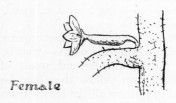

Female

Pinch out Shoots

Shoot pinched out

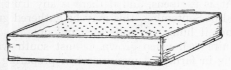

A = Drainage hole & crock.
B = Rough Stuff for Drainage.
C = Seeds at correct level.
D = Space between top of soil and top of box.
E = Sheet of Glass.
F = Piece of brown paper.

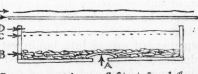

Cross section of finished box

Varieties

Stonor's Outdoor. A heavy cropper ; early ; fruit of good size
Hundredfold. A good outside variety. Very heavy cropping.
Orange Sunrise. A yellow variety ; excellent flavour.
Stonor's Exhibition. Smooth-skinned ; bright colour ; early.
Moneymaker. Vigorous ; heavy cropper ; firm.
The Amateur. The best bush type of tomato.

CUCUMBERS

Cucumbers are usually grown in glass-houses, though they can be grown in frames and on ridges outside. It is only proposed in this volume to describe briefly frame culture.

FRAME CUCUMBERS : The frames should be on soil that is well drained, as, because they need heavy watering, there must be perfect drainage to take the excess water away.

Seed sowing.—Plants are raised in a heated glass-house at a temperature of, say, 70 degrees. It is possible to raise them also in a hot-bed, providing a bottom heat of 75 degrees is obtained.

General cultivation.—The frames where the cucumbers are to be grown should be ready by the end of April. A hot-bed should have been made in the frame two weeks previously, by placing the horse manure a foot deep in the soil. A six-inch layer will be required, and this should be watered and trodden down firmly. A six-inch layer of sifted soil is placed on top of this, and the frame and light are then put into position. A four-foot square frame will accommodate one plant, which, of course, should be planted in the middle. Be very careful not to disturb the roots when planting, and, after watering well with tepid water, close the frame down for four days. Growth should commence quite soon, and a little air may then be given. Keep the soil and the plant moist by regular, gentle waterings, but never let the ground get sodden. As the plant grows, the original growths can be pinched back so as to get them to break. Four growths can then be trained, one into each corner of the frame, and, as they reach this, they should be stopped. Be sure to remove the male blooms as they appear, as otherwise the female will become pollinated and the cucumbers will be bitter.

Should the sun be too hot, and the leaves get scorched, cover the frame light with a straw mat during the daytime. During the middle of the summer, it will be necessary to syringe the plants well during the middle of the day, and again about tea-time. After the second syringing the frame should be closed down.

Remove the cucumbers as they become ready, and, if the growths become too crowded, remove the older ones that have fruited, training the younger ones in their place.

Manures.—The original dressing of farmyard manure and the addition of liquid manure added to water when watering, once or twice every week, when the plant is in full bearing. Dried blood is useful if it should be necessary to give a nitro-genous feed. This can be sprinkled lightly around the plants before watering.

Varieties

Lockie's Perfection.   Good shape ; very dark green.
Butcher's Disease Resisting.   Strong constitution.
Rollisson's Telegraph.   Heavy cropping ; dark green.

RIDGE CUCUMBERS

Just as delicious as indoor and frame cucumbers if properly grown. Raise plants under glass in April to plant out end of May or sow in pots and plunge in soil under cloche outside in April. Make ridge by taking out shallow trench, adding about 6 inches of fermenting manure, rotted compost, rotting leaves, etc., and putting soil back on top to form a slight ridge. Ridges should be 3 feet apart and plants 2 feet 6 inches apart on the ridges. Stop plant once when it has grown seven leaves. Hoe regularly ; give good soaking of water 2 or 3 times a week according to the weather, and one feed a week with weak liquid manure. Mulch ridges with straw, peat or lawn mowings.

Harvesting.—Ugly and distorted fruits should be removed at once and others cut three times a week as they develop.

Varieties

Stockwood Ridge ⎱
Bedfordshire Prize ⎰ Good types and heavy croppers.
Crystal Apple. Round like an apple.
Hampshire Giant is the best outdoor variety.

LETTUCE

People seem to be eating lettuce all the year round nowadays Unfortunately many of these used to come from abroad, but it should be possible in an ordinary garden to keep up the supply over a long period, especially if there are continuous cloches.

Soil.—Soil should be well drained, rich in organic material so that moisture is retained easily during the warm months. It is for this reason that it is a good thing to fork damp peat into the top 2 or 3 inches of soil. All lettuces should be grown as individuals, and the best results are often obtained on a sandy loam.

There are two main types of lettuce – the cos and the cabbage – but it is proposed here to treat them as one.

Seed sowing.—(1) Towards the end of August, seed should be sown thinly in a specially prepared seed-bed, using only the varieties that will live through the winter. When these plants are fit to handle, they are planted out in rows 1 foot apart and 10 inches apart in the rows.

(2) If you have frames, the next sowing is made about the middle of October. When the plants are large enough, they are pricked out into other frames, 2 inches apart. These lettuces are then planted out, in the open, early in the new year.

(3) The next sowing is made at the beginning of November, in frames, seeds being dropped in separately half an inch apart. Light soil is sifted over them, and the lights are put on the frames. During fine weather the lights can be removed, though they should be put back again during wet periods. Water the soil well before you sow the seed, as you must not water once the plants are through. During frosts, shut the

lights down, and cover with mats if necessary, but during warm periods air may be given.

(4) For summer lettuces, seed may be sown in the open, either in the seed-bed or where they are to grow, from the beginning of March onwards. Small sowings can be made at fortnightly intervals during March and April, or at three-weekly intervals from the middle of April onwards. The earlier sowings must be in a sheltered position in drills 8 inches apart, the seedlings being thinned out to 2 inches apart as soon as possible. Later on, sowings may be done in the open garden in rows a foot apart, the plants being thinned out to 10 inches apart. The thinnings can always be transplanted in other parts of the garden as and when necessary.

General cultivation.—Constant cultivation between lettuce rows is always necessary. Always handle lettuce plants carefully, as they are damaged very easily. When transplanting, never allow the roots to get dry, and so do not leave them out of the ground longer than necessary. Take every opportunity of planting up odd bits of land and " popping in " lettuce plants between other crops if there is room. When transplanting, do not bury the plants ; on the other hand, see that they are planted firmly. Cos lettuces often have to be tied round with raffia in order to make them heart properly. As a general rule, too, this type of lettuce needs far more watering than the cabbage lettuce.

Manuring.—For the lettuces that are planted out early in the new year, give 2 ozs. of fine meat meal or fish manure, ½ oz. of steamed bone flour, and ½ oz. sulphate of potash per square yard.

In addition to the liberal dressing of farmyard manure that all lettuces appreciate, the following fertiliser should be applied in the spring : .3 ozs. of Cornish fish manure. As the plants get near to hearting, 1 oz. of Chilean potash nitrate may be applied per square yard, on the surface of the ground, and lightly hoed in. This is sometimes applied at intervals of a fortnight, ½ oz. being given at each dressing. Liquid manure per the " Bottle " may be used instead.

Varieties
CABBAGE LETTUCES

(1) FOR SCWING IN OCTOBER IN COLD FRAMES OR UNDER CONTINUOUS CLOCHES :

May Queen, alternative name, **May King.**

Rosy Spring, good for the North, resistant to Mildew.

(2) FOR SOWING IN LATE SUMMER FOR NOVEMBER CUTTING, OR FOR SOWING IN THE AUTUMN TO STAND THE WINTER OUT OF DOORS :

Imperial, clear green leaves, solid heart.

Arctic King, good for the North, though small.

Stanstead Park, very hardy, leaves stained reddish-brown, very coarse.

(3) VARIETIES FOR SOWING IN THE AUTUMN TO OVERWINTER IN THE OPEN AND HEART IN THE SPRING, BUT WHICH WILL NOT DO FOR LATE SUMMER SOWINGS AND CUTTING IN NOVEMBER :

Green Winter, dull clear leaves, edged with yellow.

Hardy Hammersmith, large but coarse.

(4) VARIETIES FOR SOWING VERY EARLY IN THE YEAR FOR HEARTING EARLY SUMMER :

Improved Trocadero, fine heart, quick maturing.

Borough Wonder, similar to above, produces large firm hearts.

(5) VARIETIES FOR SOWING IN THR SPRING AND SUMMER ONLY :

All the Year Round, (badly named for not a winter lettuce), firm heart, good flavour.

Webb's Wonderful, the biggest crisp or iceberg lettuce known. Should be more grown.

Continuity. A brownish lettuce of excellent quality, usually, however, not liked because of its colour.

COS LETTUCES

Lobjoit's Green Cos. La dark green, self-folding. A summer lettuce which will stand the winter under cloches or in frames.

Hick's Hardy Winter White. A winter lettuce sown in the autumn for hearting and cutting in the spring. Needs tying up in order to make it heart.

SEMI-COS

Said to be a cross between a cabbage and a cos lettuce.

Winter Density. Glossy dark green leaves, can be sown in the autumn for cutting in spring or sown in the spring for cutting later.

Osmaston Gem. An excellent type of semi-cos. Large, crisp, delicious.

RADISH

Radishes are often treated as a catch crop, as they are quick to mature. Aim at growing small, crisp, tender radishes, and not large ones that are full of " pith."

Soil.—Radishes like a soil that is open and contains plenty of humus. They never grow well on land rich in nitrogen, so do not manure specially for them. On the other hand, they do badly on starved land.

Seed sowing.—It is possible to sow seed broadcast, or to sow them in rows 6 inches apart. Whatever you do, do not sow the seed deeply – an inch is quite deep enough. But after sowing do make the soil firm ; you never get good firm radishes on loose soil. The first sowings are made during December in a sheltered, sunny place. Choose a " Short Top " type. This seed is broadcast, and the bed is then covered with straw to a depth of four inches. When the seed has germinated, the straw should be raked off, and replaced when there is any sign of frost or snow. Finally the litter is removed altogether. It is convenient to have these beds no wider than 4 feet, so that all the operations may be done without treading on the beds. The next sowing may be made in a frame on a hot-bed. Actually it is quite convenient to do this between other crops. For instance, if you have lettuces in a frame, you can take a crop of radishes from in between them without interfering with the growth of the lettuce at all. Do not make the mistake of thinking that radishes ought to be grown close together ; they usually need to be 2 inches apart from one another. Radishes always appreciate lots of damp horticultural peat forked into the ground as the provided organic matter and helps to hold moisture. Use it at a bucketful to the square yard forked into the top 2–3 inches only.

Sowings can be made outside in the open at any time during the spring and summer. Sow thinly, sow shallowly, thin out early, and do not let the bed get dry.

Varieties

WINTER :
Black Spanish Long and **Black Spanish Round.**

LONG :
Icicle. A pure white radish.
Wood's Frame. Bright red ; very firm.

OVAL:
French Breakfast. Red with white tip.
French Breakfast Early Forcing. The frame variety.

ROUND :
Red Turnip. Bright colour.
Red Turnip Short Top Forcing. Bulbs very quickly ; has very
few leaves ; for sowing very early in the year or in frames or
under cloches in January.
Scarlet Globe. Really scarlet ; short tap-root.
Sparkler. The upper half of the root is bright scarlet, and the
lower portion pure white ; very dainty.

ENDIVE

Quite a useful salad plant, especially where winter salads
are required.

Soil.—As for lettuce.

Seed sowing.—If you need endive in the summer, it is
possible to sow out of doors at the beginning of April. If you
are aiming for autumn and winter crops, then sow at the
beginning of June and July *in situ.* The plants may be raised
by sowing in a seed-bed, rows 6 inches apart.

General cultivation.—When necessary the plants are put
out into their permanent position in rows 15 inches apart, and
12 inches apart in the rows.

When the plants are full grown, they should be blanched.
This is either done by tying the plants up individually, so as
to blanch the heart, or a tile may be laid over the plant, so as
to blanch the centre. Plants may be taken up bodily, with a
ball of soil attached to the roots, and plant them in a dark
shed. The ideal method is to place cloches which have been
white-washed over the plants when they are growing, and
close the ends. Blanching usually takes 3 weeks to a
month.

Varieties

Paris Market. Finely cut leaves ; develops a good heart.
Green Batavian. Broad lettuce-like leaves ; excellent.
Rouen. Very finely curled leaves.

MUSTARD AND CRESS

This can either be sown in boxes under glass, in frames, or out of doors.

Soil.—The soil should be on the light side, and for boxes the compost usually consists of equal proportions of good loam and leaf mould. Sufficient sand is added to make the compost porous. The soil should be made firm, the seeds being then sown on the surface. These should not be covered with soil.

Sow the cress three days before the mustard, as it is slower in germination. Be very careful in watering – the young seedlings damp off easily. It is better to soak the soil before sowing the seed.

Cut the mustard and cress when about $1\frac{1}{2}$ inches long. Do not pull up by the roots, as it is very difficult to wash the soil off afterwards.

HERBS

PARSLEY

Parsley will grow as well in light soils as it will in heavy clays. In both cases the soil needs deep working and well manuring. Light soils need firming.

Seed sowing.—For cutting in summer, sow in March ; for cutting in winter, sow in June ; for cutting in the spring, sow in August.

Rake the soil down to a very fine tilth, and sow the seeds in rows 12 inches apart ; 1 inch deep. Thin the plants to 6 inches apart. For the winter sowings, rows need only be 10 inches apart, and the plants thinned to 3 inches apart. The seed usually takes 6 weeks to germinate. Germination will be aided if when the soil is dry the drills are well watered. As the plants take so long to come through, it is usual to sow radish seed in the drills at the same time. This enables hoeing to be done far earlier, as the rows can be seen.

A good tip, with reference to the winter crop, is to remove all the large leaves during the middle of September, as this enables large numbers of new leaves to grow for winter use.

In hard winters it may be necessary to cover the parsley with frames.

Varieties

Fern-Leaved. Finely cut leaves ; useful for garnishing.
New Dark Green Winter. Stands the winter well.
Myatt's Garnishing. Closely curled ; dark green.

MINT

Mint will grow in practically any soil, and quite likes a north border. It is usually propagated by dividing the roots. These can be planted in the spring or autumn, in rows 12 inches apart. The beds should never be kept down for more than a year, as if the plants are not active, rust develops very quickly. It is very easy to lift up the roots in the winter-time, and to plant them in a green-house so as to force them on early. A few roots can be planted in pots or boxes, and taken indoors for the same purpose.

Varieties

Spearmint is usually grown, though the **Black and White Peppermint** are liked by some people.

SAGE

This is usually propagated by soft wood cuttings made in May, or the plants can be layered in July.

Plant out 18 inches apart each way. Hoe regularly. Do not be tempted to raise sage from seed, as this variety flowers profusely and is less valuable.

THYME

Thyme is propagated by dividing the roots early in April, or by taking cuttings at the beginning of September. It is possible to sow seed in April in drills 8 inches apart, the seedlings being thinned to that distance. Sow in a dry warm position, or use as an edging to paths.

Directly the flowers show, the plants should be cut, and the stems and leaves taken inside to dry. Sufficient growths should be left on the plants to keep them going.

Types.
Lemon Thyme and **Common Thyme.**

UNUSUAL VEGETABLES

If you are keen on vegetables, and want to grow variety, you will be quite interested in some of the more unusual vegetables. It is impossible to give very full details about their culture in such a book, but if you are at all excited about the thought of new vegetables, you will no doubt follow the matter up. Some of the most interesting are : Asparagus Pea, Sugar Pea or Mange-Tout Pea, Celeriac, Cardoons, Maize, the Potato Onion, the Tree Onion, Hamburg Parsley, Soya Beans, Chinese Cabbage, Couve Tronchuda, Scorzonera, Spinach Beet.

Notes on Unusual Vegetables
Asparagus Pea. Sow as for dwarf peas in the spring. The whole pod should be eaten when it is young and succulent.

Sugar Pea (or Mange-Tout Pea). Sow as for dwarf Peas in the spring. The peas are not shelled but eaten pod and all.

Celeriac. A turnip looking Celery. Raise plants as for Celery. Plant out 1 foot square. Give plenty of water. Not planted in trenches.

Cardoons. Are grown like enormous Celery plants in trenches. Raise under glass. Plant out as for Celery. Blanch.

Sweet Corn. Eaten as Cobs. Seed sown in March under glass or under cloches. Planted out early May, 1 foot square. Sunny position. Best venture—John Innes hybrid.

Potato Onion. Plant bulbs in well manured land. Rows 18 inches apart. Plant 9 inches apart. Young bulbs are formed clustering around old ones.

Tree Onion. Plant as for Potato Onion. Small onions are produced on the tops of the stems. A number of stems being thrown up from the bulb.

Hamburg Parsley. Leaves are like ordinary parsley and the root like a White Carrot. Sow seeds in March, drills 18 inches apart. Thin plants to 9 inches.

Soya Beans. Grow like French Beans. Either cook bean pod whole when young or thresh out beans when old and cook these.

Chinese Cabbage. Sow seed end of March. Used as Greens. Chili, a good light leaved variety. Chee-Hoo, a dark leaved variety.

Couve Tronchuda (or Seakale Cabbage). Useful for autumn. Grow as for Cabbage. Plant out 2 feet square. Fleshy ribs may be used as Seakale.

Scorzonera. Sow outside at the beginning of April. Good variety. Improved Long Black. A root crop. (For cultivation *see* Salsify.)

Seakale Spinach. Has very broad leaves with thick white mid ribs. Sow April.

Note. – The fullest details on these and other Unusual Vegetables are given in the book *The A B C of Vegetable Growing* by the same author, published by the English Universities Press.

COLD FRAMES

Every garden, however small, should have at least one frame, as this is of the greatest use in raising plants, in protecting plants throughout the winter, and in growing some of the more tender plants during the summer.

When giving directions in the various chapters for the growing of plants, frames are mentioned from time to time. These should be placed in a position where they can get the greatest amount of sunshine. They should also rest on a hard, dry bottom which is capable of allowing for good drainage. If you are only going to use them for housing pot plants or plants in boxes, then a layer of ashes in the bottom of the frames will be necessary. If, on the other hand, you are going to use the frames for raising plants, either by sowing seed or by striking cuttings, soil will be placed in the frames, and this should be a lightish loam. A good plan is to place a 4-inch or so layer of rotted leaves in the bottom, and the sandy soil of 4-inch depth on the top. See that the soil is firm, especially in the corners, and then on top of all put a thin layer of sharp silver sand.

There are all kinds of frames on the market to-day : wooden frames, and those made of steel ; single frames and double-sided frames ; frames that have removable lights, and frames whose lights lift up on hinges.

For early vegetable culture the Dutch frame is now much to

the fore. This consists of one large single pane of glass, instead of a very large number of smaller ones with the two cross bars.

Whatever frames or lights you have, be sure they are either made of seasoned wood or of steel, and make certain they are draught-proof and rain-proof. Paint them every year, and give them three good coats of white lead paint. Cedar wood frames do not need painting. For vegetables convenient frames are usually 12 feet long and 4 feet wide, thus taking three 4-foot lights. For ordinary work, the frame lights can be 6 feet by 4 feet, the frames, of course, being made to suit.

It may be necessary to shade the frames in a hot summer, and canvas can be used for this. In the same way, protection may have to be given from the frost, and canvas, again, or Archangel mats come in useful. Straw can be used if necessary, though it is apt to make the glass dirty when taken on and off.

HOT-BEDS

If you want to get plants on earlier, or give them some protection by " bottom " heat, hot-beds may be made.

About 8 inches of old and new horse dung is mixed, levelled and trodden down firmly in the bottom of a frame, so that it is at least 8 inches thick. On top of the manure about 9 inches of special soil should be placed, this being raked level. This soil should consist, if possible, of rotted leaves, sieved through an eighth-of-an-inch sieve and mixed with an equal part of sandy loam. It can be seen that the soil in the frame must be dug out deep enough to allow of this being done. The soil is pressed down with a flat board, and can then be used as desired.

CONTINUOUS CLOCHES

Continuous Cloches are easy to use for they fit in with any normal gardening scheme. They fit over the rows of plants and it is a question of bringing the greenhouse to the plants instead of trying to grow plants in a greenhouse. Most people find them far more useful than frames for they are, as it were, automatically ventilated, and can be placed wherever desired. The cloches seem to trap the sun's rays and bottle them up for the plants, but of course they can't manufacture them, so it is always better to put them where the maximum sunshine can be assured.

Cloches enable plants to be grown in the winter and spring when otherwise the cold wet weather would prevent this. Seeds often fail to germinate properly in the early spring because the soil is cold, but if Continuous Cloches are put into position 14 days before seed growing the soil is warmed and the seeds grow perfectly. In fact, the germination of seeds under Continuous Cloches is usually over 90 per cent.

Seeds are sown at the same depth under cloches as in the open but less seed can be used. As there is little hoeing to be done the rows may be close together without any sacrifice of quality or size. Under the Barn Cloches it is usual to fit 2 or 3 rows under 1 cloche row. There is no difficulty in providing water for cloche plants for if watering should be necessary this can be done over the cloches and the water then seeps down and reaches the roots without any difficulty. Cloches make it possible for the gardener to take 3 or 4 crops off a piece of ground in one year.

It is necessary to treat the ground liberally under cloches, especially in regard to composted vegetable refuse. The growing of numerous crops per year under these glass tents tends to exhaust the humus and this must be replaced each season. In addition it is usually advisable to fork into the top 2 or 3 inches of soil, horticultural peat, which can act as a sponge, and help the little seedlings as they grow. In dry soil the peat should be thoroughly soaked before being used.

It isn't possible in a book of this size to give full directions for growing crops under cloches, but the Author's book, *Continuous Cloche Culture* does provide for this need.

There will be found below, however, a few notes on what can be done and those who are keen on cloches should read the other literature available.

French Beans. First sowing mid March for harvesting June. Last sowing August for harvesting Oct.-Nov.
Broad Beans. First sowing January for harvesting in June.
Runner Beans. First sowing, mid March for harvesting mid July. Last sowing June for harvesting Oct.-Nov.

Cabbage First sowing end January for harvesting May and June.

     Subsequent sowings Feb.–March.

Carrots First sowing January for harvesting May.

     Last sowing June.

Cauliflowers. January for harvesting July and August.

Endive. First sowing June for harvesting October.

New Potatoes. First planting February, harvested May.

Lettuce. For spring use, sow January.

     For winter use sow mid August.

Onions. First sowing January, harvested September. (Spring sown onions).

     First sowing July, harvested following August (Autumn sown onions).

Peas. First sowing January for harvesting mid May.

     Last sowing July.

Radishes. First sowings January for harvesting in March.

Spinach. First sowings, Prickly, January and September.

Sweet Corn. First sowings April for harvesting in July.

Tomatoes. First sowing March for harvesting in July and Aug.

Turnips. First sowings mid March for harvesting in May.

     Subsequent sowings :

      Winter turnips, July and August.

      Summer turnips, once a month till end of June.

CHAPTER XIII

FRUIT

*We are going to grow fruit in our garden and so we will have
a kind of Committee on the subject. We shall discuss :—*

1. How the Root Stock is just as important as the variety.
2. How we can have a succession of apples from August to May.
3. How useful cordons are and take up little room.
4. What pears have the best flavour.
5. The best way of growing stone fruits.
6. How it is necessary to have definite pollinators, especially
   for cherries.

MANY people are of the opinion that it is impossible to grow
fruit except on certain soils and in certain districts, but there
is no reason why all gardens should not contain a few fruit
trees, provided they are given the care and attention they
deserve.

THE APPLE

There are very few people who dislike apples, and nowadays
they are on sale all the year round. They can be grown either
in grass, or in cultivated land, and will do quite well also on
walls and fences. It should be possible, in a moderate-sized
garden, to keep up a supply of apples from, say, August to the
following May.

Soil.—Apples will grow on practically all soils, providing
they are well drained. Beware of shallow soils overlying limestone, or over one of the " ironstones," commonly called
" foxbench " in the north. Make certain the apples will have
a free root run by breaking up a hard substratum like this
before planting the tree.

Stocks.—Apples are grafted or budded on to Root Stocks,
which are really a " wild " form of this fruit. Some stocks
have a dwarfing effect. The tree will be small, but will crop
heavily from the time it is planted. Another stock will have

an invigorating effect, and cause the tree to grow away vigorously.   Such a tree may not crop for eight or nine years, and may, in a small garden, grow very large and be unmanageable.

> The most dwarfing stock is known as Type IX.   This is suitable for cordons or small bush trees, but should not be used for weak varieties.
>
> Type II is not quite so dwarfing as a rule in its effect as Type IX. Should be used for bush or pyramid trees.   Will cause early fruitfulness.
>
> Type I is perhaps the best stock for a permanent strong growing bush tree.   Not suitable for small gardens as it will make too big a tree, as a rule.
>
> Type XVI a stock used for large permanent trees.   Useful, possibly, for half standards, or even standards.
>
> These Paradise stocks were classified and numbered by the East Malling Research Station.

Planting.—The land where the trees are to grow should be perfectly clean before the trees are planted.   Be sure to fork out all the perennial weeds, as it is impossible to do this once the trees are in.   Do not make the mistake of digging in farmyard manure, either when preparing the land or in the hole where the tree is to be put.   Any dung that is to be used must be put on as a mulch, on top of the ground, after planting, and not in the ground beforehand.   Make certain that the soil is well drained.   Apples will not grow well in soil that gets waterlogged in the winter.

Make a hole, usually a circular one, about 3 feet wide and not more than 9 inches deep.   Fork up the bottom of the hole, and arrange that there is a little mound 2 or 3 inches high in the centre of the hole, on which the base of the tree may rest.   The roots should then be spread evenly round, so that they are radiating from the centre of the tree – something like the spokes on a wheel.   In this way the tree will be more firmly anchored, and the soil on all sides of the tree will have a chance of being " tapped " for plant foods.

When the tree was dug up in the nursery, in all probability some of the roots were damaged.   The damaged portions should be cut off cleanly with a knife, the cut being made in such a way that it faces the ground when planted. Place the tree in position, and then put on the roots a spadeful or two of soil. Tread this down firmly ; put on another layer of soil, tread again, and continue doing this until you reach the level of the ground. It is quite a good plan to look for the " soil mark " made in the nursery, and to plant to this depth and no deeper. You need to be very careful not to bury the union of the stock and scion – that is, the place where the tree was grafted or budded. If you plant too deeply, the scion – that is, the variety – may send out roots which will prevent the stock from having its full effect. It is foolish to take all the trouble to buy the tree on the right stock, and then to plant it so deeply that it grows on its own roots. *See* page 189.

When the trees arrive, unpack them and see that they are what you have ordered. If you are not ready to plant, then heel them in – this is merely the process of digging a hole, putting the roots in the ground, throwing earth on them, and treading down firmly. Trees will keep in this way for several weeks. Should the weather be frosty, then it may be better to keep the trees in their straw bundle in a shed, and wait for more favourable conditions.

In the case of bush trees, stakes should be driven in the ground at an angle of 45 degrees, and the tree should be tied to this. Put a band of sacking, 3 inches wide and 9 inches long, round the stem, and with tarred string bind the " sackinged " part to the stake. By doing this the tree is not injured, and yet is kept firmly in the ground. It is impossible for the tree to settle down and make new roots if it is rocking about in the soil.

Half standards should be staked with double stakes and a cross bar. The stem, again, being wrapped round with sacking and this part being tied to the cross bar (*see* diagram on p. 188).

If you are planting in grass, on a lawn or in a pasture, then you carry out exactly the same procedure, except that you bury the turf upside down above the roots and not below them, placing a little more soil on the top of them to level up.

Whatever you do, plant firmly, and be quick about it. Do not dig the hole out weeks beforehand and let them either

TWO WAYS OF STAKING

FRUIT TREES

Half-Standard

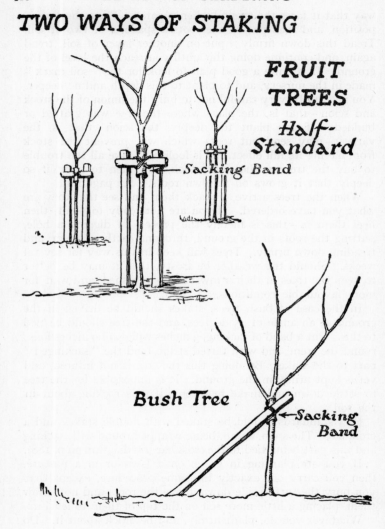

Sacking Band

Bush Tree

← Sacking Band

HOW A GRAFT IS MADE

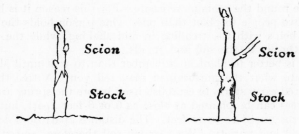

Scion

Stock

Scion

Stock

Stock and Scion placed together

After a year — Stock and Scion have united

The Importance of Depth in Planting

CORRECT DEPTH

PLANTED TOO LOW

Scion

Position of Graft

Stock

Scion growth depends on Stock Roots only

The Scion has rooted above the graft

Scion roots

Position of graft

get dried out if there should be a sunny period or full of wate: if it should rain hard. If you shake the tree slightly while the soil is being put into position, you will find that the latter will settle round the roots more easily. For this reason it is better for two people to plant than one. One person holds the tree, and helps with the treading in and shaking, while the other one throws in the soil and treads.

It is better to plant in November than to wait until March, despite what the nurseryman may tell you. A tree that is planted early starts to establish itself before the spring arrives.

Trees can be planted as close as 6 or 8 feet apart, but as a rule they need 10 to 12 feet. The distance apart does depend on soil and variety. With strong soil therefore, and strong-growing varieties, a greater distance than 12 feet may be required.

Pruning.—One of the most difficult things to explain in the book is pruning. It is fairly easy to demonstrate when you have got the tree in front of you, and the audience around you, but to write about it, or to try and illustrate it with a drawing, is almost impossible. It is necessary to give a few hints, and they will perforce be simple ones.

First of all it is perfectly safe to say that on the whole it is better not to prune at all than to prune too severely. You will get some sort of a crop, if you do not prune, but you can easily get no crop at all – at any rate, for years and years – if you prune too hard.

The question is often asked, " Should one prune at the same time as planting ? " Some people say " Yes," and others say " No." Good advice seems to be as follows : plant your tree in November, get it firmly established, and then prune it the following early March. In this way you do not lose a year's growth, and you get the tree shaping well. For the first five or six years of a tree's life you ought to prune to form good strong branches. You want these evenly distributed, and so as to produce what may be called a " goblet " shaped tree. We will take it that the reader has bought two-year-old trees, which should have, say, a stem 2 feet high on which are already growing three one-year-old branches (*see* diagram opposite) ;

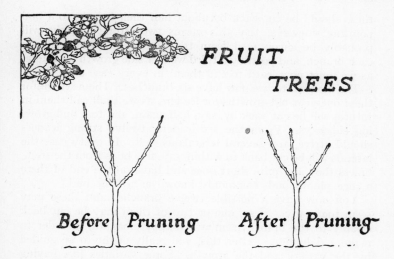

FRUIT TREES

Before Pruning   After Pruning

FIRST WINTER

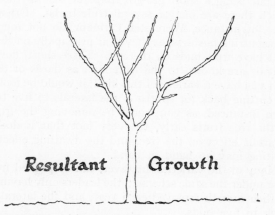

Resultant   Growth

SECOND WINTER

these should be cut back by about half their length, to a bud pointing sideways. By this means two strong growths will probably be encouraged from the two highest buds left on each branch, and possibly a third weaker side growth (or lateral as we must now learn to call them) in every case also.

The next winter we now have six branches. The next winter these one-year-old growths (or leaders, as we shall call them in future) will be cut back by, say, half again, and to a bud growing sideways. From the six leaders, twelve strong leaders should arrive, and several laterals as well. In every case the laterals will be cut back to within, say, five buds from the stem, unless they are quite short ones and have on the end of them a nice plump bud, commonly known as a fruit bud.

You now have a possible twelve branches and these may seem too many. If so, one or two of them may be cut back cleanly to the branch from which they emanate, in order to make a reduction. After this, you really ought to be guided by the variety and the growth. Some varieties like having their laterals cut back in this way, and on them they quickly form fruit buds. These are known as varieties that spur easily (a spur being a short growth from the side of the branch on which there are one or several fruit buds). Other varieties, like, for instance, Worcester Permain, do not much care for this spurring business, as they bear principally on short laterals that have fruit buds on the end. These short, flower-bearing laterals are known to the fruit man as dards or dods.

If you have a variety of this kind, it would be foolish to keep on cutting back (or spurring) the laterals to five buds as has been instanced, as you would be removing the fruiting part. If the tree fruits early, the very fact that it does so has a dwarfing effect on the tree, and the dwarfing effect and early fruiting may go hand in hand.

Many of the varieties, however, can be pruned from year to year under the same scheme ; the leaders only having a quarter of their growth removed each year, and the laterals being cut back to five buds.

When a tree has been pruned, the leader cuts should all be at the same height all over the tree. Look out when you are

Pegging down strawberry runners into pots which have been sunk into the soil close to the strawberry rows.

Applying hydrated lime to the surface of the ground at 5-6 ounces to the sq. yard. Lime washes through so quickly that it is important to make it a surface dressing.

pruning and see that the leaders are cut to the same level, even if it means cutting some harder than others.

With half standards and standards it is a good plan to prune severely for the first five or six years, and then to leave the tree alone. All that has to be done afterwards is to remove the dead wood, the crossing branches, the rubbing branches, and to see that the centre of the tree is kept open. This scheme may be carried out with the bush trees also, if it is desired. For detailed methods of pruning *see* Author's ABC of Fruit Growing.

General routine.—Every year the tree will receive a wash in the winter. At the present time this means the spraying on, with as great a force as possible, of a tar distillate wash, using either a $7\frac{1}{2}$ or a 10 per cent. solution, depending on whether the tree is fairly free from moss and lichen or no. Other routine sprayings will probably be – the use of lime-sulphur, just before the blossom opens and after the blossom falls, and perhaps a spraying with nicotine. Di-nitro-ortho-cresol applied as late as February may take the place of the tar distillate wash, or be used in addition. (For further details of pest and fungus control *see* Chapter XV).

When the apples are about the size of walnuts, they should be thinned out, leaving no fruit closer than 6 or 9 inches the one from the other. People hate doing this, because it seems that you are taking three-quarters of the crop off the tree, but it is well worth while, as the remaining apples are able to grow to perfection, and the tree itself does not get too exhausted in any one year. This makes for annual cropping, and not for the biennial cropping that is all too common in many varieties.

If you get a cluster of apples on a spur, be sure and remove the centre one, known as the King apple, as this is never so good as the others surrounding it.

If you have dessert varieties, and you want to see them highly coloured, it is not a bad plan to shorten back some of the laterals which tend to shade the tree about the beginning of August.

Pick at the right time – that is, when the seeds in the apple are turning brown. A good test is to lift the fruit carefully in the palm of the hand, and if the stalk comes away readily,

G

without any twisting or pulling, then it is ready. Of course early varieties will be picked earlier than late varieties. Never pick by squeezing the apple between the thumb and forefinger – this only bruises the fruit, spoils its appearance, and prevents it from keeping well.

Manuring.—It is very difficult in the small space that can be spared to go into the question of manuring thoroughly. The general principals are, however, as follows : in cultivated land see that the ground has sufficient potash ; 2 ozs. of sulphate of potash per square yard every year should keep things right. It has not yet been shown that apples in the open suffer from lack of phosphates. The manure should be applied during the month of December. If the tree, when it has settled down, has borne a heavy crop, then it is as well to give nitrogen in the form of, say, nitro-chalk during the middle of January. Normally, in cultivated land, if the tree is growing well, nitrogen should not be added.

If you are growing trees on grass, by the time trees are firmly established and the grass is growing up to the stems, it is as well to fear nitrogen starvation, and so to apply 2 ozs. of nitro-chalk per square yard in June, and another similar dressing at the end of September.

You can recognise potash starvation from the brownish-grey scorched edges you get on the leaves–at any rate, in severe cases– and nitrogen starvation from the yellow colour of the foliage.

Organic matter is not considered of great importance in apple growing, but for trees growing in grass it is a very good plan to cut down the grass before it has seeded and gather it round the base of the trees ; this acts as a mulch and when rotted down provides food.

Storing.—Apples, at any rate the keeping varieties, can be stored so as to keep up a supply throughout the winter. After picking, they should be stood out in the open for some time, to " sweat." They should be kept in a room or shed where a constant and low temperature can be guaranteed. For the first fortnight or so after they have been put in, see that there is plenty of ventilation, and then close the ventilators and doors. If you are building a special shed for the purpose, see that the walls and roof are properly insulated, and that double doors and ventilators are supplied. The ventilation should always be high up. A thatched roof is very useful for ensuring an equitable temperature. Make the storehouse vermin proof. Every year clean it out thoroughly and spray with formaldehyde, using a 2 per cent. solution. In this way you start with a clean store, free from fungus diseases.

Apples that store well are : *Cookers* : Lane's Prince Albert, Bramley seedling, and Newton Wonder. *Dessert* : Allington Pippin, Rival, King of the Pippins, Cox's Orange Pippin, Laxton's Superb, Blenheim Orange, Upton Pine, Belle de Boskoop, St. Cecilia, Duke of Devonshire, May Queen, and Easter Orange.

Varieties

There are a host of varieties, which are apt to bewilder a new-comer to gardening. The following are those which are comparatively easy to grow, and which should suit a small garden.

COOKING VARIETIES :

Grenadier. Can be picked the fourth week in July. Will keep until September. Large ; " flattish " ; green, turning yellow.

Rev. W. Wilkes. Can be picked the first week in August. Will keep until November. Large, creamy yellow fruit, dotted with minute scarlet specks ; abundant bearer.

Lord Derby. Can be picked the second week of September. Will keep until November. Very large, deep green fruit, changing to yellow when ripe. An upright grower ; excellent for mincemeat.

Lane's Prince Albert. Can be picked the fourth week in September. Will keep until December. A large striped, heavy cropping variety. Spreading in growth ; can be pruned hard.

Edward VII. Can be picked first week in October. Will keep until May. Somewhat conical, dark green apple. A free bearer.

Newton Wonder. Can be picked the first week in October. Will keep until February. A large handsome, reddish-yellow apple ; after Christmas can be used for dessert. A very strong grower ; should not receive hard pruning. Buy on a No. IX stock.

Encore. Can be picked on or about the end of October and will keep until June. A largish green fruit, acid in flavour. Probably the best keeping apple there is. Makes a big tree ; does not need hard pruning.

DESSERT VARIETIES :

Advance. Can be picked, usually, on August 1st. Must be used immediately. Round to conical apple ; bright crimson ; of fair flavour when eaten straight from the tree. Valuable because it is one of the first juicy apples in season.

Beauty of Bath. Early August. Must be used immediately. A small, flat, prettily striped apple. Gather before ripe, and store in a cool place. The fruit is apt to rot.

Worcester Pearmain. Fourth week of August. Will keep until November. A conical-shaped scarlet apple. A very regular annual bearer. Quite palatable when ripe – those you buy in shops are usually not so. Is apt to bear on short laterals.

James Grieve. To be picked about September 1st. Will keep until November. A lemon-yellow, red-striped medium-sized apple. Flesh very juicy. Will stand hard pruning.

Laxton's Exquisite. Ready for picking the fourth week in August. Will keep until October. Fruit, golden yellow, striped red. A fairly upright grower ; crops freely.

Charles Ross. To be picked the third week in September. Will keep until early December. Very large, coloured, delicious apple. Does well on chalk sub-soils. Very fertile.

Ellison's Orange. Picked early October. Will keep until early November. A very heavy cropper ; similar in shape and colour to Cox's Orange. Very useful for the Midland and northern counties. There is a suspicion of aniseed in the flavour.

Laxton's Superb. Ready to pick the first week of October. Will keep until March. Rather larger than a Cox. The skin is yellow, and slightly flushed all over ; red on the exposed side. A healthy, strong grower.

In order to obtain succession, the following varieties may be recommended, and are quite suitable when grown as cordons. They are all dessert varieties, each of them having a distinct and different flavour.

Owen Thomas, for August.
Everard, for September.
Ellison's Orange, for October.
Egremont Russet, for November.
Cox's Orange Pippin, for Nov.-Dec.
Laxton's Superb, for Dec.-Jan.
Blenheim Orange, for February.
St. Cecilia, for March.
Duke of Devonshire, for April.
May Queen, for May.
Easter Orange will keep right on until June.

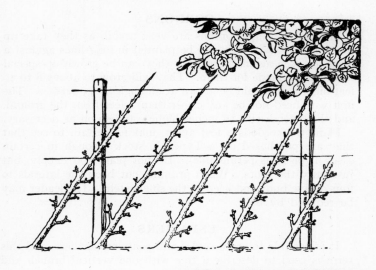

CORDON APPLES

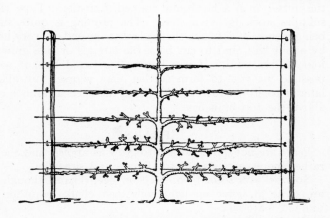

ESPALIER APPLE TREE

CORDONS

In small gardens, cordons are very useful, as they take up such little room. They can be planted in long lines against a fence, or even against a wall, or they can be grown up special wire fencing made for them. They will grow to about 8 to 10 feet high, and should be grown at an angle of 45 degrees. The first wire need not be any closer than 2 feet from the ground, and the second wire 18 inches higher, and so on as necessary.

Plant the cordons 2 feet apart, making certain to see that they are purchased on a Type IX stock (though in certain cases Type II is permissible). Do not plant too deeply, but just bury the roots. When pruning, cut back the laterals to four or five buds and keep to the single stem. The leader may be reduced by half.

ESPALIERS

It is possible to grow apples and pears as espaliers, and this term is used to describe a tree with one vertical branch and several tiers of horizontal branches growing from it at right angles. A tree having four tiers of branches will be called by the nurseryman a horizontal-trained, four-tier. Type II is a suitable stock for such trees. The pruning is quite simple, being merely to cut back the leaders at the end of every branch by about half, and to cut back the laterals or side growth to four or five buds. If you buy a four-tiered tree, it will be possible for you to form further tiers yourself, by allowing laterals to grow out from the side of the vertical branch a foot above the top branches.

PEARS

Pears are not quite so easy to grow as apples, and they are rather more particular as to climate and situation.

Soil.—Pears seem to do well on deep loams, though they are quite at home on light soils over chalk, or other well-drained material.

Stocks.—For bush trees the Quince stock should be used. The Type A has a dwarfing effect on the pear, and is the most popular stock for this purpose. Type C may be used for cordons.

Planting.—All the rules given for apple planting apply to pears also. Be very careful not to bury the union of the root stock and scion, as pear scions root very easily. The varieties Conference and Beurré Hardy do not seem to scion root readily. (*See* page 189.)

Pruning.—On the whole, pears bear on naturally formed spurs on the older wood. They also will form fruit buds on those artificially created at the base of the previous years' shoots. Fruit buds of pears are very easily distinguishable, as they are plump and fat, whereas the wood buds are thin and pointed. The laterals can be cut back to four or five buds in nearly every case, the leaders or end growths of branches being reduced by half, or, in cases of strong growth, by a quarter.

General routine.—There is not the same need to spray pears with a tar distillate wash as there is with apples, as the only insect eggs that this will destroy are those of the aphis, and this is seldom a bad pest. It is a good plan, on the other hand, to spray them with such a wash every three years in order to keep the bark clean. Pears are very subject to scab, especially varieties like Williams, and you will have to lime-sulphur spray before and after the blossom sets, as for apples. Some people dust with copper lime, once or twice, at intervals of a fortnight, even after the last lime-sulphur spraying. All varieties except Conference will need to be thinned rigorously.

Manuring.—On the whole, manuring can be similar to apples, though there is little evidence that potash is as great a necessity to pears as it is to apples. Pears should be done well, and quite a good scheme would be to give them 3 ozs. or fish manure or meat and bone meal, and 2 ozs. steamed bone flour, per square yard in January. Later on, in March, should there be any signs of a heavy crop, it may be necessary to give 4 ozs. of a good fish manure per square yard.

Storing.—Far more care must be taken in gathering and storing pears than perhaps in any other kind of fruit. If the fruits are gathered too early they shrivel, and if gathered too late they are soon overripe. The fruit should really be stored in single layers on shelves or trays, in a temperature of round about 40 degrees F. The light should always be excluded from the fruit. Examine the pears from day to day, and use them as they are ready – they soon go " sleepy " after this.

Varieties

There are a very large number of varieties, and perhaps the easiest to grow are:

Conference. Season, October. A large long pear. Heavy cropper, self-fertile.

Fertility. Season, October. Dull yellow; almost covered with brown russet. Should be thinned heavily when it grows a nice-sized fruit. A very heavy, regular cropper.

Pitmaston Duchess. Season, October–November. Very large. Pale yellow, marbled with brown russett. Crops well; of quite good flavour when properly grown.

William's Bon Chrétien. Season, September. Golden yellow, with russet dots and faint red stripes. Quite the best of the early pears. Must be gathered green, and ripened in store.

Dr. Jules Guyot. Early September. Pale yellow, with a slight red flush. Gather early and store in a cool place. Must be double-worked. A regular and heavy cropper.

Laxton's Superb. Season, October. One of the new pears, but one well worth while growing. Yellow with a russety flush. Large. Should be eaten two or three days after gathering.

Other pears that are not quite such regular bearers, and that are more difficult to grow for one reason or another, are the following (they are included because they each of them have an excellent and distinctive flavour) : Beurré Superfin, which requires to be eaten when the skin seems fairly firm. Doyenne du Comice, which should be pollinated by Glou Morceau. Doyenne George Boucher ; keeps until March ; considered to be a late Comice. Josephine de Malines ; keeps until the end of January ; quite the most reliable fruit in its season. Madame Lye Ballet ; should be grown in a warm situation and rich soil.

Cooking Pears.—The best cooking pear to grow is Catillac, which makes a fine spreading tree. The pear is large, its colour being green with a dull red flush.

PLUMS

In practically every book you take up, you will see it stated that all stone fruits need liberal quantities of lime. This is largely a fallacy, but has grown from year to year because so often soils that suit plums either overlie limestone or have a chalky sub-soil. As a matter of fact you can get what is known as lime-induced chlorosis through too much lime – that is, a yellowing of the leaf, which certainly does not improve the tree's growth or yielding capacity.

It should be possible to grow plums in most gardens, providing the greatest care is taken over the pollination problem.

Soil.—Plums will grow well in any soils that are derived from calcareous formations. The heavy marly loams are particularly suitable, but they are known to thrive on lighter soils providing sufficient organic material can be given.

Stocks.—Perhaps the best stock for the small plum tree is the Common Plum. Czar will not grow on this stock, but Victoria does well on it. Myrobolan is a stronger stock than the Common Plum, and all varieties seem to grow well on it. Useful for half standards or standards.

Planting.—Plums can be planted at any time during the autumn and winter, though it is better to move them and put them in the ground directly the leaves have fallen. As they are, on the whole, shallow rooting, they will need staking. For other particulars as to planting *see* Apples.

Pruning.—Perhaps the most popular way of growing plums is on a clean stem 3 or 4 feet high. This is called a half standard. Because of its height, it makes pruning and the picking of fruit easy to do. For the first five or six years it is a good plan to cut the leaders or end growths back by half. It is necessary to form good strong branches on which the weight of fruit will have to be borne. If this is not done, there is a tendency when the plums swell for the branches to break off. This, naturally, not only ruins the shape of the tree and decreases its bearing capacity, but it may let in the dreaded disease " silver leaf." After this period, there is little pruning to do. All that need be done is to cut out the dead wood, the

G*

rubbing wood, and to attempt to keep the tree open. Some varieties, like Pond's Seedling and Czar, being upright growing, may easily become crowded in the centre. Other varieties, like Victoria and Early Rivers, will tend to droop on to the ground, and so must have their drooping parts cut back to a side growth or lateral growing in an upward direction.

Whatever you do, be sure to clean up all saw cuts with a knife, leaving the cut surface clean and smooth. Go over all such cuts, painting them with thick white lead paint, as this is the only thing that will prevent the entry of disease spores.

Some stocks tend to sucker, and, as these appear from the ground, they should be removed by making a cut with a sharp spade below ground.

Methods of training.—Plums may be grown as bush trees, as half standards, as cordons, or as fan-trained trees. The fan-trained trees grown on walls are very popular, and a good method of training is to arrange that the main branches in the first place are about 2 feet apart. As these branches get older, young growths may be take up from, say, half-way down them, the old growth being cut off and the new one trained in its place. Of course on the older growths will be formed side shoots, and the stronger of these can be spurred back to within 6 inches. They will often thus fruit the second year.

General routine.—Spray the trees in the winter, preferably December with a tar distillate wash, using 1 gallon to 16 gallons of water. If the plums have been badly attacked with red spider (this is shown by the fact that the plum leaves assume autumn tints much earlier in the year than they should, and when you examine the leaves there seems to be a little white down on the underneath) you will have to spray with D.N.C. at 1 gallon to 11½ gallons of water.

The weight of a heavy crop may easily break young branches, and so these should be shored up. Put a pole in the centre of the tree, and tie the laden branches up to this, the whole effect being something like a maypole. Another method is to hook a laden branch on one side of the tree on to a similar branch on the other, and thus make each branch bear the weight of the other.

Never allow a tree to bear too heavily. In many years it will be necessary to remove half the plums when they are the size of filberts, and in some years you may have to take off three-quarters of them. The plums you leave behind will grow much larger, and the tree will in consequence bear regularly.

Manuring.—Plums need far more nitrogen than apples, and, because they grow rapidly in what is often a dry time of the year, this is best applied in an organic form. Give them liberal dressings of well-rotted compost or farmyard manure, and this means 1 cwt. to 8 square yards. In addition to this, give 5 ozs. of meat and bone meal, or fish manure, and 2 ozs. of sulphate of potash, both per square yard.

Varieties

Rivers Early Prolific. Cooking. Ready end of July. Small, round, deep purple. Used as dessert when fully ripened. Partly self-fertile. Pollinator: Cambridge Gage or Jefferson.

Early Laxton. Fruit small, yellow with a red flush. The earliest of modern plums to ripen. Excellent for cooking and canning.

Czar. Culinary. Early August. Round, almost black. May be used for dessert when ripe. Self-fertile.

Pershore Egg. Culinary. August. Oval; yellow, with a white bloom. Good for canning and bottling. Self-fertile.

Victoria. Dessert. Early September. Large, oval; red. Very fertile and reliable. Liable to " silver " leaf. If grown against a wall, gets red spider badly, unless regularly syringed. Self-fertile.

Pond's Seedling. Cooking. Mid-September. Large, oval; dark red with blue bloom. Very fertile; excellent for walls. Self sterile, the pollinator being Czar.

Belle de Louvain. Cooking. End of August. Large; reddish-purple. Excellent for walls, partly self-fertile.

Monarch. Dessert. End of September, early October. Large; rich dark purple. A regular cropper; fruit does not crack when wet. Self-fertile.

Giant Prune. Cooking. End of September. Grows vigorously and crops regularly. Fruit rather like Pond's. Self-fertile.

Cambridge Gage. This, though similar to the old greengage, is self-fertile and a free cropper. The old greengage was self-sterile and cropped but seldom.

Laxton's Gage. An oval yellow gage. Crops heavily. Shaped like the Victoria. Self-fertile.

DAMSONS

Damsons are grown in exactly the same way as plums, though they are often used as wind breaks. The two best varieties, perhaps, are:

The Shropshire Prune. Season, October. A heavy late bearer, growth weeping.

Merryweather. September. Very large, oval, black. The largest damson grown.

CHERRIES

It is generally considered necessary to grow dessert cherries on grassland, and certainly most of the cherry orchards one finds in Kent and other counties have their trees growing in well-kept and well-cropped grass. In the private garden, dessert cherries are often grown as espaliers on walls, but it should be possible to grow bush cherries and cordons as well. At any rate, there is no reason at all why Morellos and the other acid cherries should not be grown just as one would grow a bush plum.

Soil.—Cherries prefer a medium loam. It should be a soil that is retentive of water. Further than this, it must be of a fair depth and be very fertile. The drainage should be thorough, and this in many cases is provided by chalk or gravel as a subsoil.

Stocks.—For standard trees the stock for sweet cherries is Gean, which makes a large tree and is very free growing. For bush trees and the like, Mahaleb is used, as this is distinctly dwarfing. At the present time Mahaleb is principally used for the Morello group.

Planting.—Bush cherries will need about 18 feet square if you are planting a number of them. Fan-trained trees will need 18 feet apart as well, while cordons can be as close as $2\frac{1}{2}$ feet.

Plant as soon as possible after the beginning of November, spreading the roots out evenly, and to their full length, in the hole. Be sure to plant firmly, and not too deeply. Whatever you do, do not bury the join of the scion – that is, the variety, and the stock. It is not usually necessary to plant any deeper than 6 inches. Early in March the following year, you can give a mulching of dung round the tree.

Pruning.—With bush trees carry out similar pruning as recommended for plums. With the fan-trained trees, a certain amount of old wood will be removed every year, and the young new wood trained in its place. (*See* illustration.)

General routine.—Be very careful to net cherries on walls, at blossoming time to prevent frost damage, and at ripening time to prevent the birds eating the fruit. With big trees this is rather impossible, though something can be done to scare the birds away by using pieces of paper, old mirrors, rattling cans, etc., tied up in the tree.

Be sure to spray the trees in the winter-time with tar distillate wash – 1 gallon to 16 gallons of water. It is not a bad plan, either, to put a grease band round the tree – " Takitak " being an example of good grease for this purpose. These should be put round about the first of October.

Manuring.—As for Plums.

Varieties

No self-fertile sweet cherries have yet been found, therefore all varieties require another near them to provide the necessary pollen. Unfortunately, if variety A will pollinate variety B, it does not mean to say that variety B will reciprocate. Thus a variety C may have to be planted to pollinate A. There are, however, several pairs that will pollinate one another equally well, and they are as follows :

Frogmore Bigarreau	and	Governor Wood
Emperor Francis	,,	Governor Wood
Elton Bigarreau	,,	Napoleon
Napoleon	,,	Bigarreau Schrecken
Bigarreau Schrecken	,,	Bedford Prolific
Bedford Prolific	,,	Napoleon
Frogmore Bigarreau	,,	Early Rivers

Bedford Prolific. **Large.** Early July. Dark crimson. **Very** hardy.

Bigarreau Schrecken. Very large. Early July. Shining black. An excellent garden fruit.

Early Rivers. Large. End of June. Shining black. Very tender ; good flavour. Needs vigorous pruning.

Elton Bigarreau. Large. Early July. Bright red and yellow. Does well on walls.

Emperor Francis. Very large. August. Firm flesh, very juicy, Does well in Scotland.

Frogmore Bigarreau. Large. Early July. Pale yellow with light red. Juicy and delicious. Very prolific and very large on a wall

Governor Wood. Large. Early July. Pale yellow with red flush. Good in the garden.

Napoleon. Large. August. Scarlet on pale yellow. Hardy and prolific. Excellent for walls.

CHAPTER XIV

SOFT FRUIT

I show how soft fruits can be grown in most gardens.

1. I give advice on growing black currants free from big bud.
2. I show with illustrations how cuttings can be taken.
3. I give the latest information on strawberry growing.
4. Autumn fruiting raspberries are a change and can easily be grown.
5. I give advice on the growing of large blackberries.
6. " London," " Norfolk " and " Lancashire " are mentioned.

THOUGH it may not always be possible to grow the fruits mentioned in the previous chapter in a small garden, there is no reason at all why some of the soft fruits should not find room there.

Some of them, like the red currant, can be grown as standards, and look quite attractive in shrub borders or as the background to herbaceous borders.

BLACK CURRANTS

Now that it is possible to keep down " Big Bud," it is certain that black currants will be more and more grown. They are very useful for cooking purposes, and for making jams, jellies, and cordials.

Soil.—Black currants grow best on a stiff clay, but even this should be well drained. The one danger is spring frosts. As they do quite well on the lighter soils of Essex and Norfolk, they should be profitable in most gardens.

Propagation.—It is very easy to propagate black currants, and all you have to do is to take cuttings 9 to 12 inches long. These should consist of one-year-old wood, and cuts at an angle of 45 degrees should be made with a sharp knife to a bud at the top and at the bottom of the cutting. *See* page 212.

Place this in some light soil, burying it, say, 8 inches. Do not remove any of the buds, and be sure to only take cuttings from healthy bushes known to be heavy croppers. If you are going to strike a number of them, the rows should be 18 inches apart, and the cuttings 3 inches apart in the rows.

Planting.—Plant at any time during the winter, using two-year-old bushes preferably. Make the rows 6 feet apart, and the bushes 4 feet apart in the rows. After planting, cut the bush down to the ground.

Pruning.—As the black currant bears on the young wood, it is a good plan to aim at removing a fifth of the bush at least every year. In this way it is kept growing vigorously and new wood is constantly provided. As the bush gets older, it may be necessary to cut away a third of the bush every year.

General routine.—Cultivate round the bushes every winter, and dig in the necessary manures. Keep the ground hoed all the summer, giving a mulching in very dry years in addition. Keep a sharp look-out for " Big Bud," and spray with lime sulphur just before the blossoms open.

Manuring.—Be sure to give plenty of farmyard manure or composted vegetable refuse every year. Apply this in the spring, digging it in. In addition to this, add 1 oz. sulphate of potash per square yard. During the summer, dressings of dried poultry manure or fish manure may be given at 2 ozs. per bush in the months of May, June, and July.

Varieties

Boskoop Giant. Throws a long bunch, and bears the largest fruit of any variety. Excellent for jam making and bottling. Is liable to " Big Bud " mite.

Mendip Cross. Bears good bunches of fair-sized berries. The heaviest cropper in some areas. Makes a large bush. Early.

Davison's Eight. Is a cross between Boskoop Giant and Baldwin, and has, perhaps, the best qualities of these two combined in it.

Daniel's September. A very late-ripening variety ; the berries are large and firm. Grows well.

Seabrook's Black. A good mid-season variety, said to be resistant to " Big Bud " mite. The fruit is of medium size, and so are the bunches.

Wellington XXX. A cross between Baldwin and Boskoop. Long trusses, large sweet berries. Vigorous, drooping.

RED AND WHITE CURRANTS

Because they bear on very short spurs on the old wood, they are both popular, grown as cordons, U-shaped trees, and as standards. On standards fruit may be grown right the way up the main stem.

Soils.—They can be grown on a much lighter soil than black currants, and, in fact, seem to prefer a light sandy soil to a heavy clay.

Propagation.—Cuttings are made from wood taken from the bushes any time between October and February. They should be about 15 inches long, and be only one year old and well ripened. Cut to a bud top and bottom, as in the case of black currants. Remove all the buds from the base of the cutting, except three or four at the top. The cutting is then put into the nursery bed, which should consist of light soil, and planted 6 inches deep. Tread down firmly afterwards, and then hoe out the footmarks. The reason the buds are removed is that you want to grow red currants on a leg. *See* page 212.

Planting.—Red currants may be planted 5 feet square, but in the case of Fay's Prolific 4 feet will do.

Pruning.—Red currants are pruned very much in the same way as bush apples. Aim at getting six or seven main branches ; try and grow these so that the tree is goblet-shaped. Then spur back by all the side growths to 2 or 3 buds, the leaders being reduced by, say, half, and cut to an outward bud.

During the summer, just as the berries start to ripen, all the side growths should be broken off by half. It is better to break them than cut them.

General routine.—Spray with a tar distillate wash, 1 in 16, every winter. Keep the ground round the bushes clean and well hoed during the summer.

Manuring.—The principal requirements of these bushes are potash coupled with small quantities of nitrogen and phosphates. You never want rank growth in red currants. Every year dig in a light dressing of farmyard manure or fish manure in the spring, and use 3 ozs. of meat and bone meal or compost per bush as well. Every four years, give each bush 2 ozs. of steamed bone flour.

Varieties

Skinner's Early. The earliest red currant. Grows a long bunch of bright red berries.

Fay's Prolific. Bears a smaller berry and a shorter bunch. The wood is very brittle. Early.

Laxton's Perfection. Bears a long bunch of large currants. The berries are pale, turning to a dull, dark red later.

Laxton's No. 1. Bears a long bunch of large berries. The bush is robust, and the berries are of a bright red colour. A very useful late currant.

Wilson's Long Bunch. Large fruit. Well coloured. A very late currant.

WHITE CURRANTS

Treated in exactly the same way as red currants.

Varieties

Transparent. Bears large yellow berries on long bunches. An excellent exhibition variety. Good for walls.

Wentworth Leviathan. Fine large fruit ; very useful for the midlands and the north.

White Versailles. Bears large berries on short bunches. Very early.

GOOSEBERRIES

Gooseberries can be grown either purely for culinary purposes or for dessert. If you have not grown a really good dessert gooseberry, you should certainly try it, and the different varieties give a wonderful range of flavours.

Soils.—Gooseberries will grow on practically any soils, providing they are well manured and well drained.

Propagation.—As for red currants. *See* page 212.

Planting.—Plant as soon as possible after the leaves have dropped, five or six feet square. Spread the roots out evenly, remove the damaged portions with a knife, cover with soil, and tread down firmly. Do not plant deeper than six inches.

Pruning.—In the first two or three years shorten the leading growths back by half, so as to form an open-centred bush. In the case of the spreading varieties, be careful to cut to an inward bud, and for the upright growing varieties to an outward bud. Once the bush is formed, the only pruning that need be done is to cut out sufficient wood to leave the bush open and from which it is easy to pick.

For dessert varieties, when you wish to grow large berries, it is possible to spur prune – i.e., cutting the laterals back to four or five buds every year.

General routine.—A spraying with a tar distillate wash, 1 in 16, every winter. Aim at clean cultivation. Do not dig round the bushes too deeply in the winter. Look out for caterpillar attack, and dust or spray with Derris.

Manuring.—Dig in a good dressing of dung or well rotted compost every spring, and in addition to this use 5 ozs. of meat and bone meal or fish manure and 1 oz. sulphate of potash per bush, or 5 ozs. of wood ash per bush.

Varieties

REDS :

Lancashire Lad. Fairly upright in growth, needs good soil. Oval large.

London. Has produced the heaviest gooseberry known. Smooth skin ; delicious.

Whinham's Industry. Makes a spreading bush. Grows well under trees. A long hairy berry.

GREENS

Keepsake. One of the earliest berries to be picked. A good-quality cooker. The berry is large, oval, and hairy.

Lancer. Makes a large spreading bush ; is vigorous, and bears an enormous crop. Skin downy, but not hairy. Excellent flavour. Very late.

Shiner. A mid-season variety. Makes a fair bush. The berry is very large, flat-sided, and smooth. Excellent flavour.

WHITES :

Careless. Grows a spreading bush. Should be heavily manured, as it is not a strong grower. Bears a large, oval, downy berry. Well flavoured. A second early.

Transparent. Makes a fair bush. Probably the largest white grown. Smooth skin. Sweet and delicious.

YELLOWS :

Leveller. The bush has a spreading habit. Rather a weak grower. Very sulphur-shy. Bears a large oval, smooth berry of good flavour. Mid-season.

Early sulphur.—An upright grower. The berry is hairy and bright transparent yellow in colour. Very early.

BUSH FRUIT CUTTINGS

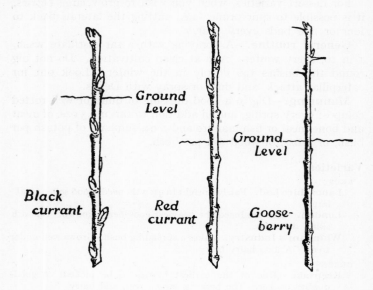

Ground
Level

Ground
Level

Black
currant

Red
currant

Goose-
berry

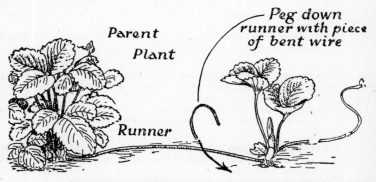

Parent
Plant

Peg down
runner with piece
of bent wire

Runner

STRAWBERRY PROPAGATION

Ringer. A spreading grower. Bears the largest yellow berry known. A variety rather difficult to get.

Gunner. A medium grower. The berries are dark olive green striped with yellow. Hairy. Richly flavoured. Mid-season.

STRAWBERRIES

Most garden owners will want to grow a few strawberries, as these need not take up a great deal of room.

Soil.—They will grow on most soils, though probably a medium heavy loam is best.

Propagation.—Runners are taken from one-year-old plants, once these have struck in the summer. The important thing is to see that the plants from which the runners are taken are perfectly healthy. The results from the experiments at the East Malling Research Station seem to show that it does not matter how many runners are taken per plant as long as the parent is free from pests and diseases. In gardens, it is possible to sink 3-inch pots, filled with a light loamy compost, into the ground. The runner plant is them placed into this, and so roots there. To assist rooting, it is advisable to " peg " the runner down by means of a piece of bent wire shaped like a hairpin. Once the young plants have rooted well, they may be removed and planted into their new quarters.

Planting.—Never plant strawberries on anything else but perfectly clean land, which should have preferably grown a well-manured crop previously. Plant in September, if possible, or at least in October, for unless you are on well-drained land in, say, the south-east, you will then have to delay the planting until early the next spring. The rows should be at least 30 inches apart, and the plants 18 inches apart in the rows. Plant with a trowel, making a hole sufficiently deep to take the full length of the roots ; see that these are spread out and not turned up. After planting, see that the soil is quite firm, but never tread on the plant itself. Be sure to hoe out the footmarks, and keep the hoe going throughout the year. Should there be a severe frost soon after planting, the young plants may tend to lift out of the ground. It is necessary then, to take the first favourable opportunity to firm them in when the land is sufficiently dry.

Support for
RASPBERRIES

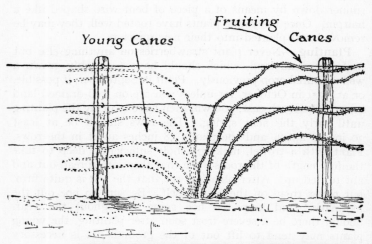

Young Canes

Fruiting

Canes

TRAINING BLACKBERRIES

General routine.—Keep the land free from weeds by periodical hand hoeing. The first year, as soon as the blooms appear, they should be pinched out, and, if you are not proposing to raise new plants, you should commence to cut the runners off. In the autumn, farmyard manure will be applied, and the rows can be lightly forked in. During all operations be sure to keep the soil up to the crown of the plant, as it tends to make new roots higher up the crown every year.

Next year, cultivation will have to start early, and a dressing of artificial be given. Directly the bloom begins to set straw should be put along the rows to prevent the fruit getting dirtied with soil. When all the fruit has been picked, remove the straw and burn it. Hand weed the plants, and start hoeing immediately afterwards, in order to clean the land for the winter.

Manuring.—Farmyard manure should be applied every year in the autumn, spread up the rows, and be forked in. In addition to this, give in the early spring 4 ozs. of meat and bone meal per yard run, together with 2 ozs. of sulphate of potash.

Varieties

(Always buy plants Virus free).

Royal Sovereign. Very early. Robust and hardy. Fruit large, and of delicious flavour. Malling 40 is the best strain.

Cambridge Favourite. Outstanding in size, appearance and quality.

Cambridge Profusion. Very juicy – a week earlier than any other variety.

Auchincruive Climax. Large, fine flavour. Strong grower ; usually gives a second crop in the autumn.

Special Note.—Before planting, runners may be treated with warm water. (*See* Chapter XV.)

RASPBERRIES

There are two main classes of raspberries – the summer fruiting and the autumn fruiting. Most people know about the former, but few seem to grow the latter.

Soil.—Raspberries seem to do best in a deeply worked loam.

Wherever they are grown they must be regularly fed, and they do like moisture. They certainly like a cool climate, and the morning mists and moisture seem to help in swelling the berries. The variety Superlative often does better on heavy soils than on light ones.

Propagation.—It is usual to propagate raspberries by means of the suckers that grow from their roots. These are sometimes known as " spawn," and are really " side canes." They often come up a foot or so from the original row, and are severed from the parent plants in autumn and planted out. One of the most difficult things to-day is to obtain raspberries free from mosaic, and, as this virus reduces the crop and the growth considerably, it is well worth while buying material from a mosaic-free cane nursery.

Planting.—It is very important to plant at the correct depth. Examine the roots, and you will soon see several large, spur-shaped buds, either above them or in them. These are the producers of next season's canes, and so they must be studied. Place these no deeper than $1\frac{1}{2}$ inches below the surface of the soil, and see that they are not damaged or broken off while planting. The rows should be 5 feet apart, and the cane 15 to 18 inches, the one from the other. Directly after planting cut the canes down to the ground. In the spring give a mulching of dung.

Pruning.—Newly planted canes should never be allowed to fruit the first year. Concentrate, then, on producing really strong canes from which fruit will be borne the year after.

After this, directly the canes have fruited they should be removed and the new canes given every chance. In the winter all the very weak canes will be cut down hard.

Should the canes grow very tall, it is usual to cut them back just after the buds at the tip have broken. Canes 5 feet high are considered by most people tall enough. This cutting back causes the canes to break lower down.

General cultivation.—In dry years it is very important to mulch the rows, either with dung or lawn mowings, etc., in May.

Fork along the rows every autumn and clean them, and in

the spring cultivate along the rows again, adding the artificials. Hoe all through the summer regularly.

Manuring.—Give farmyard manure, or well rotted compost every year. In addition give meat and bone meal or fish manure at the rate of, say, 8 ozs. per yard run, as well as 1 oz. of sulphate of potash per yard run also. It is not necessary to put the manure exactly along the row, as the feeding roots spread out considerably.

Varieties

Lloyd George. This is certainly not one of the best flavoured raspberries, but is a tall grower and a very free cropper. An autumn fruiter as well as a summer cropper ; the fruit being bright red, and large. The New Zealand strain is Virus free.

Malling Promise. An early variety bearing large delicious fruits. A very strong grower.

Malling Enterprise. Bears one of the largest berries. Bright red in colour. Fruit of good flavour. Mid season.

Malling Jewell. Recommended to those people who cannot grow Enterprise. It has every promise of being a heavy cropper, having the same delicious flavour as the other " Mallings."

Norfolk Giant. A late variety. A strong and vigorous grower, bearing solid and firm fruit. Excellent for canning, bottling and jam making.

Amber Queen. The best yellow variety. The berries look very attractive, and are particularly well flavoured. They are orange-yellow in colour.

AUTUMN FRUITING VARIETIES

The only difference in the treatment of autumn-fruiting raspberries from their cousins, the summer-fruiting varieties, is that the pruning is done at a different time of the year. The fruit is borne on the canes produced in the same season, and so the pruning has to be delayed until the spring. The berries are gathered in September and October, and sometimes in November.

Varieties

Queen Alexandra. Large, dark red fruit of excellent flavour. Does not make too much cane.

Haytor. Bears firm juicy berries in thick clusters. A very dwarf grower.

BLACKBERRIES

Blackberries would be grown far more if people only realised how profitable they were, and how well they would grow in almost any corner.

Soil.—The Parsley-Leaved blackberry seems to prefer a rich deep soil, but the Himalayan Giant grows well on quite poor soils.

Propagation.—Select young canes the third week in August, and layer these with the terminal buds still intact. The tips should be buried 4 or 5 inches deep, and it is usual to make a hole 6 inches deep and to put in the bottom of this an inch thickness of leaf mould or fine soil. Then fill in the hole and press down.

When layered in this way the plants are ready for lifting towards the end of November, but if not sufficiently rooted should be left until early April. Sever the plant 6 inches above ground level and on the side of the parent plant.

Planting.—Dig the soil deeply, and make certain that it is free from perennial weeds. Plant in a sheltered situation, and, if you are going to put in large numbers of them, see that the rows are 7 feet apart, and the plants 16 feet apart in the rows. This refers to the Himalayan, as the Cut-Leaved variety can be planted closer. Try and get the planting done during the month of November.

Pruning.—Every year the old canes that have finished fruiting are cut down to the ground and the new canes are tied up in their place.

General routine.—Cultivate continually among the plants by hoeing. Flood the soil, if necessary, from time to time, in droughty summers.

Keep the young canes tied into position and out of the way, to prevent them getting damaged. (*See* drawing page 214).

Manuring.—Every year, in the autumn, dig in the farm-yard manure, or well-rotted compost. The following should be added in February and be forked in : 4 ozs. of meat and bone meal or fish manure per square yard.

Varieties

Himalayan Giant. A very large blackberry, producing large clusters of fine fruit ; one plant is capable of bearing over 30 lb. of fruit per year. Can bear fruit on the old wood for several years as well as the new.

Bedford Giant. Earlier than the Himalayan Giant, the fruit being large. Preferred by many as being better flavoured. Self fertile.

John Innes. The latest to ripen. A long picking season.

LOGANBERRIES

Loganberries can be treated in exactly the same way as blackberries. They are gross feeders, and will need heavy manuring every year. The loganberry is said to be the result of a cross between the raspberry and blackberry. The fruit is firm and keeps a long time when gathered, and it is especially valuable for tarts and jams.

CHAPTER XV

THE COMMONER PESTS AND DISEASES

Having been a County Adviser for some ten years, I know how much people are worried about these. I want to help you to:—

1. Appreciate the difference between biting and sucking insects.
2. Realise that prevention is better than cure and to show you what precautions to take.
3. Keep down slugs and snails by the use of a poison bait.
4. Get rid of Black Fly on Broad Beans.
5. Control Club Root, which I know ravages thousands of gardens.
6. Kill the Woolly Aphis (or American Blight) on Apple trees.

ONE of the most difficult things to do in a gardening book of this kind is to deal simply and thoroughly with the subject of pests and diseases. In the first place one does not want to frighten garden owners unduly by giving a long list of troubles which may ruin their plants. On the other hand it would be foolish to pretend that it is not necessary to take every precaution to keep such troubles away.

However carefully one may choose the pests and diseases that normally occur, there are always sure to be some omitted which the reader hopes – in vain – to find in such a chapter. It must be remembered that this is only an A B C of gardening, and so those who are really troubled, or particularly interested in the subject, should procure literature such as the Ministry of Agriculture offers, which gives greater detail and covers a wider sphere.

ORDINARY PRECAUTIONS

Whatever kinds of plants are being grown there are certain general rules which must be observed. The soil must be properly tilled in order to allow as deep rooting as is necessary.

The drainage should be perfect, so that no stagnant water can lie among the roots. Hoeing should be carried out regularly. In this way the weeds are kept down, and as many of them are alternate " hosts " to both pests and diseases, it can be seen how important this is. The surface mulch that hoeing produces, also helps to conserve the moisture and so keeps the plant growing healthily. After all, this is what one must aim at.

The plant is far more likely to be attacked if it is weak and " sickly." A good strong robust plant may easily get over troubles of this kind on its own, while a sickly " brother " will " go down " very quickly.

To this end one must see that the soil is in the right condition. Most plants dislike acid soil, and so lime has to be applied regularly to prevent such acidity. On the other hand there are plants, as has already been mentioned, that hate lime, and so will grow in a more healthy manner without it.

Be sure to manure correctly. Plants that have been given too heavy doses of nitrogen, for instance, are apt to be soft and so succumb to both fungi and insects. Give potash, where potash is needed, in order to keep the plants " hard." See that there is sufficient organic matter in the soil to hold the moisture and allow for bacterial activity.

When thinning or planting out has to be done, see that it is done early enough. Do not let plants get long and lanky because they are too crowded together. In the same way, when planting, give sufficient room for development, and see that the plants are put in neither too deeply nor too shallowly. Further, plant at the right time. Not so early, for instance, that they get damaged by spring frosts, and not so late that they are cut off by the autumn frosts before they have grown to maturity. Some plants will need protection during the winter ; others that flower early may need a slight covering during the spring. Learn to give protection when it is needed and not to coddle plants unnecessarily.

Do not allow refuse to collect in odd corners of the garden ; too often hedge bottoms, for instance, are regular breeding grounds for all kinds of insects. You cannot afford to neglect any portion of the garden in this way. Burn all the rubbish, hedge prunings, fruit-tree prunings, etc., that will not rot down and provide you with an organic form of manure.

When you are making a heap of leaves, lawn-mowings, and so on, sprinkle the heap regularly with sulphate of ammonia, calcium cyanamide, or Adco. This ensures that the heap rots down quickly, does not smell, cannot breed pests or diseases, and yet provides a much more valuable manure than it would if left alone.

It may be necessary to remove portions of the plants that are particularly attractive to insects – such as the pinching out of the growing point of broad beans – or to take away the bottom leaves as they turn yellow – as in the case of Brussels sprouts – in order to do away with the potential home of insects or fungi. In this latter case, there is the additional aid in that more light can reach the plant.

CONTROLLING INSECT PESTS

As a class, insects for our purposes, may be divided into two large groups : first, those that do damage by actually biting and nibbling the fruits, flowers, or foliage ; secondly, those that injure any part of the tree or plant by puncturing the tissue and sucking the sap. Typical examples of biting insects are the caterpillars, while aphides (or green fly) are perhaps the commonest type of sucking insects.

When an insect actually nibbles a leaf or stem, it is quite possible to put some poison there in order to act as a kind of protective layer. Immediately the poison is eaten, of course, the insect dies.

In the case of the sucking pests, this is impossible. Most of them have long pointed " noses " which they push into the plant tissue and so suck from the inside. A protective poison layer is useless here, and so spraying must be done to actually kill the insect when it is present.

Washes are used either to block up their breathing pores or to paralyse them.

It may be necessary in the case of the biting insects to be careful about poison. If, for instance, you wish to eat the vegetable or fruit soon after you have had to spray, it is not a good plan to cover them with poison. In this case a non-poisonous product like Derris has to be employed.

CONTROLLING DISEASES

There are a large number of fungi, and these, depending on the type of disease, may live on any particular part of a tree or plant. It is a good plan to think of a fungus as a small minute plant, growing as it does on the food produced by another. For instance, these black spots we often find on apples and pears are due to a fungus disease called scab. This disease will live on the leaves, on the buds, on the young wood, and on the apples. To control it you have to spray when the " spores " of scab are just starting to blow about ; before they have a chance of germinating and starting to grow you kill them with lime sulphur. In addition to this you put a protective layer of sulphur all over the leaves, so that if any spore does come along it will not have much chance of developing there.

In the same way other fungi, like the mildews and the rusts, develop.

Our aim as gardeners must be to control these troubles in the early stage, and to do the job thoroughly. There must be no half measures and no quarter !

In some cases it may be necessary to spray even before the trouble arises, and to do such spraying as a regular routine, as a kind of insurance.

PREVENTION – BETTER THAN CURE

In the introductory paragraphs mention has been made of how important it is to grow the plant as hard and as healthy as possible. In addition to this there are chemicals that can be applied, either on the ground or on the plant itself, which act as a deterrent and keep the pests away.

A typical example is the use of naphthalene for such insect troubles as the carrot and onion fly. The smell of naphthalene drives away the females when they come to lay their eggs, and so these vegetables are saved.

Fruit trees are given protection from the ravages of the winter moth caterpillars by having a band of grease put round their trunks. This sticky band catches the female moths as they crawl up to lay their eggs. It is convenient that the male should have wings and the females none !

TRAPPING

This is another method of catching and destroying the insect enemies. Various traps are used for the different marauders one is up against. For instance, carrots or cut potatoes, when buried in the ground 2 inches deep and " spitted " on a stick, act as traps for wire-worms. When they have been down a day or two the bait is removed, the wire-worms pulled out of their host plant and dropped into a little can of paraffin.

Slugs can be trapped under the halves of oranges or grape-fruit after the fruit pulp has been removed. Earwigs are trapped if an upturned pot, full of straw, is placed on a bamboo.

There are methods of trapping apple blossom weevils, etc., when bands of corrugated cardboard or of sacking are tied around the trunks of trees for them to hibernate in.

BAITS

In some cases it is necessary to put down some tempting provender that the insect much likes, and then to poison this with some form of arsenic. Under glass the tomato moth, for instance, is baited with a pleasant sugary mixture in a jam-jar.

Wasps may be collected in the same way if a jam-jar full of fruit juice or sugar and water is hung up in the branches of fruit trees. A piece of paper may be tied tightly over the top, and a hole the size of a pencil made in the middle. The wasps clamber through this, but can never get out.

Slugs and leather-jackets are baited with bran and Paris green. Not more than 1 lb. of Paris green is put with 20 lbs. of bran.

FUMIGANTS

Under glass it is quite common to fumigate either by a chemical reaction such as that giving hydrocyanic gas or by means of a special fumigating machine to cause fumes of sulphur or nicotine to permeate the whole house.

In the soil it is possible to use fumigants as well, though these are rather expensive. The most common example is the use of carbon bisulphide against the root form of woolly aphis. Paradichlor-benzine is sometimes dug in against wire-worm and other pests, and this, by giving off fumes, does give control.

HINTS ON HOW TO GET THE BEST RESULTS

Having discussed in a general way what can be done towards the control of pests and diseases in the garden, we must now turn to the individual troubles one by one. Before doing so, there are one or two important points which the reader must notice.

In the notes that follow, instructions are given on spraying, dusting, and the like, and it is no use blaming the author if satisfactory controls are not experienced if the instructions are not followed to the last letter.

All remedies must be applied in the right manner. Do not just leave such important jobs to somebody else. Either do them yourself or personally supervise them.

See that the remedies are applied in the correct form : the dilution must be most carefully done ; soft water may have to be used ; a " spreader " may have to be introduced.

Be sure you are using the right type of remedy. Do not think that any wash will kill any pest. Think of the damage it does to the plant and the way it does it, and spray accordingly.

Apply the remedy at the correct time. It is no good waiting until the pest has multiplied exceedingly, or has got into curled leaves, and so is difficult to get at, before you do something about it. With both pests and diseases there is a right time to do the job.

Learn to recognise the trouble in its early stages. Do not be one of those ignorant people who call everything they find damaging their plants a " blight." If you can recognise the trouble, you can look up the control in a work of this character.

H

See that you have a garden medicine cupboard. Do not wait until the troubles are there before rushing out to try and get the right chemicals to control them. Keep the ordinary remedies by you, under lock and key, so that they are available at any moment. Purchase the best grade of materials at the cheapest possible price. Do not put up with imitations. Buy from recognised firms, and see that you get exactly the article you require.

GENERAL PESTS

SLUGS

Slugs may be found in most gardens at all times of the year – except perhaps during heavy frosts, when they burrow well down into the ground. Their round, jelly-like eggs will be found in rubbish heaps, in the soil, and laid at the roots of many bushy plants. They do more damage in wet weather than during dry periods.

They feed mainly during the night, above ground, but under the soil level they can do damage during any part of the day or night.

Control.—Use a poison bait. 20 lbs. of bran should be damped with a gallon of water and 1 lb. of Paris green stirred in. This mixture is a sufficient dressing for one acre of garden. It may be necessary to give more than one dressing in the season. Heavy rains will wash the Paris green off and prevent the bait from being effective. Spread the mixture early in the evening, and the slugs will be killed overnight.

Powder Meta fuel and mix a saltspoonful of this powder with a handful of bran or damp tea leaves. Put in heaps the size on an egg cup about the affected plants on the ground.

In the winter, equal parts of copper sulphate and ground lime should be mixed together and dug into the ground between the top and bottom spit at the rate of $\frac{1}{2}$ oz. to the square yard.

Other points for successful slug control are : keep the ground regularly hoed ; do not allow rubbish to accumulate ; never leave cabbage stalks, etc., lying about.

WIRE-WORMS

Wire-worms are yellow or yellowish-brown creatures with a hard smooth skin and a brown head. They have biting jaws and three pairs of legs, one on each of the first three rings of their bodies. They may be up to an inch in length. These facts are mentioned so that readers may not confuse them with centipedes, which have one pair of legs on each segment, and millipedes which have two pairs to each segment. Wire-worms are the larvae of the click beetle, and can live in the ground for over seven years, feeding on the roots of plants. When fully grown they can be about an inch in length. The click beetles are brown in colour, and when turned over right themselves by skipping while making a sound from which their name is derived. The beetles are generally found in June and July. The wire-worms burrow their way into the roots of plants like carrots – they can riddle potatoes with holes, and in fact attack the roots of most plants.

Control.—Whizzed naphthalene may be dug in, at the rate of 3 ozs. per square yard, as a method of driving them away.

Obtain para-di-chlor-benzine from the chemist and break it up into portions about the size of a French bean and make holes 6 inches deep with a dibber, or pointed stick, 2 feet apart all over the affected ground. Drop the small portion of para-di-chlor-benzine in the bottom of each hole and fill in. The wire-worms will come to the surface and die.

Trapping is also effective, and pieces of carrot or linseed cattle cake spitted on a stick, may be inserted in the soil 2 inches deep. Every week the traps can be removed by means of the stick, and the wire-worms can easily be picked out and put into a small tin of paraffin.

Peas and beans are sometimes attacked.

When turf is dug up to make a garden, the sods should be dug in and gammexane dust should be worked in at 4 ozs. to the square yard.

LEATHER-JACKETS

These grubs are wrinkled, brown, and have rather a tough skin. There is no obvious head and they have no legs. The

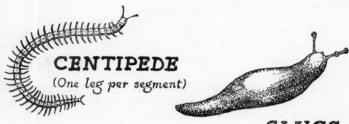

CENTIPEDE
(One leg per segment)

SLUGS

MILLIPEDE
(Two legs per segment)

Carrot-Fly

Chrysanthemum Leaf-Miner

Grub in the Leaf

Pale Patches in the leaf made by Grub

WIRE-WORM

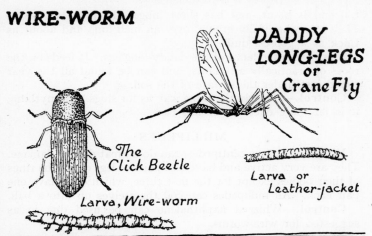

DADDY LONG-LEGS or Crane Fly

The Click Beetle

Larva, Wire-worm

Larva or Leather-jacket

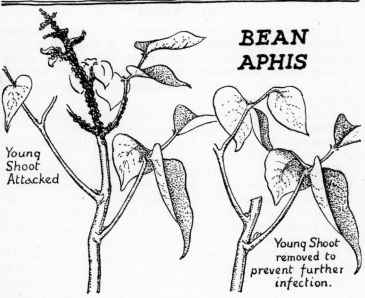

BEAN APHIS

Young Shoot Attacked

Young Shoot removed to prevent further infection.

H*

tail end is blunt, and has short, finger-like processes on it. They are, when fully grown, over an inch long and about as thick as a goose's quill.

This pest is the larva of the daddy-longlegs. It feeds on the roots of practically all plants, and can be found all the year round just under the surface of the soil.

Control.—Exactly the same way as for slugs. If anything, it is far more effective in this case.

MILLIPEDES

Millipedes, unlike centipedes, can do a great deal of damage. They are very active and have two pairs of legs on all the rings of their bodies except for the first three, which only have one pair each. All millipedes can coil themselves up into a ball.

Control.—Whizzed naphthalene can be used dug in as suggested for wire-worms.

EEL-WORM

Though eel-worms are very minute and cannot be seen except under a high-powered microscope, it is as well to warn readers. One type attacks the roots and another stems, causing galling and stunted and distorted growth. Another attacks tubers of potatoes, producing little cysts like little round galls on the roots.

Among flowers, eel-worm is unfortunately common in narcissi bulbs, on chrysanthemums, and in phlox.

Control.—Do not grow the same crop on the same piece of land year after year.

With bulbs, try and get a guarantee when buying them that they have been heated in a warm-water bath at 110 degrees F. for twenty minutes. Before taking cuttings from chrysanthemums, the stools should be treated in exactly the same way. With phlox, it is best to obtain cuttings from washed roots, as the eel-worm is known to live in the stem and leaf.

It is not easy for the amateur to recognise eel-worm infected plants, and so the following remarks may be helpful : Bulbs attacked by eel-worms are soft, when the attack is far advanced. In the initial stages if a bulb is cut open brown rings of attacked scale leaves will be found. As the leaf grows it will be yellow and stunted. With chrysanthemums, parts of older leaves turn light green, then brown and finally black, when they die off ; sometimes they become twisted and malformed. The eel-worm always rises upwards, and so the bottom leaves show the symptoms first.

CHAFER BEETLES

There are three kinds of chafer beetles, which attack the roots of many plants. They are about $\frac{1}{2}$ to $1\frac{1}{2}$ inches and are reddy-brown in colour. The largest is the common May bug, which so often flies indoors when they swarm in May. The larva is a greyish white grub, which lives in the ground for three years in this state.

Control.—If the beetles are eating the leaves of plants, spray with arsenate of lead and a spreader (*see* usual formula page 249). For the grubs, dig in whizzed naphthalene at the rate of 1 oz. to the square yard early in the spring.

ANTS

A poison bait for ants may be prepared in the following manner :

Soak a small sponge with the mixture given below and place small pieces which have been broken off on the beds or wherever the ants abound. Care should be taken with the bait as sodium arsenite is poisonous.

Dissolve 2 lbs. sugar in 1 pint of water, adding $\frac{1}{10}$ oz. of tartaric acid, and boil for half an hour. Dissolve $\frac{1}{10}$ oz. sodium arsenite in 2 ozs. of hot water. Allow both mixtures to cool and then mix them thoroughly and add 3 ozs. of sugar or honey. Ants can be killed by liquid derris.

VEGETABLE PESTS

BEAN APHIS

Commonly known as black fly, black dolphin, or black blight. The black flies settle on the tops of the plants and multiply so rapidly that they cover them as a black sticky mess. If left alone, this soon spreads down to the pods.

The plant is stunted, and there is, in consequence, a tremendous loss of crop. These pests winter on the spindle-berry-tree and on docks, so it is a good thing to destroy these as far as possible.

Control.—Directly the pest is seen, spray or dust with Derris.

CABBAGE CATERPILLARS

These may be the caterpillars of the cabbage moth or the cabbage white butterfly. In the former case they are usually brown, and in the latter case green. They eat and foul the leaves, and can do a great deal of damage in a short time.

Control.—Spray or dust with Liquid Derris. Hand picking is first class, of course, but tedious.

CABBAGE ROOT MAGGOT

All cabbages, cauliflowers, and the like are attacked by this pest. The fly, which much resembles a small house fly, lays an egg, on or near the stem, which hatches out into a maggot. This tunnels into the root and stem, checks the growth, and often causes the plants to fall over.

Control.—Make up a solution of mercuric chloride (corrosive sublimate). Mix 1 oz. of this in $\frac{1}{2}$ gallon of hot water, and add to it 12 gallons of cold water. Pour a cupful of the diluted solution into each hole at planting-out time. Should this not have been done, and an attack is seen, it is a good plan to pour the solution about the plant directly the first signs of the trouble are apparent. Calomel dust can be used also but does not give as good results as mercuric chloride.

MEALY CABBAGE APHIS

This is a bluey mauve little insect, very much like the black fly on broad beans. It gets on the under sides of cabbage and sprout leaves, and in the case of the latter makes the young sprouts very unpleasant.

Control.—Give a good spraying with Liquid Derris, using

as much force as possible. See that the undersides of the
leaves are thoroughly wetted.

CABBAGE ROOT GALL

This is due to the weevil commonly known as turnip root
gall weevil. A round knob or gall will be found on the roots
of members of the cabbage family in the autumn. These,
when cut open, will be seen to contain a maggot. This should
not be confused with the cabbage root maggot which does its
damage principally in June and July. Anyway, in the latter
case there is no gall produced. In the same way the galls must
not be mixed up with the swellings by the club root disease,
in which the swellings contain rather objectionable slime.

Control.—Be sure and burn all the roots that contain this
maggot. Digging naphthalene into the ground, at 1 oz. to the
square yard, is said to act as a deterrent.

CARROT FLY

Carrots that are attacked by this pest flag, and, when
pulled up, grubs will be found in the roots, any time from the
end of May onwards. The fly that causes the trouble is very
small, shiny, and of a blackish, green colour. It has a yellow
head and yellow legs.

Control.—Sow whizzed naphthalene along the rows, a few
days before thinning, at $\frac{1}{2}$ oz. to the yard row. Do this again
twice, at fourteen-day intervals, afterwards. Never leave
thinned carrots lying about. Firm the ground around the
carrots after this operation.

CELERY FLY

Numbers of blisters can be produced on the leaves by the
maggot of this fly. If the blister is opened, a little white grub
will be found inside. The fly lays its eggs on the young plants,
usually before they are put out into the trenches, say from
mid-April until early June.

Control.—In the case of slight attacks the blisters may be
pinched and the maggots killed. A very good control can be
obtained if the plants are sprayed with nicotine and soft soap

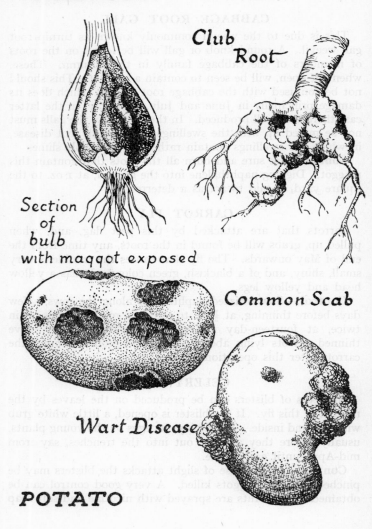

ONION FLY

Club
Root

Section
of
bulb
with maggot exposed

Common Scab

Wart Disease

POTATO

WOOLLY APHIS Attack on Apple

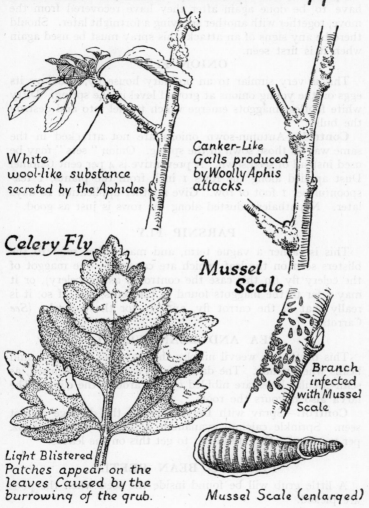

White wool-like substance secreted by the Aphides

Canker-Like Galls produced by Woolly Aphis attacks.

Celery Fly

Mussel Scale

Branch infected with Mussel Scale

Light Blistered Patches appear on the leaves Caused by the burrowing of the grub.

Mussel Scale (enlarged)

(*see* formula page 248) twice, at fourteen-day intervals before the plants are set out in their permanent position. This will have to be done again after they have recovered from the move, together with another spraying a fortnight later. Should there be any signs of an attack, this spray must be used again when it is first seen.

ONION FLY

This is very similar to an ordinary house fly, and lays its eggs on the young onions at ground level in the spring. Dirty white footless maggots emerge which tunnel into and destroy the bulbs.

Control.—Autumn-sown onions are not attacked in the same way as those sown in the spring. Onion " sets " may be used instead of seed sown. A preventive is 4 per cent Calomel Dust applied along the rows 1 inch from the plants, 1 teaspoonful per 1 foot of row. Give another application 10 days later. Naphthalene dusted along the rows is just as good.

PARSNIP FLY

This is rather a vague term, and may either refer to the blisters seen on the leaf, which are caused by the maggot of the celery fly (in this case the control is as for celery), or it may refer to the maggots found in the roots, and, if so, it is really that of the carrot fly, and so, for the control. (*See* Carrots.)

PEA AND BEAN WEEVIL

This beetle-like weevil nibbles the leaves of both peas and beans when young. The damage can easily be recognised, as semi-circular holes are nibbled out all around the edges. The larva also devours the roots.

Control.—Spray with Derris directly the damage is first seen. Sprinkle calcium cyanamide along the rows at 1 oz. per yard run. Be careful not to get this on the leaves.

PEA AND BEAN BEETLE

A little grub will be found inside the seed when the pods are picked.

Control.—Do not purchase either peas or beans with small holes in them. It is a good plan to fumigate infested seed by putting them into an airtight tin which contains ⅛ oz. of carbon bisulphide to 12 lbs. of seed. ·

TURNIP FLEA BEETLE

This little black beetle eats the leaves of turnips, radishes, and members of the cabbage family. This pest usually appears in large numbers in a dry summer.

Control.—Dust with Derris or P. P. Plus during the middle of the day. This may have to be done three times, at intervals of three days, the first as soon as the seedlings appear. Stimulate growth by applying Chilean potash nitrate at the rate of 1 oz. per yard run.

VEGETABLE DISEASES

CELERY RUST OR LEAF SPOT

This is often confused with celery fly, as only too often the leaves are attacked by both these troubles. In the case of the rust, discoloured patches appear on the leaf ; these increase in size until the whole leaf turns black and wilts. When examined carefully, minute black spots will be found on the infected leaves. These contain the " seed " of the fungus.

Control.—Give a thorough spraying with a Bordeaux mixture, just before the first earthing up. Instructions for making Bordeaux are given in the tables on page 249. Spray again fourteen days later, and even a third time if necessary. There are colloidal copper sprays on the market – like Bouisol – which are quite useful also.

CLUB ROOT

This disease, known as finger-and-toe or anbury, will attack the roots of any member of the cruciferae family (i.e. cabbage, cauliflower, turnip, radish, wallflowers, stocks, and weeds like shepherd's purse and charlock). The root swells and becomes knotted and distorted. The swellings contain rotted evil-

H**

smelling material. The plants are dwarf, look sickly, and never come to anything.

Control.—The first thing to do is to raise clean, healthy plants, so the seed-bed has to be watered with corrosive sublimate (mercuric chloride), using 1 oz. of the chemical to 12 gallons of water. As mercuric chloride is difficult to dissolve in cold water, it is a good plan to use ½ gallon of hot water first of all, and then to add the rest of the water to make up the correct solution. Soak the seed-bed a day or so before sowing the seed, and again fourteen days after the seed has been put in. In this way you can guarantee that you have raised plants free from the disease. If your garden or allotment is badly infected also, pour an eighth of a pint of a similar solution into every hole that is made at planting out time.

General Remarks.—Club root is always on acid soil, so see that the land is well limed. Corrosive sublimate is *very poisonous*, and must be used with care. In addition to this, as its name suggests, it will eat away metal vessels if the liquid is left in them too long. Do not use vessels that have contained the solution for household purposes afterwards.

PEA MILDEW

Peas are often attacked by mildew, which can be recognised by the white downy appearance of the leaves. The disease is usually worse in dry years and on light soils. It is seldom that the early varieties are attacked.

Controls.—Be sure to cultivate deeply, so as to give a good root run. Mulch the rows to help to retain the moisture in the soil. Burn the infected haulm. It is possible to spray with colloidal sulphur, or dust with a fine sulphur dust.

POTATO BLIGHT

This is perhaps the most serious disease of potatoes, and is usually first seen in June or July. A delicate brown and white mould will be found on the under-surface of the leaves, which go brown and die back from the edges. This spreads rapidly, especially if the weather is damp. The leaves eventually become black, and the whole haulm is destroyed.

The spores from the diseased leaves fall on to the ground and infect the potatoes. Even at lifting-time infection may take place, and so tubers, after they have been stored, may be found to be diseased.

Control.—Spray in July, either towards the beginning, for the south, or towards the end, for the north. Spray again three weeks later, and yet another spraying is often advisable. Use a Bordeaux mixture (*see* formula page 249).

POTATO: COMMON SCAB

A surface scab appears on the skin of the potato, but this never goes deep into the tuber.

Control.—Put plenty of lawn-mowings or other fresh organic material into the holes or drills at planting-out time.

POTATO WART DISEASE

This produces abnormal, black cauliflower-looking growths on the potato. If this disease is seen, it should be reported to the police immediately.

Control.—Grow immune varieties of potatoes only.

TURNIP: CLUB ROOT

For description *see* Cabbage.

Control.—Soak the ground where the seed is to be sown with a mercuric chloride solution as for cabbages.

FLOWER PESTS

CAPSID BUGS

These are known sometimes as tarnished plant bugs or bishop flies. Some people mistake it for a large green fly, or even a little green beetle. It has wings and can fly, and runs about very quickly. It attacks Asters, Dahlias, Chrysanthemums, and Erigeron. The leaves are " pitted," the stems are scarred, and the flowers may be distorted. In bad attacks plants often do not flower at all.

Control.—Spray with nicotine and soft soap (*see* formula page 248) directly the pest is seen, and again ten days later. Drench the plants thoroughly. It may be necessary to spray several times.

EARWIGS

Earwigs usually attack Chrysanthemums, Dahlias, and Sweet Peas. The earwig climbs up and gets into the flower, and may do damage.

Control.—Use a poison bait consisting of breadcrumbs and Paris green ; ½ lb. of Paris green is sufficient for 5 lbs. of breadcrumbs. Damp the crumbs, and stir in the Paris green gradually ; spread the mixture in the affected areas. Invert flower-pots stuffed with straw on to bamboos inserted among the plants usually attacked and remember to empty them regularly.

CUCKOO SPIT

A white froth will be found on the leaves and stems of flowering plants, and if examined carefully will be found to contain a yellow-green insect which becomes the frog hopper.

Control.—Spray with nicotine and soft soap (usual formula page 248), using a good deal of force.

GREEN FLY

This pest, commonly known as the blight, is really one of the aphides. It is often very bad on roses, though other plants are also attacked.

Control.—Spray with nicotine and soft soap or Liquid Derris (usual formulas pages 248, 249) directly the pest is seen.

LEAF MINER

The leaves are tunnelled by a little grub producing yellowish irregular continuous markings. This damage often occurs in the cutting stage, and, when bad, may reduce the vigour of the crop considerably.

Control.—Dip the cuttings in a nicotine and soft soap solution before striking them. Spray with nicotine and soft soap when the trouble is first seen, and again, as necessary, every ten days until under control. Pick off badly diseased leaves and burn them.

THRIPS

These are minute, black, long-shaped creatures which get into the flowers of many plants and on to the leaves as well. They not only do a certain amount of damage themselves, but they can transmit virus also. Their presence can be detected very often, if the plant is tapped over a white handkerchief. The little creatures drop off, and can be seen against the dense whiteness of the linen.

Control.—Spray with nicotine and soft soap (usual formula page 248), using a good deal of force.

CATERPILLARS

These may be found on various flowering plants from time to time and will eat away much of the foliage and even the blossom.

Control.—Spray with Liquid Derris.

FLOWER DISEASES

CHRYSANTHEMUM RUST

Little reddy-brown tufted spots appear on the under surface of the leaves in the first place. These gradually spread until the leaves turn brown and die.

Control.—Spray the under and upper sides of the leaves with an equal mixture of proprietary colloidal copper and colloidal sulphur. Pick off and burn all badly infested leaves.

CHRYSANTHEMUM MILDEW

White powdery patches appear on the leaves and stems.
Control.—Spray with colloidal sulphur.

HOLLYHOCK RUST

Hard orange pustules appear on the leaves and stems.
Control.—Never keep old plants in the garden ; cut off the attacked leaves and burn them. Spray with Bordeaux mixture (usual formula page 249).

ROSE BLACK SPOT

In the first place you will notice purple irregular shaped spots on the leaves and then on the young stems. These soon turn black, and in bad cases the bush can be defoliated.

Control.—Spray with Bordeaux mixture or colloidal copper, using a spreader (*see* formula page 249). Spray directly there are any signs of spots and again fourteen days later. Next season, spray just before the buds open, and again directly the young leaves are developed. Collect and burn all diseased leaves.

ROSE RUST

In this case orange galls, covered with orange powder, are found on the under surface of the leaves. In very bad attacks the stems can die back and partial defoliation may take place.

Control.—Cut out diseased stems and burn them. For leaf damage, spray as above, when the disease is first seen, and again ten days later. Next year, spray when the leaves are unfolding, as a preventive. Cut out the diseased parts and burn them.

ROSE MILDEW

Mildew can be recognised by the white powdery substance that is found on the young stems, leaves, and thorns. There are usually two attacks, the first just after the leaves are fully open, and the second at the end of June. In bad cases the plants may lose their leaves and so be weakened.

Control.—Spray with colloidal sulphur directly there is any sign of the trouble. Cut out diseased shoots in pruning.

MILDEWS

Many plants are attacked by mildew, and the white " furry " substances will be seen on the leaves and stems.

Control.—Spray with colloidal sulphur according to the instructions given by the makers on the container.

FRUIT PESTS

APPLE: SAW-FLY

A maggot will be found in the apple which has entered from the side, and not through the eye or calyx. The eggs are laid in May.

Control.—Drench the tree with nicotine and soft soap seven days after 90 per cent. of the blossoms have fallen.

APPLE: SUCKER

This is a little insect which creeps into the unopened blossom and quickly ruins it. It has a flattened body.

Control.—Spray the trees with a tar distillate wash in the winter and kill all the eggs.

APPLE: APHIS

Various kinds of " green fly " which can curl up the leaves and even stunt and malform the young apples.

Control.—Spray the trees in winter with a tar distillate wash.

APPLE: CAPSID BUG

A little green bug which resembles a large green fly. It will nibble the apples and prevent them from getting to any size, and will bite the end of young shoots, causing them to break into three or four. It sucks at the leaves, perforating them.

Control.—Soak the tree towards the end of February with a $7\frac{1}{2}$ per cent solution of di-nitro-ortho-cresol, usually known as D.N.C. This yellow liquid is unpleasant to handle but does smother to Capsid eggs which are laid on the branches.

APPLE: RED SPIDER

The leaves get their autumn tints much earlier than they should, and, if the underneath side is examined, it will be found to be covered with microscopic spider mites in their webs. They are transparent red creatures.

Control.—Spray with D.N.C. as for capsid bugs.

APPLE : BLOSSOM WEEVIL

A greyey-white maggot will be found inside the brown unopened flower. In bad cases nearly every flower may be ruined in this way.

Control.—Put a band of corrugated paper, with the corrugations inside, around the trunk of the tree in June. The weevils will hibernate here. Take it off in September. Throw the weevils into paraffin. Spray with a 20% D.D.T. wash as the buds " break." Use ¾ lb. to 25 galls. water.

APPLE : CATERPILLARS

There are a large number of caterpillars that eat the leaves and mark the fruit, but for our purpose it will be good enough to classify them under one heading.

Control.—Spray with a tar distillate wash in December, using a 10 per cent solution. See that the whole tree is washed thoroughly. When the leaves start to unfold in the spring and caterpillars are seen, you can spray with arsenate of lead to poison them.

APPLE : WOOLLY APHIS

(Sometimes known as A :ERICAN BLIGHT)

The aphis cover themselves with a white woolly substance, as a protection. They suck the sap from the bark, eventually causing a swelling, and the spores of " canker " are likely to get into the wounds they make.

Control.—Spray with a Tar Oil wash in December. Paint affected areas with Liquid Derris, using a stiff brush.

APPLE : MUSSEL SCALE

Attacks all kinds of fruit trees, but principally the apple. The larvae cover themselves with a mussel-shell-like scale as a protection, hence the name. This also sucks the sap from the bark.

Control.—Spray with a tar oil winter wash during the dormant season, or if only a slight attack, scrub off with a stiff brush dipped in a caustic soda solution. (*See* Brown Rot, page 247).

CHERRIES : GREEN FLY

This pest will attack both the shoots and leaves, and though I have called them green fly, as this is the gardener's name for all aphides, they are more often black in colour.

Control.—Spray with a 7½ per cent tar distillate wash in December. Spray with Liquid Derris when first seen in summer.

CURRANTS : GREEN FLY

Again an aphis which gets on the underneath of leaves and sucks the sap. The leaves turn red, and look as if they are blistered.

Control.—Spray with a 6 per cent tar distillate wash in December ; this kills all the eggs.

CURRANTS : BIG BUD MITE

It is only on black currants that the buds get big and swollen, and it is in these that the mites breed. In red and white currants the buds die when attacked by the mite.

Control.—Spray, when the leaves are the size of a two-shilling piece, with lime sulphur, using 1 gallon to 13 gallons of water.

GOOSEBERRIES : CATERPILLARS

Caterpillars often swarm on gooseberry bushes, and soon devour every leaf.

Control.—Spray or dust with Derris directly they are first seen. This acts like magic, and the caterpillars die immediately.

PEARS : APHIS (GREEN FLY)

As for apples.

PEARS : CATERPILLARS

As for apples.

PLUMS: APHIS

Seem to swarm down on the under surface of the leaves and on the young growths and cover them with a mealy mauve-looking mass.

Control.—Spray with a tar distillate wash in December.

PLUMS: CATERPILLARS

Tar distillate wash as for aphis, and lead arsenate as for apples.

RASPBERRIES: BEETLE

It is not so much the beetle that worries growers, but the maggot which gets into the fruit. The beetles can be seen laying their eggs in the open blossoms, and it is then that they should be killed.

Control.—Spray with Derris when the majority of the blossoms are open. If spraying is impossible, dust two or three times with Derris.

STRAWBERRIES: GREEN FLY

The leaves become curled and turn reddish in colour.

Control.—Put the young plants in warm water at exactly 110 degrees F. for twenty minutes. Cool immediately afterwards in cold water. Spray, if seen in the field, with nicotine and soft soap. Nico-sulphur dust can be used as an alternative.

STRAWBERRIES: MITE

The leaves become small and the whole plant looks stunted Use the warm water treatment as for aphis.

STRAWBERRIES: RED SPIDER

A very tiny minute yellow insect which can be seen on the under sides of the leaves with a magnifying glass.

Control.—Use the warm water treatment before planting as for aphis. In cases of bad subsequent attack, spray with weak lime sulphur and a spreader.

DISEASES OF FRUIT

APPLE : SCAB

Brown spots are seen on the leaves, and eventually on the fruit. These turn black later. When the fruits are badly attacked, the skin may be severely cracked.

Control.—Spray with lime sulphur 1 in 30 and a spreader just before the blossoms open, and lime sulphur 1 in 60 just after the blossoms have fallen. With sulphur-shy varieties, like Stirling Castle, use Bordeaux mixture instead.

APPLE : CANKER

Sunken areas around the buds ; dying back of young shoots. Seems to eat away the old branches and form an ugly gnarled-looking wound.

Control.—Be sure and keep down aphis and red spider, as these may be carriers of the disease. With a sharp knife pare out the diseased parts and burn them. Cover over the cleaned-up wound with thick white lead paint, or use " Medo."

APPLE : BROWN ROT

Both apples, plums and cherries are attacked by this disease. The fruit is attacked during the summer, the spores usually entering a small wound. The fruit goes brown, rotten, and discoloured. Rings of purplish pustules appear with a powdery surface. The attacked fruit shrinks in size, and deep wrinkles appear on the skin. These mummified fruits may hang on the trees during the winter.

Control.—Remove the mummified fruits directly they are seen and burn them. Spray with the usual Tar Distillate Wash in December, and follow with caustic soda 1 lb., soft soap 1 lb. to 10 gallons of water before the buds start to open, say, in late February.

GOOSEBERRY : DIE BACK

The branches die back one after the other when attacked by this disease.

Control.—Cut out all the dead and affected wood and burn it. Spray with copper sulphate, using 1 lb. to 25 gallons of water, just before the buds burst.

GOOSEBERRY : MILDEW

Has in the past been a very serious disease. White patches appear on the shoots, leaves, and finally the berries, and these turn a brown colour eventually.

Control.—Be sure and burn all the diseased shoots when pruning in the winter. Give the bushes a good spraying early in April, and again four weeks later, with ammonium polysulphide, using a quarter of a gallon of this liquid to 50 gallons of water.

PEARS : SCAB

(*See* Apple.)

PLUMS : SILVERLEAF

The leaves turn from green to a silvery colour, and the branches eventually die. In the winter, when the branches are dead, a greyish purple fungus will be found on the bark.

Control.—By a Government order all the silvered wood must be sawn off and burnt before July 15th of every year.

RASPBERRIES : MOSAIC

A Virus disease which causes the leaves to become mottled and in bad cases crinkled. It exhausts the plant and reduces the crop.

Control.—No method of control is known. Purchase virus-free canes.

QUANTITIES FOR THE VARIOUS WASHES RECOMMENDED

CONTACT WASHES

(1) **Nicotine and soft soap**

   1 oz. of nicotine   10 gallons of water
   1 lb. of soft soap

(2) **Derris and soft soap**

 1 lb. of Derris   50 gallons of water
 4 lbs. of soft soap

POISON SPRAYS

Arsenate of lead

 1 lb. arsenate of lead paste 20 gallons of water

FUNGUS SPRAYS

(1) **Bordeaux**

 4 lbs. of quicklime   100 gallons of water
 6 lbs. of copper sulphate

This is the best formula to use for celery blight and potato blight.

In the case of apples and pears use the following :

 6 lbs. quick lime   100 gallons of water
 4 lbs. copper sulphate

(2) **Cheshunt Compound** (hardly a spray, but is used to control " damping off " in seedlings).

 2 parts finely powdered copper sulphate
 11 parts finely powdered ammonium carbonate
   (use 1 oz. to 2 gallons of water)

GLOSSARY

COMMON TERMS USED IN GARDENING

ARTIFICIALS

Chemical manures. Used in powder or pellet form. Sometimes referred to as " chemicals."

ARCHANGEL MATS

Special mats that can be bought at a Nurseryman's or Sundriesman's for covering frames or tender plants. Russian mats are similar.

BLANCHING

By excluding light, certain parts of vegetables, like seakale and celery can be kept white. This prevents them from being bitter and makes them more tender.

BLEEDING

Sap exuding from unhealed wounds.

CORDON

A tree with one branch only, which carries fruit spurs all the way up the stem.

CHLOROSIS

The loss of the green colouring matter in leaves. May be due to lack of nitrogen in the soil or to a disease.

CROWN

A large bud found at the top of a root, as in the case of the strawberry or lily of the valley. Found also at the end of a rhizome, as on the horseradish and seakale. In chrysanthemums, it is the first bud to form at the end of the main growth which causes new branches to be sent out.

CANES

In raspberries, the growths that come up from the roots on which the fruit is borne. The bamboos used for staking plants are often known as canes also.

DISBUDDING

In chrysanthemums, the removal of the buds found in the axils of the leaves so as to leave one plump bud at the end of each branch. In potatoes, it may mean the removal of the sprouts from a tuber you propose to plant.

DOUBLE - WORKED

One variety budded or grafted on to the Stock, and another variety grafted on to this. Often done in the case of varieties of pears that do not " take " on quince.

ESPALIER

A tree grown against a wall, fence, or wire, which is grown so as to have a number of horizontal cordons.

FORKING OVER

A fork is used, generally in the spring and summer, to break up the lumps of soil and to level the ground.

FRIABLE

Getting the soil into such a condition that the particles can be separated easily. Sand may be said to be in a friable condition always.

GREEN MANURING

A crop which is sown purely for the purpose of digging it in while it is young and fresh.

HUMUS

A brownish black " jam " or " jelly " derived from decomposed vegetables and animal material. Vegetable refuse, grass, straw, and other decaying matter when dug into the ground adds humus.

HYBRID

A cross-bred plant which is produced when the stigma of one species (the female part) is fertilised with the pollen (male part) of another. If this is done in the case of two varieties, this is known as cross-pollination.

LATERAL

A shoot growing out from the side of a branch.

LOAM

Soil which consists of approximately equal parts of clay and sand. If the clay predominates, it may be described as a heavy loam, and if the sand predominates it is described as a light loam.

MULCH OR MULCHING

The placing of a layer of material on the surface of the soil, around plants, to prevent the moisture from the ground being evaporated. Farmyard manure, rotted leaves, and lawn-mowings are often used. A dust mulch can be produced by hoeing.

ROOT CUTTINGS

Small pieces of root, or sometimes of rhizome, by which certain plants can be propagated. Common examples among flowers are anchusas and delphiniums, and in vegetables, seakale and horse-radish. In the latter case the root cuttings are often known as thongs.

REVERSION

Normally used to describe a virus disease in black currants. The true meaning of the word is really a throw back to an older type.

RUNNERS

Growths which come out from a plant, like the strawberry, and root at the various " joints " as they grow along the ground.

SEED BED

A piece of ground which has been specially prepared and finely raked ready for seed sowing.

SETTING BLOOM

When the pollen has fertilised the flower and the seed-pod starts to form ; in some cases this, of course, is the fruit, e.g. tomato and apple.

SPUR

A short side growth on which fruit buds are produced.

SPRIT

A short growth from the eye of a potato. This is usually formed when potatoes are put to sprout before planting.

STAGGERED

Often used in the case of sowings when these are placed into position alternately in two rows.

STOCK

The root system of a bush or tree on to which the variety has been budded or grafted, e.g. the paradise stock for apples, and the rugosa stock for roses.

STOPPING

The pinching out of the growing point of a plant.

SUCKER

The growth which comes up from the roots. Is useful in the case of black currants, but should be dug up and destroyed in the cases of roses and plums, for example.

TILTH

Fine tilth denotes land cultivated down to a fine condition, with every soil particle as small as a grain of wheat.

WATERLOGGING

The spaces in between the particles of soil are filled with water.

INDEX

255

Garden Planning

RICHARD SUDELL
F.I.L.A.

"Here at last is a really useful book on planning the ordinary small or medium-sized garden which most of us own. It is a practical book for practical people who understand that to start right is the key to success."

ALLOTMENT AND HOME GARDEN

"Page after page of well-thought-out designs, nearly all for the average small site, help the garden planner in a practical and refreshingly modern way."

DAILY EXPRESS

50 complete plans   **8s. 6d. net**